Advances in Pattern Recognition

For further volumes:
http://www.springer.com/series/4205

Marco Treiber

An Introduction to Object Recognition

Selected Algorithms for a Wide Variety of Applications

 Springer

Marco Treiber
Siemens Electronics Assembly Systems
    GmbH & Co. KG
Rupert-Mayer-Str. 44
81359 Munich
Germany
Ma.Treiber@web.de
Marco.Treiber@siemens.com

Series editor
Professor Sameer Singh, PhD
Research School of Informatics
Loughborough University
Loughborough, UK

ISSN 1617-7916
ISBN 978-1-4471-2578-5   ISBN 978-1-84996-235-3 (eBook)
DOI 10.1007/978-1-84996-235-3
Springer London Dordrecht Heidelberg New York

British Library Cataloguing in Publication Data
A catalogue record for this book is available from the British Library

Printed on acid-free paper

Springer is part of Springer Science+Business Media (www.springer.com)

TO MY FAMILY

Preface

Object recognition (OR) has been an area of extensive research for a long time. During the last decades, a large number of algorithms have been proposed. This is due to the fact that, at a closer look, "object recognition" is an umbrella term for different algorithms designed for a great variety of applications, where each application has its specific requirements and constraints.

The rapid development of computer hardware has enabled the usage of automatic object recognition in more and more applications ranging from industrial image processing to medical applications as well as tasks triggered by the widespread use of the internet, e.g., retrieval of images from the web which are similar to a query image. Alone the mere enumeration of these areas of application shows clearly that each of these tasks has its specific requirements, and, consequently, they cannot be tackled appropriately by a single general-purpose algorithm. This book intends to demonstrate the diversity of applications as well as to highlight some important algorithm classes by presenting some representative example algorithms for each class.

An important aspect of this book is that it aims at giving an *introduction* into the field of object recognition. When I started to introduce myself into the topic, I was fascinated by the performance of some methods and asked myself what kind of knowledge would be necessary in order to do a proper algorithm design myself such that the strengths of the method would fit well to the requirements of the application. Obviously a good overview of the diversity of algorithm classes used in various applications can only help.

However, I found it difficult to get that overview, mainly because the books dealing with the subject either concentrate on a specific aspect or are written in compact style with extensive usage of mathematics and/or are collections of original articles. At that time (as an inexperienced reader), I faced three problems when working through the original articles: first, I didn't know the meaning of specific vocabulary (e.g., what is an object *pose*?); and most of the time there were no explanations given. Second, it was a long and painful process to get an understanding of the physical or geometrical interpretation of the mathematics used (e.g., how can I see that the given formula of a metric is insensitive to illumination changes?). Third, my original goal of getting an overview turned out to be pretty tough, as often the authors want to emphasize their own contribution and suppose the reader is already familiarized with the basic scheme or related ideas. After I had worked through an article, I often ended up with the feeling of having achieved only little knowledge gain, but having written down a long list of cited articles that might be of importance to me.

I hope that this book, which is written in a tutorial style, acts like a shortcut compared to my rather exhausting way when familiarizing with the topic of OR. It should be suitable for an introduction aimed at interested readers who are not experts yet. The presentation of each algorithm focuses on the main idea and the basic algorithm flow, which are described in detail. Graphical illustrations of the algorithm flow should facilitate understanding by giving a rough overview of the basic proceeding. To me, one of the fascinating properties of image processing schemes is that you can visualize what the algorithms do, because very often results or intermediate data can be represented by images and therefore are available in an easy understandable manner. Moreover, pseudocode implementations are included for most of the methods in order to present them from another point of view and to gain a deeper insight into the structure of the schemes. Additionally, I tried to avoid extensive usage of mathematics and often chose a description in plain text instead, which in my opinion is more intuitive and easier to understand. Explanations of specific vocabulary or phrases are given whenever I felt it was necessary. A good overview of the field of OR can hopefully be achieved as many different schools of thought are covered.

As far as the presented algorithms are concerned, they are categorized into global approaches, transformation-search-based methods, geometrical model driven methods, 3D object recognition schemes, flexible contour fitting algorithms, and descriptor-based methods. Global methods work on data representing the object to be recognized as a whole, which is often learned from example images in a training phase, whereas geometrical models are often derived from CAD data splitting the objects into parts with specific geometrical relations with respect to each other. Recognition is done by establishing correspondences between model and image parts. In contrast to that, transformation-search-based methods try to find evidence for the occurrence of a specific model at a specific position by exploring the space of possible transformations between model and image data. Some methods intend to locate the 3D position of an object in a single 2D image, essentially by searching for features which are invariant to viewpoint position. Flexible methods like active contour models intend to fit a parametric curve to the object boundaries based on the image data. Descriptor-based approaches represent the object as a collection of descriptors derived from local neighborhoods around characteristic points of the image. Typical example algorithms are presented for each of the categories. Topics which are not at the core of the methods, but nevertheless related to OR and widely used in the algorithms, such as edge point extraction or classification issues, are briefly discussed in separate appendices.

I hope that the interested reader will find this book helpful in order to introduce himself into the subject of object recognition and feels encouraged and well-prepared to deepen his or her knowledge further by working through some of the original articles (references are given at the end of each chapter).

Munich, Germany   Marco Treiber
February 2010

Acknowledgments

At first I'd like to thank my employer, Siemens Electronics Assembly Systems GmbH & Co. KG, for giving me the possibility to develop a deeper understanding of the subject and offering me enough freedom to engage myself in the topic in my own style. Special thanks go to Dr. Karl-Heinz Besch for giving me useful hints how to structure and prepare the content as well as his encouragement to stick to the topic and go on with a book publication. Last but not least, I'd like to mention my family, and in particular my wife Birgit for the outstanding encouragement and supporting during the time of preparation of the manuscript. Especially to mention is my 5-year-old daughter Lilian for her cooperation when I borrowed some of her toys for producing some of the illustrations of the book.

Contents

1 Introduction 1
  1.1 Overview 1
  1.2 Areas of Application 3
  1.3 Requirements and Constraints 4
  1.4 Categorization of Recognition Methods 7
  References 10

2 Global Methods 11
  2.1 2D Correlation 11
    2.1.1 Basic Approach 11
    2.1.2 Variants 15
    2.1.3 Phase-Only Correlation (POC) 18
    2.1.4 Shape-Based Matching 20
    2.1.5 Comparison 22
  2.2 Global Feature Vectors 24
    2.2.1 Main Idea 24
    2.2.2 Classification 24
    2.2.3 Rating 25
    2.2.4 Moments 25
    2.2.5 Fourier Descriptors 27
  2.3 Principal Component Analysis (PCA) 31
    2.3.1 Main Idea 31
    2.3.2 Pseudocode 34
    2.3.3 Rating 35
    2.3.4 Example 35
    2.3.5 Modifications 37
  References 38

3 Transformation-Search Based Methods 41
  3.1 Overview 41
  3.2 Transformation Classes 42
  3.3 Generalized Hough Transform 44
    3.3.1 Main Idea 44
    3.3.2 Training Phase 44

	3.3.3	Recognition Phase	45
	3.3.4	Pseudocode	46
	3.3.5	Example	47
	3.3.6	Rating	49
	3.3.7	Modifications	50
3.4		The Hausdorff Distance	51
	3.4.1	Basic Approach	51
	3.4.2	Variants	59
3.5		Speedup by Rectangular Filters and Integral Images	60
	3.5.1	Main Idea	60
	3.5.2	Filters and Integral Images	61
	3.5.3	Classification	63
	3.5.4	Pseudocode	65
	3.5.5	Example	66
	3.5.6	Rating	67
		References	67
4		**Geometric Correspondence-Based Approaches**	69
4.1		Overview	69
4.2		Feature Types and Their Detection	70
	4.2.1	Geometric Primitives	71
	4.2.2	Geometric Filters	74
4.3		Graph-Based Matching	75
	4.3.1	Geometrical Graph Match	75
	4.3.2	Interpretation Trees	80
4.4		Geometric Hashing	87
	4.4.1	Main Idea	87
	4.4.2	Speedup by Pre-processing	88
	4.4.3	Recognition Phase	89
	4.4.4	Pseudocode	90
	4.4.5	Rating	91
	4.4.6	Modifications	91
		References	92
5		**Three-Dimensional Object Recognition**	95
5.1		Overview	95
5.2		The SCERPO System: Perceptual Grouping	97
	5.2.1	Main Idea	97
	5.2.2	Recognition Phase	98
	5.2.3	Example	99
	5.2.4	Pseudocode	99
	5.2.5	Rating	100
5.3		Relational Indexing	101
	5.3.1	Main Idea	101
	5.3.2	Teaching Phase	102
	5.3.3	Recognition Phase	104

	5.3.4	Pseudocode	105
	5.3.5	Example	106
	5.3.6	Rating	108
5.4	LEWIS: 3D Recognition of Planar Objects		108
	5.4.1	Main Idea	108
	5.4.2	Invariants	109
	5.4.3	Teaching Phase	111
	5.4.4	Recognition Phase	112
	5.4.5	Pseudocode	113
	5.4.6	Example	114
	5.4.7	Rating	115
	References		116

6 Flexible Shape Matching 117
  6.1 Overview 117
  6.2 Active Contour Models/Snakes 118
    6.2.1 Standard Snake 118
    6.2.2 Gradient Vector Flow Snake 122
  6.3 The Contracting Curve Density Algorithm (CCD) 126
    6.3.1 Main Idea 126
    6.3.2 Optimization 128
    6.3.3 Example 129
    6.3.4 Pseudocode 130
    6.3.5 Rating 130
  6.4 Distance Measures for Curves 131
    6.4.1 Turning Functions 131
    6.4.2 Curvature Scale Space (CSS) 135
    6.4.3 Partitioning into Tokens 139
  References 143

7 Interest Point Detection and Region Descriptors 145
  7.1 Overview 145
  7.2 Scale Invariant Feature Transform (SIFT) 147
    7.2.1 SIFT Interest Point Detector: The DoG Detector 147
    7.2.2 SIFT Region Descriptor 149
    7.2.3 Object Recognition with SIFT 150
  7.3 Variants of Interest Point Detectors 155
    7.3.1 Harris and Hessian-Based Detectors 156
    7.3.2 The FAST Detector for Corners 157
    7.3.3 Maximally Stable Extremal Regions (MSER) 158
    7.3.4 Comparison of the Detectors 159
  7.4 Variants of Region Descriptors 160
    7.4.1 Variants of the SIFT Descriptor 160
    7.4.2 Differential-Based Filters 162
    7.4.3 Moment Invariants 163
    7.4.4 Rating of the Descriptors 164

7.5   Descriptors Based on Local Shape Information   164
       7.5.1   Shape Contexts   164
       7.5.2   Variants   168
7.6   Image Categorization   170
       7.6.1   Appearance-Based "Bag-of-Features" Approach   170
       7.6.2   Categorization with Contour Information   174
References   181

8   Summary   183

Appendix A   Edge Detection   187

Appendix B   Classification   193

Index   199

Abbreviations

BGA	Ball Grid Array
CCD	Contracting Curve Density
CCH	Contrast Context Histogram
CSS	Curvature Scale Space
DCE	Discrete Curve Evolution
DoG	Difference of Gaussian
EMD	Earth Mover's Distance
FAST	Features from Accelerated Segment Test
FFT	Fast Fourier Transform
GFD	Generic Fourier Descriptor
GHT	Generalized Hough Transform
GLOH	Gradient Location Orientation Histogram
GVF	Gradient Vector Flow
IFFT	Inverse Fast Fourier Transform
LoG	Laplacian of Gaussian
MELF	Metal Electrode Leadless Faces
MSER	Maximally Stable Extremal Regions
NCC	Normalized Cross Correlation
NN	Neural Network
OCR	Optical Character Recognition
OR	Object Recognition
PCA	Principal Component Analysis
PCB	Printed Circuit Board
PDF	Probability Density Function
POC	Phase-Only Correlation
QFP	Quad Flat Package
SIFT	Scale Invariant Feature Transform
SMD	Surface Mounted Devices
SNR	Signal-to-Noise Ratio
SVM	Support Vector Machine

Chapter 1
Introduction

Abstract Object recognition is a basic application domain of image processing and computer vision. For many decades it has been – and still is – an area of extensive research. The term "object recognition" is used in many different applications and algorithms. The common proceeding of most of the schemes is that, given some knowledge about the appearance of certain objects, one or more images are examined in order to evaluate which objects are present and where. Apart from that, however, each application has specific requirements and constraints. This fact has led to a rich diversity of algorithms. In order to give an introduction into the topic, several areas of application as well as different types of requirements and constraints are discussed in this chapter prior to the presentation of the methods in the rest of the book. Additionally, some basic concepts of the design of object recognition algorithms are presented. This should facilitate a categorization of the recognition methods according to the principle they follow.

1.1 Overview

Recognizing objects in images is one of the main areas of application of image processing and computer vision. While the term "object recognition" is widely used, it is worthwhile to take a closer look what is meant by this term. Essentially, most of the schemes related to object recognition have in common that one or more images are examined in order to evaluate which objects are present and where. To this end they usually have some knowledge about the appearance of the objects to be searched (the model, which has been created in advance). As a special case appearing quite often, the model database contains only one object class and therefore the task is simplified to decide whether an instance of this specific object class is present and, if so, where. On the other hand, each application has its specific characteristics. In order to meet these specific requirements, a rich diversity of algorithms has been proposed over the years.

The main purpose of this book is to give an introduction into the area of object recognition. It is addressed to readers who are not experts yet and should help them to get an overview of the topic. I don't claim to give a systematic coverage or even less completeness. Instead, a collection of selected algorithms is presented attempting to highlight different aspects of the area, including industrial applications (e.g., measurement of the position of industrial parts at high precision) as well as recent research (e.g., retrieval of similar images from a large image database or the Internet). A special focus lies on presenting the general idea and basic concept of the methods. The writing style intends to facilitate understanding for readers who are new to the field, thus avoiding extensive use of mathematics and compact descriptions. If suitable, a link to some key articles is given which should enable the interested reader to deepen his knowledge.

There exist many surveys of the topic giving detailed and systematic overviews, e.g., the ones written by Chin and Dyer [3], Suetens et al. [12], or Pope [9]. However, some areas of research during the last decade, e.g., descriptor-based recognition, are missing in the older surveys. Reports focusing on the usage of descriptors can be found in [10] or [7]. Mundy [6] gives a good chronological overview of the topic by summarizing evolution in mainly geometry-based object recognition during the last five decades. However, all these articles might be difficult to read for the inexperienced reader.

Of course, there also exist numerous book publications related to object recognition, e.g., the books of Grimson [4] or Bennamoun et al. [1]. But again, I don't feel that there exists much work which covers many aspects of the field and intends to introduce non-experts at the same time. Most of the work either focuses on specific topics or is written in formal and compact style. There also exist collections of original articles (e.g., by Ponce et al. [8]), which presuppose specific knowledge to be understood. Hence, this book aims to give an overview of older as well as newer approaches to object recognition providing detailed and easy to read explanations. The focus is on presenting the key ideas of each scheme which are at the core of object recognition, supplementary steps involved in the algorithm like edge detection, grouping the edge pixels to features like lines, circular arcs, etc., or classification schemes are just mentioned or briefly discussed in the appendices, but a detailed description is beyond the scope of this book. A good and easy to follow introduction into the more general field of image processing – which also deals with many of the aforementioned supplementary steps like edge detection, etc. – can be found in the book of Jähne [5]. The book written by Steger et al. [11] gives an excellent introductory overview of the superordinated image processing topic form an industrial application-based point of view. The Internet can also be searched for lecture notes, online versions of books, etc., dealing with the topic.[1]

Before the presentation of the algorithms I want to outline the wide variety of the areas of application where object recognition is utilized as well as the different requirements and constraints these applications involve for the recognition methods. With the help of this overview it will be possible to give some criteria for a categorization of the schemes.

---

[1]See, e.g., http://www.icaen.uiowa.edu/~dip/LECTURE/lecture.html or http://homepages.inf. ed.ac.uk/rbf/CVonline/ or http://www.ph.tn.tudelft.nl/Courses/FIP/noframes/fip.html (last visited January 26, 2010).

1.2 Areas of Application

One way of demonstrating the diversity of the subject is to outline the spectrum of applications of object recognition. This spectrum includes industrial applications (here often the term "machine vision" is used), security/tracking applications as well as searching and detection applications. Some of them are listed below:

- *Position measurement*: mostly in industrial applications, it is necessary to accurately locate the position of objects. This position information is, e.g., necessary for gripping, processing, transporting or placing parts in production environments. As an example, it is necessary to accurately locate electrical components such as ICs before placing them on a PCB (printed circuit board) in placement machines for the production of electronic devices (e.g., mobile phones, laptops, etc.) in order to ensure stable soldering for all connections (see Table 1.1 for some example images). The $[x, y]$-position of the object together with its rotation and scale is often referred to as the object *pose*.
- *Inspection*: the usage of vision systems for quality control in production environments is a classical application of machine vision. Typically the surface of industrial parts is inspected in order to detect defects. Examples are the inspection of welds or threads of screws. To this end, the position of the parts has to be determined in advance, which involves object recognition.
- *Sorting*: to give an example, parcels are sorted depending on their size in postal automation applications. This implies a previous identification and localization of the individual parcels.
- *Counting*: some applications demand the determination of the number of occurrences of a specific object in an image, e.g., a researcher in molecular biology might be interested in the number of erythrocytes depicted in a microscope image.
- *Object detection*: here, a scene image containing the object to be identified is compared to a model database containing information of a collection of objects.

Table 1.1 Pictures of some SMD components which are to be placed at high accuracy during the assembly of electronic devices

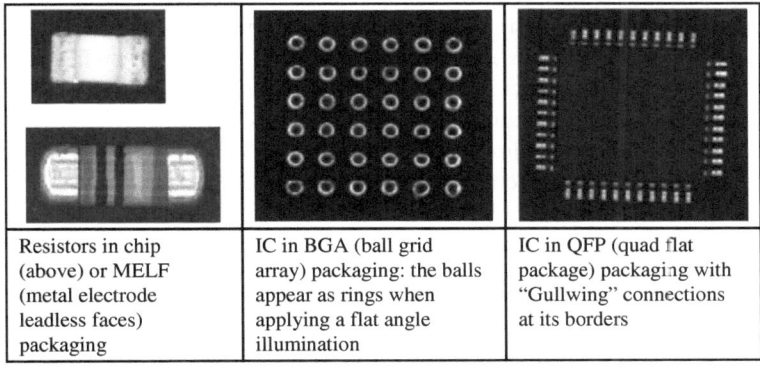

Resistors in chip (above) or MELF (metal electrode leadless faces) packaging	IC in BGA (ball grid array) packaging: the balls appear as rings when applying a flat angle illumination	IC in QFP (quad flat package) packaging with "Gullwing" connections at its borders

Table 1.2 Example images of scene categorization

Scene categorization: typical images of type "building," "street/car," or "forest/field" (from *left* to *right*)

A model of each object contained in the database is often built in a training step prior to recognition ("off-line"). As a result, either an instance of one of the database objects is detected or the scene image is rejected as "unknown object." The identification of persons with the help of face or iris images, e.g., in access controls, is a typical example.

- *Scene categorization*: in contrast to object detection, the main purpose in categorization is not to match a scene image to a single object, but to identify the object class it belongs to (does the image show a car, building, person or tree, etc.?; see Table 1.2 for some example images). Hence categorization is a matter of classification which annotates a semantic meaning to the image.
- *Image retrieval*: based on a query image showing a certain object, an image database or the Internet is searched in order to identify all images showing the same object or similar objects of the same object class.

1.3 Requirements and Constraints

Each application imposes different requirements and constraints on the object recognition task. A few categories are mentioned below:

- *Evaluation time*: especially in industrial applications, the data has to be processed in real time. For example, the vision system of a placement machine for electrical SMD components has to determine the position of a specific component in the order of 10–50 ms in order to ensure high production speed, which is a key feature of those machines. Of course, evaluation time strongly depends on the number of pixels covered by the object as well as the size of the image area to be examined.
- *Accuracy*: in some applications the object position has to be determined very accurately: error bounds must not exceed a fraction of a pixel. If the object to be detected has sufficient structural information sub-pixel accuracy is possible, e.g., the vision system of SMD placement machines is capable of locating the object position with absolute errors down to the order of 1/10th of a pixel. Again, the number of pixels is an influence factor: evidently, the more pixels are covered by the object the more information is available and thus the more accurate the component can be located. During the design phase of the vision system, a trade-off

between fast and accurate recognition has to be found when specifying the pixel resolution of the camera system.

- *Recognition reliability*: of course, all methods try to reduce the rates of "false alarms" (e.g., correct objects erroneously classified as "defect") and "false positives" (e.g., objects with defects erroneously classified as "correct") as much as possible. But in general there is more pressure to prevent misclassifications in industrial applications and thus avoiding costly production errors compared to, e.g., categorization of database images.
- *Invariance*: virtually every algorithm has to be insensitive to some kind of variance of the object to be detected. If such a variance didn't exist – meaning that the object appearance in every image is identical – obviously the recognition task would be trivial. The design of an algorithm should aim to maximize sensitivity with respect to information discrepancies between objects of different classes (inter-class variance) while minimizing sensitivity with respect to information discrepancies between objects of the same class (intra-class variance) at the same time. Variance can be introduced by the image acquisition process as well as the objects themselves, because usually each individual of an object class differs slightly from other individuals of the same class. Depending on the application, it is worthwhile to achieve invariance with respect to (see also Table 1.3):

- *Illumination*: gray scale intensity appearance of an object depends on illumination strength, angle, and color. In general, the object should be recognized regardless of the illumination changes.
- *Scale*: among others, the area of pixels which is covered by an object depends on the distance of the object to the image acquisition system. Algorithms should compensate for variations of scale.
- *Rotation*: often, the rotation of the object to be found is not known a priori and should be determined by the system.
- *Background clutter*: especially natural images don't show only the object, but also contain background information. This background can vary significantly for the same object (i.e., be uncorrelated to the object) and be highly structured. Nevertheless, the recognition shouldn't be influenced by background variation.
- *Partial occlusion*: sometimes the system cannot rely on the fact that the whole object is shown in a scene image. Some parts might be occluded, e.g., by other objects.
- *Viewpoint change*: in general, the image formation process projects a 3D-object located in 3D space onto a 2D-plane (the image plane). Therefore, the 2D-appearance depends strongly on the relative position of the camera to the object (the viewpoint), which is unknown for some applications. Viewpoint invariance would be a very desirable characteristic for a recognition scheme. Unfortunately, it can be shown that viewpoint invariance is not possible for arbitrary object shapes [6]. Nevertheless, algorithm design should aim at ensuring at least partial invariance for a certain viewpoint range.

Table 1.3 Examples of image modifications that can possibly occur in a scene image containing the object to be recognized (all images show the same toy nurse)

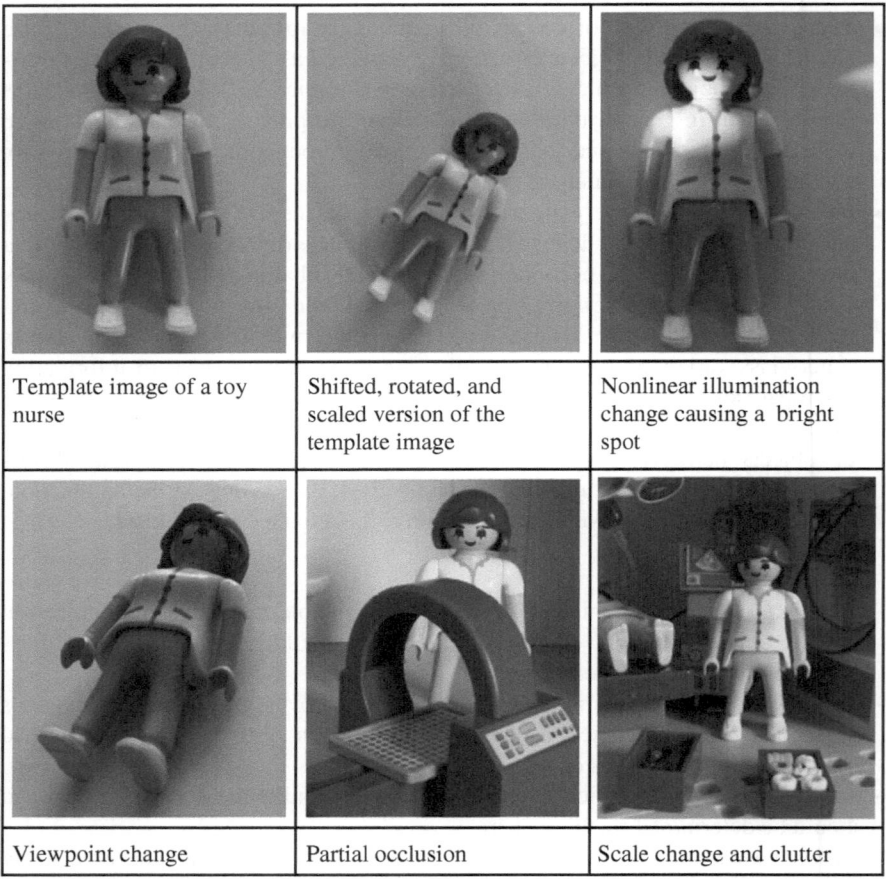

Template image of a toy nurse	Shifted, rotated, and scaled version of the template image	Nonlinear illumination change causing a bright spot
Viewpoint change	Partial occlusion	Scale change and clutter

Please note that usually the nature of the application determines the kinds of variance the recognition scheme has to cope with: obviously in a counting application there are multiple objects in a single image which can cause much clutter and occlusion. Another example is the design of an algorithm searching an image database, for which it is prohibitive to make assumptions about illumination conditions or camera viewpoint. In contrast to that, industrial applications usually offer some degrees of freedom which often can be used to eliminate or at least reduce many variances, e.g., it can often be ensured that the scene image contains at most one object to be recognized/inspected, that the viewpoint and the illumination are well designed and stable, and so on. On the other hand, industrial applications usually demand real-time processing and very low error rates.

1.4 Categorization of Recognition Methods

The different nature of each application, its specific requirements, and constraints are some reasons why there exist so many distinct approaches to object recognition. There is no "general-purpose-scheme" applicable in all situations, simply because of the great variety of requirements. Instead, there are many different approaches, each of them accounting for the specific demands of the application context it is designed for.

Nevertheless, a categorization of the methods and their mode of operation can be done by means of some criteria. Some of these criteria refer to the properties of the model data representing the object, others to the mode of operation of the recognition scheme. Before several schemes are discussed in more detail, some criteria are given as follows:

- *Object representation*: Mainly, there are two ways information about the object can be based on: *geometry* or *appearance*. Geometric information often refers to the object boundaries or its surface, i.e., the *shape* or silhouette of the object. Shape information is often object centered, i.e., the information about the position of shape elements is affixed to a single-object coordinate system. Model creation is often made by humans, e.g., by means of a CAD-drawing. A review of techniques using shape for object recognition can be found in [13], for example. In contrast to that, appearance-based models are derived form characteristics of image regions which are covered by the object. Model creation is usually done in a training phase in which the system builds the model automatically with the help of one or more training images. Therefore data representation is usually viewpoint centered in that case meaning that the data depends on the camera viewpoint during the image formation process.
- *Scope of object data*: Model data can refer to *local* properties of the object (e.g., the position of a corner of the object) or *global* object characteristics (e.g., area, perimeter, moments of inertia). In the case of local data, the model consists of several data sections originating from different image areas covered by the object, whereas in global object representations often different global features are summarized in a global feature vector. This representation is often only suitable for "simple objects" (e.g., circles, crosses, rectangles, etc. in 2D or cylinders, cones in the 3D case). In contrast to that, the local approach is convenient especially for more complex and highly structured objects. A typical example is industrial parts, where the object can be described by the geometric arrangement of primitives like lines, corners. These primitives can be modeled and searched locally. The usage of local data helps to achieve invariance with respect to occlusion, as each local characteristic can be detected separately; if some are missing due to occlusion, the remaining characteristics should suffice for recognition.
- *Expected object variation*: Another criterion is the variance different individuals of the same object class can exhibit. In industrial applications there is very

little intra-class-variance, therefore a rigid model can be applied. On the opposite side are recognition schemes allowing for considerable deformation between different instances of the same object class. In general the design of a recognition algorithm has to be optimized such that it is robust with respect to intra-class variations (e.g., preventing the algorithm to classify an object searched for as background by mistake) while still being sensitive to inter-class variations and thereby maintaining the ability to distinguish between objects searched for and other objects. This amounts to balancing which kind of information has to be discarded and which kind has to be studied carefully by the algorithm. Please note that intra-class variation can also originate from variations of the conditions during the image formation process such as illumination or viewpoint changes.

- *Image data quality*: The quality of the data has also a significant impact on algorithm design. In industrial applications it is often possible to design the vision system such that it produces high-quality data: low noise, no background clutter (i.e. no "disturbing" information in the background area, e.g., because the objects are presented upon a uniform background), well-designed illumination, and so on. In contrast to that, e.g., in surveillance applications of crowded public places the algorithm has to cope with noisy and cluttered data (much background information), poor and changing illumination (weather conditions), significant lens distortion.

- *Matching strategy*: In order to recognize an object in a scene image a matching step has to be performed at some point in the algorithm flow, i.e., the object model (or parts of it) has to be aligned with the scene image content such that either a similarity measure between model and scene image is maximized or a dissimilarity measure is minimized, respectively. Some algorithms are trying to optimize the parameters of a transformation characterizing the relationship between the model and its projection onto the image plane of the scene image. Typically an affine transformation is used. Another approach is to perform matching by searching correspondences between features of the model and features extracted from the scene image.

- *Scope of data elements used in matching*: the data typically used by various methods in their matching step, e.g., for calculation of a similarity measure, can roughly be divided into three categories: raw intensity pixel values, low-level features such as edge data, and high level features such as lines or circular arcs. Even combinations of lines and/or cones are utilized. As far as edge data is concerned, the borders of an object are often indicated by rapid changes of gray value intensities, e.g., if a bright object is depicted upon a dark background. Locations of such high gray value gradients can be detected with the help of a suitable operator, e.g., the Canny edge detector [2] (see Appendix A for a short introduction) and are often referred to as "edge pixels" (sometimes also the term "edgels" can be found). In a subsequent step, these edge pixels can be grouped to the already mentioned high-level features, e.g., lines, which can be grouped again. Obviously, the scope of the data is enlarged when going from pixel intensities to high-level features, e.g., line groups. The enlarged scope of the latter leads to increased information content, which makes decisions based on this data more reliable. On the other hand, however, high-level features are more difficult to detect and therefore unstable.

Some object recognition methods are presented in the following. The focus thereby is on recognition in 2D-planes, i.e., in a single-scene image containing 2D-data. This scene image is assumed to be a gray scale image. A straightforward extension to color images is possible for some of the methods, but not considered in this book. For most of the schemes the object model also consists of 2D-data, i.e., the model data is planar.

In order to facilitate understanding, the presentation of each scheme is structured into sub-sections. At first, the main idea is presented. For many schemes the algorithm flow during model generation/training as well as recognition is summarized in separate sub-sections as well. Whenever I found it helpful I also included a graphical illustration of the algorithm flow during the recognition phase, where input, model, and intermediate data as well as the results are depicted in iconic representations if possible. Examples should clarify the proceeding of the methods, too. The "Rating" sub-section intends to give some information about strengths and constraints of the method helping to judge for which types of application it is suitable. Another presentation from a more formal point of view is given for most of the schemes by implementing them is pseudocode notation. Please note that the pseudocode implementation may be simplified, incomplete, or inefficient to some extent and may also differ slightly from the method proposed in the original articles in order to achieve better illustration and keep them easily understandable. The main purpose is to get a deeper insight into the algorithm structure, not to give a 100% correct description of all details.

The rest of the book is arranged as follows: Global approaches trying to model and find the object exclusively with global characteristics are presented in Chapter 2. The methods explained in Chapter 3 are representatives of transformation-search-based methods, where the object pose is determined by searching the space of transformations between model and image data. The pose is indicated by minima of some kind of distance metric between model and image. Some examples of geometry-based recognition methods trying to exploit geometric relations between different parts of the object by establishing 1:1 correspondences between model and image features are summarized in Chapter 4. Although the main focus of this book lies on 2D recognition, a collection of representatives of a special sub-category of the correspondence-based methods, which intend to recognize the object pose in 3D space with the help of just a single 2D image, is included in Chapter 5. An introduction to techniques dealing with flexible models in terms of deformable shapes can be found in Chapter 6. Descriptor-based methods trying to identify objects with the help of descriptors of mainly the object appearance in a local neighborhood around interest points (i.e., points where some kind of saliency was detected by a suitable detector) are presented in Chapter 7. Finally, a conclusion is given in Chapter 8.

Please note that some of the older methods presented in this book suffer from drawbacks which restrict their applicability to a limited range of applications.

However, due to their advantages they often remain attractive if they are used as building blocks of more sophisticated methods. In fact, many of the recently proposed schemes intend to combine several approaches (perhaps modified compared to the original proposition) in order to benefit from their advantages. Hence, I'm confident that all methods presented in this book still are of practical value.

References

1. Bennamoun, M., Mamic, G. and Bouzerdoum, A., *"Object Recognition: Fundamentals and Case Studies"*, Springer, Berlin, Heidelberg, New York, 2002, ISBN 1-852-33398-7
2. Canny, J.F., "A Computational Approach to Edge Detection", *IEEE Transactions on Pattern Analysis and Machine Intelligence,* 8(6):679–698, 1986
3. Chin, R.T. and Dyer, C.R., "Model-Based Recognition in Robot Vision", *ACM Computing Surveys,*18:67–108, 1986
4. Grimson, W.E., *"Object Recognition by Computer: The Role of Geometric Constraints"*, MIT Press, Cambridge, 1991, ISBN 0-262-57188-9
5. Jähne, B., *"Digital Image Processing"* (5th edition), Springer, Berlin, Heidelberg, New York, 2002, ISBN 3-540-67754-2
6. Mundy, J.L., "Object Recognition in the Geometric Era: A Retrospective", *Toward Category-Level Object Recognition, Vol. 4170 of Lecture Notes In Computer Science*, 3–28, 2006
7. Pinz, A., "Object Categorization", *Foundations and Trends in Computer Graphics and Vision*, 1(4):255–353, 2005
8. Ponce, J., Herbert, M., Schmid, C. and Zisserman, A., *"Toward Category-Level Object Recognition"*, Springer, Berlin, Heidelberg, New York, 2007, ISBN 3-540-68794-7
9. Pope, A.R., "Model-Based Object Recognition: A Survey of Recent Research", *University of British Columbia Technical Report 94–04*, 1994
10. Roth, P.M. and Winter, M., "Survey of Appearance-based Methods for Object Recognition", *Technical Report ICG-TR-01/08 TU Graz*, 2008
11. Steger, C., Ulrich, M. and Wiedemann, C., *"Machine Vision Algorithms and Applications"*, Wiley VCH, Weinheim, 2007, ISBN 978-3-527-40734-7
12. Suetens, P., Fua, P. and Hanson, A.: "Computational Strategies for Object Recognition", *ACM Computing Surveys*, 24:5–61, 1992
13. Zhang, D. and Lu, G., "Review of Shape Representation and Description Techniques", *Pattern Recognition,*37:1–19, 2004

Chapter 2
Global Methods

Abstract Most of the early approaches to object recognition rely on a global object model. In this context "global" means that the model represents the object to be recognized as a whole, e.g., by one data set containing several global characteristics of the object like area, perimeter, and so on. Some typical algorithms sharing this object representation are presented in this chapter. A straightforward approach is to use an example image of the model to be recognized (also called template) and to detect the object by correlating the content of a scene image with the template. Due to its simplicity, such a proceeding is easy to implement, but unfortunately also has several drawbacks. Over the years many variations aiming at overcoming these limitations have been proposed and some of them are also presented. Another possibility to perform global object recognition is to derive a set of global features from the raw intensity image first (e.g., moments of different order) and to evaluate scene images by comparing their feature vector to the one of the model. Finally, the principal component analysis is presented as a way of explicitly considering expected variations of the object to be recognized in its model: this is promising because individual instances of the same object class can differ in size, brightness/color, etc., which can lead to a reduced similarity value if comparison is performed with only one template.

2.1 2D Correlation

2.1.1 Basic Approach

2.1.1.1 Main Idea

Perhaps the most straightforward approach to object recognition is 2D cross correlation of a scene image with a prototype representation of the object to be found. Here, the model consists of a so-called template image, which is a prototype representation of the gray value appearance of the object. Model generation is done in a training phase prior to the recognition process. For example, the template image is set to a reference image of the object to be found. 2D correlation is an example of an appearance-based scheme, as the model exclusively depends on the (intensity) appearance of the area covered by the "prototype object" in the training image.

The recognition task is then to find the accurate position of the object in a scene image as well as to decide whether the scene image contains an instance of the model at all. This can be achieved with the help of evaluating a 2D cross correlation function: the template is moved pixel by pixel to every possible position in the scene image and a normalized cross correlation (NCC) coefficient ρ representing the degree of similarity between the image intensities (gray values) is calculated at each position:

$$\rho(a,b) = \frac{\sum\limits_{x=0}^{W}\sum\limits_{y=0}^{H}\left(I_S\left(x+a,y+b\right)-\overline{I_S}\right)\cdot\left(I_T\left(x,y\right)-\overline{I_T}\right)}{\sqrt{\sum\limits_{x=0}^{W}\sum\limits_{y=0}^{H}\left(I_S\left(x+a,y+b\right)-\overline{I_S}\right)^2\cdot\sum\limits_{x=0}^{W}\sum\limits_{y=0}^{H}\left(I_T\left(x,y\right)-\overline{I_T}\right)^2}} \tag{2.1}$$

where $\rho(a,b)$ is the normalized cross correlation coefficient at displacement $[a,b]$ between scene image and template. $I_S(x,y)$ and $I_T(x,y)$ denote the intensity of the scene image and template at position $[x,y]$, $\overline{I_S}$, and $\overline{I_T}$ their mean and W and H the width and the height of the template image. Because the denominator serves as a normalization term ρ can range from -1 to 1. High-positive values of ρ indicate that the scene image and template are very similar, a value of 0 that their contents are uncorrelated, and, finally, negative values are evidence of inverse contents.

As a result of the correlation process a 2D function is available. Every local maximum of this matching function indicates a possible occurrence of the object to be found. If the value of the maximum exceeds a certain threshold value t, a valid object instance is found. Its position is defined by the position of the maximum.

The whole process is illustrated by a schematic example in Fig. 2.1: There, a 3×3 template showing a cross (in green, cf. lower left part) is shifted over an image of 8×8 pixel size. At each position, the value of the cross-correlation coefficient is calculated and these values are collected in a 2D matching function (here of size 6×6, see right part. Bright pixels indicate high values). The start position is the upper left corner; the template is first shifted from left to right, then one line down, then from left to right again, and so on until the bottom right image corner is reached. The brightest pixel in the matching function indicates the cross position.

In its original form correlation is used to accurately find the $[x,y]$-location of a given object. It can be easily extended, though, to a classification scheme by calculating different cross correlation coefficients ρ_i; $i \in \{1,..,N\}$ for multiple templates (one coefficient for each template). Each of the templates represents a specific object class i. Classification is achieved by evaluating which template led to the highest $\rho_{i,\max}$. In this context i is often called a "class label".

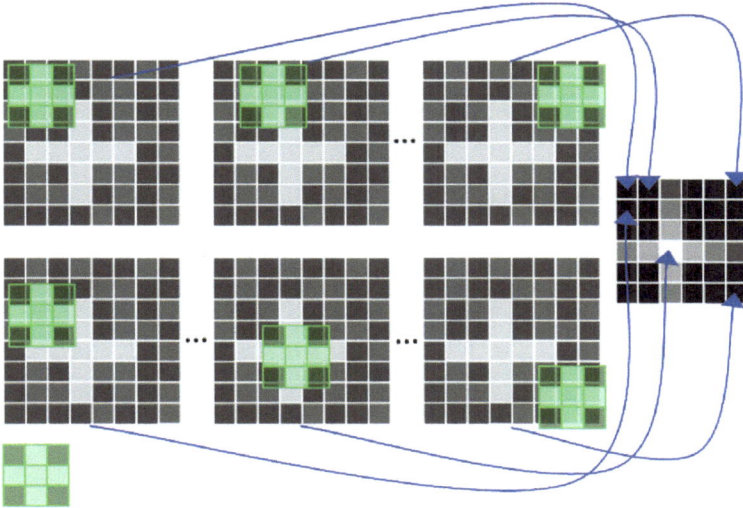

Fig. 2.1 Illustration of the "movement" of a template (*green*) across an example image during the calculation process of a 2D matching function

2.1.1.2   Example

Figure 2.2 depicts the basic algorithm flow for an example application where a toy nurse has to be located in a scene image with several more or less similar objects. A matching function (right, bright values indicate high ρ) is calculated by correlating a scene image (left) with a template (top). For better illustration all negative values of ρ have been set to 0. The matching function contains several local maxima, which are indicated by bright spots. Please note that objects which are not very similar to the template lead to considerable high maxima, too (e.g., the small figure located bottom center). This means that the method is not very discriminative and therefore runs into problems if it has to distinguish between quite similar objects.

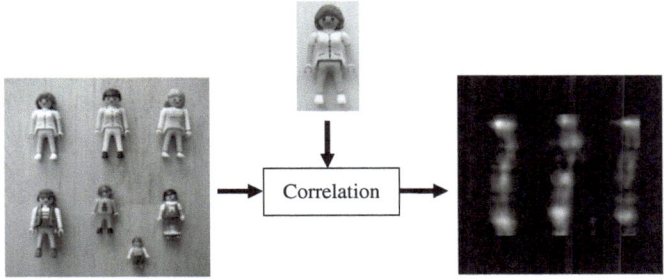

Fig. 2.2 Basic proceeding of cross correlation

2.1.1.3 Pseudocode

```
function findAllObjectLocationsNCC (in Image I, in Template T,
in threshold t, out position list p)

// calculate matching function
for b = 1 to height(I)
   for a = 1 to width(I)
      if T is completely inside I at position (a,b) then
         calculate NCC coefficient ρ(a,b,I,T) (Equation 2.1)
      else
         ρ(a,b) ← 0
      end if
   next
next

// determine all valid object positions
find all local maxima in ρ(a,b)
for i = 1 to number of local maxima
   if ρi(a,b) ≥ t then
      append position [a,b] to p
   end if
next
```

2.1.1.4 Rating

This simple method has the advantage to be straightforward and therefore easy to implement. Additionally it is generic, i.e., the same procedure can be applied to any kind of object (at least in principle); there exist no restrictions about the appearance of the object.

Unfortunately, there are several drawbacks. First, the correlation coefficient decreases significantly when the object contained in the scene image is a rotated or scaled version of the model, i.e., the method is not invariant to rotation and scale.

Second, the method is only robust with respect to linear illumination changes: The denominator of Equation (2.1) is a normalization term making ρ insensitive to linear scaling of contrast; brightness offsets are dealt with by subtracting the mean image intensity. However, often nonlinear illumination changes occur such as a change of illumination direction or saturation of the intensity values.

Additionally, the method is sensitive to clutter and occlusion: as only one global similarity value ρ is calculated, it is very difficult to distinguish if low maxima values of ρ originate from a mismatch because the searched object is not present in the scene image (but perhaps a fairly similar object) or from variations caused by nonlinear illumination changes, occlusion, and so on.

To put it in other words, cross correlation does not have much discriminative power, i.e., the difference between the values of ρ at valid object positions and some mismatch positions tends to be rather small (for example, the matching function displayed in Fig. 2.2 reveals that the upper left and a lower middle object lead to similar correlation coefficients, but the upper left object clearly is more similar to the template).

Furthermore the strategy is not advisable for classification tasks if the number of object classes is rather large, as the whole process of shifting the template during calculation of the matching function has to be repeated for each class, which results in long execution times.

2.1.2 Variants

In order to overcome the drawbacks, several modifications of the scheme are possible. For example, in order to account for scale and rotation, the correlation coefficient can also be calculated with scaled and rotated versions of the template. Please note, however, that this involves a significant increase in computational complexity because then several coefficient calculations with scaled and/or rotated template versions have to be done at every $[x, y]$-position. This proceeding clearly is inefficient; a more efficient approach using a so-called principal component analysis is presented later on. Some other variations of the standard correlation scheme aiming at increasing robustness or accelerating the method are presented in the next sections.

2.1.2.1 Variant 1: Preprocessing

Instead of the original intensity image it is possible to use a gradient image for correlation: The images of the training as well as the recognition phase are preprocessed by applying an edge detection filter (e.g., the canny filter [3], see also Appendix A); correlation is then performed with the filtered images (cf. Fig. 2.3).

This stems from the observation that in many cases characteristic information about the object is located in the outer shape or silhouette of the 3D object resulting in rapid changes of the gray values in the image plane. The Canny filter responds to these changes by detecting the gray value edges in the images. The main advantage

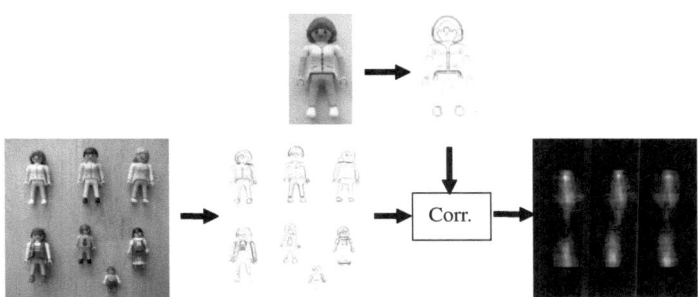

Fig. 2.3 Basic proceeding of cross correlation with preprocessing

is that discriminative power is enhanced as now relatively thin edge areas must overlap in order to achieve high values of ρ. As a consequence the correlation maxima are now sharper, which leads to an increased accuracy of position determination. Robustness with respect to nonlinear illumination changes is increased significantly, too.

Furthermore, partly occluded objects can be recognized up to some point as ρ should reach sufficiently high values when the thin edges of the non-occluded parts overlap. However, if heavy occlusion is expected better methods exist, as we will see later on.

Example

The algorithm flow can be seen in Fig. 2.3. Compared to the standard scheme, the gradient magnitudes (here, black pixels indicate high values) of scene image and template are derived from the intensity images prior to matching function calculation. Negative matching function values are again set to 0. The maxima are a bit sharper compared to the standard method.

Pseudocode

```
function findAllObjectLocationsGradientNCC (in Image I, in
Template T, in threshold t, out position list p)

// calculate gradient images
I_G ← gradient magnitude of I
T_G ← gradient magnitude of T

// calculate matching function
for b = 1 to height(I_G)
  for a = 1 to width(I_G)
     if T_G is completely inside I_G at position (a,b) then
        calculate NCC coefficient ρ(a,b,I_G,T_G) (Equation 2.1)
     else
        ρ(a,b) ← 0
     end if
  next
next

// determine all valid object positions
find all local maxima in ρ(a,b)
for i = 1 to number of local maxima
  if ρ_i(a,b) ≥ t then
     append position [a,b] to p
  end if
next
```

2.1.2.2   Variant 2: Subsampling/Image Pyramids

A significant speedup can be achieved by the usage of so-called *image pyramids* (see, e.g., Ballard and Brown [1], a book which also gives an excellent introduction to and overview of many aspects of computer vision). The bottom level 0 of the pyramid consists of the original image whereas the higher levels are built by subsampling or averaging the intensity values of adjacent pixels of the level below. Therefore at each level the image size is reduced (see Fig. 2.4). Correlation initially takes place in a high level of the pyramid generating some hypotheses about coarse object locations. Due to the reduced size this is much faster than at level 0. These hypotheses are verified in lower levels. Based on the verification they can be rejected or refined. Eventually accurate matching results are available. During verification only a small neighborhood around the coarse position estimate has to be examined. This proceeding results in increased speed but comparable accuracy compared to the standard scheme.

The main advantage of such a technique is that considerable parts of the image can be sorted out very quickly at high levels and need not to be processed at lower

Fig. 2.4 Example of an image pyramid consisting of five levels

levels. With the help of this speedup, it is more feasible to check rotated or scaled versions of the template, too.

2.1.3 Phase-Only Correlation (POC)

Another modification is the so-called *phase-only correlation* (POC). This technique is commonly used in the field of image registration (i.e., the estimation of parameters of a transformation between two images in order to achieve congruence between them), but can also be used for object recognition (cf. [9], where POC is used by Miyazawa et al. for iris recognition).

In POC, correlation is not performed in the spatial domain (where image data is represented in terms of gray values depending on x and y position) as described above. Instead, the signal is Fourier transformed instead (see e.g. [13]).

In the Fourier domain, an image $I(x, y)$ is represented by a complex signal: $F_I = A_I(\omega_1, \omega_2) \cdot e^{\theta_I(\omega_1, \omega_2)}$ with amplitude and phase component. The amplitude part $A_I(\omega_1, \omega_2)$contains information about how much of the signal is represented by the frequency combination (ω_1, ω_2), whereas the phase part $e^{\theta_I(\omega_1, \omega_2)}$ contains (the desired) information where it is located. The cross spectrum $R(\omega_1, \omega_2)$ of two images (here: scene image $S(x, y)$ and template image $T(x, y)$) is given by

$$R(\omega_1, \omega_2) = A_S(\omega_1, \omega_2) \cdot A_T(\omega_1, \omega_2) \cdot e^{\theta(\omega_1, \omega_2)} \tag{2.2}$$

$$\text{with } \theta(\omega_1, \omega_2) = \theta_S(\omega_1, \omega_2) - \theta_T(\omega_1, \omega_2) \tag{2.3}$$

where $\theta(\omega_1, \omega_2)$ denotes the phase difference of the two spectra. Using the phase difference only and performing back transformation to the spatial domain reveals the POC function. To this end, the normalized cross spectrum

$$\hat{R}(\omega_1, \omega_2) = \frac{F_S(\omega_1, \omega_2) \cdot \overline{F_T(\omega_1, \omega_2)}}{\left| F_S(\omega_1, \omega_2) \cdot \overline{F_T(\omega_1, \omega_2)} \right|} = e^{\theta(\omega_1, \omega_2)} \tag{2.4}$$

(with $\overline{F_T}$ being the complex conjugate of F_T) is calculated and the real part of its 2D inverse Fourier transform $\hat{r}(x, y)$ is the desired POC function. An outline of the algorithm flow can be seen in the "Example" subsection.

The POC function is characterized by a sharp maximum defining the x and y displacement between the two images (see Fig. 2.5). The sharpness of the maximum allows for a more accurate translation estimation compared to standard correlation. Experimental results (with some modifications aiming at further increasing accuracy) are given in [13], where Takita et al. show that the estimation error can fall below 1/100th of a pixel. In [13] it is also outlined how POC can be used to perform rotation and scaling estimation.

Fig. 2.5 Depicting 3D plots of the correlation functions of the toy nurse example. A cross correlation function based on intensity values between a template and a scene image is shown in the *left* part, whereas the POC function of the same scene is shown on the *right*. The maxima of the POC function are much sharper

2.1.3.1 Example

The algorithm flow illustrated with our example application can be seen in Fig. 2.6. Please note that in general, the size of the template differs from the scene image size. In order to obtain equally sized FFTs (fast Fourier transforms), the template image can be padded (filled with zeros up to the scene image size) prior to FFT. For illustrative purposes all images in Fourier domain show the magnitude of the Fourier spectrum. Actually, the signal is represented by magnitude and phase component in Fourier domain (indicated by a second image in Fig. 2.6). The POC function, which is the real part of the back-transformed cross spectrum (IFFT – inverse FFT), is very sharp (cf. Fig. 2.5 for a 3D view) and has only two dominant local maxima which are so sharp that they are barely visible here (marked red).

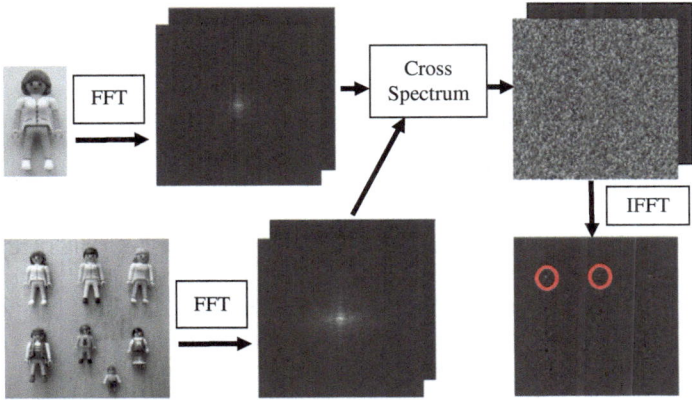

Fig. 2.6 Basic proceeding of phase-only correlation (POC)

2.1.3.2 Pseudocode

```
function findAllObjectLocationsPOC (in Image S, in Template
T, in threshold t, out position list p)

// calculate fourier transforms
F_S ← FFT of S // two components: real and imaginary part
F_T ← FFT of T // two components: real and imaginary part

// POC function
calculate cross spectrum R̂(ω₁,ω₂,F_S,F_T) (Equation 2.4)
r̂(x,y) ← IFFT of R̂(ω₁,ω₂)

// determine all valid object positions
find all local maxima in r̂(x,y)
for i = 1 to number of local maxima
    if r̂_i(x,y) ≥ t then
        append position [x,y] to p
    end if
next
```

2.1.4 Shape-Based Matching

2.1.4.1 Main Idea

Steger [12] suggests another gradient-based correlation approach called "shape-based matching". Instead of using gradient magnitudes, the similarity measure is based on gradient orientation information: an image region is considered similar to a template if the gradient orientations of many pixels match well. The similarity measure s at position $[a, b]$ is defined as

$$s(a,b) = \frac{1}{W \cdot H} \sum_{x=0}^{W} \sum_{y=0}^{H} \frac{\langle \mathbf{d}_S(x+a,y+b), \mathbf{d}_T(x,y) \rangle}{\|\mathbf{d}_S(x+a,y+b)\| \cdot \|\mathbf{d}_T(x,y)\|} \qquad (2.5)$$

where the operator $\langle \cdot \rangle$ defines the dot product of two vectors. $\mathbf{d}_S$ and $\mathbf{d}_T$ are the gradient vectors of a pixel of the scene image and the template, respectively (consisting of the gradients in x- and y-direction). The dot product yields high values if $\mathbf{d}_S$ and $\mathbf{d}_T$ point in similar directions. The denominator of the sum defines the product of the magnitudes of the gradient vectors (denoted by $\|\cdot\|$) and serves as a regularization term in order in improve illumination invariance.

The position of an object can be found if the template is shifted over the entire image as explained and the local maxima of the matching function $s(a, b)$ are extracted (see Fig. 2.7 for an example).

Often a threshold s_{min} is defined which has to be exceeded if a local maximum shall be considered as a valid object position. If more parameters than translation are to be determined, transformed versions of the gradient vectors $t(\mathbf{d}_T)$ have to be used (see Chapter 3 for information about some types of transformation). As a

Fig. 2.7 Basic proceeding of shape-based matching

consequence, s has to be calculated several times at each displacement $[a, b]$ (for multiple transformation parameters t).

In order to speed up the computation, Steger [12] employs a hierarchical search strategy where pyramids containing the gradient information are built. Hypotheses are detected at coarse positions in high pyramid levels, which can be scanned quickly, and are refined or rejected with the help of the lower levels of the pyramid.

Additionally, the similarity measure s doesn't have to be calculated completely for many positions if a threshold s_{min} is given: very often it is evident that s_{min} cannot be reached any longer after considering just a small fraction of the pixels which are covered by the template. Hence, the calculation of $s(a, b)$ can be aborted immediately for a specific displacement $[a, b]$ after computing just a part of the sum of Equation (2.5).

2.1.4.2 Example

Once again the toy nurse example illustrates the mode of operation, in this case for shape-based matching (see Fig. 2.7). The matching function, which is based on the dot product $\langle \cdot \rangle$ of the gradient vectors, reflects the similarity of the gradient orientations which are shown right to template and scene image in Fig. 2.7, respectively. The orientation is coded by gray values. The maxima are considerably sharper compared to the standard method. Please note also the increased discriminative power of the method: the maxima in the bottom part of the matching functions are lower compared to the intensity correlation example.

2.1.4.3 Pseudocode

```
function findAllObjectLocationsShapeBasedMatching (in Image
S, in Template T, in threshold t, out position list p)

// calculate gradient images
d_S ← gradient of S     // two components: x and y
d_T ← gradient of T     // two components: x and y
```

```
// calculate matching function
for b = 1 to height(d_S)
    for a = 1 to width(d_S)
        if d_T is completely inside d_S at position (a,b) then
            calc. similarity measure s(a,b,d_S,d_T)  (Equation 2.5)
        else
            s(a,b) ← 0
        end if
    next
next

// determine all valid object positions
find all local maxima in s(a,b)
for i = 1 to number of local maxima
    if s_i(a,b) ≥ t then
        append position [a,b] to p
    end if
next
```

2.1.4.4 Rating

Compared to the correlation of intensity values, shape-based matching shows increased robustness to occlusion and clutter. Missing parts of the object lead to uncorrelated gradient directions in most cases, which in total contribute little to the sum of Equation (2.5). Please note that in the presence of occlusion or clutter usually gradient orientation information is much more uncorrelated compared to intensity values, which explains the increased robustness. An additional improvement can be done if only pixels are considered where the norm $\|\mathbf{d}_S\|$ is above a pre-defined threshold.

Moreover, the fact that the dot product is unaffected by gradient magnitudes to a high extent leads to a better robustness with respect to illumination changes. The proposed speedup makes the method very fast in spite of still being a brute-force approach. A comparative study by Ulrich and Steger [15] showed that shape-based matching achieves comparable results or even outperforms other methods which are widely used in industrial applications. A commercial product adopting this search strategy is the HALCON® library of MVTec Software GmbH, which offers a great number of fast and powerful tools for industrial image processing.

2.1.5 Comparison

In the following, the matching functions for the toy nurse example application used in the previous sections are shown again side by side in order to allow for a comparison. Intensity, gradient magnitude, gradient orientation (where all negative correlation values are set to zero), and phase-only correlation matching functions are shown. All matching functions are calculated with identical template and scene image. For each of the methods, only translation of the template is considered when calculating the matching function. Please note that the figure in the upper right part of the scene image is slightly rotated and therefore doesn't achieve very high similarity values for all correlation methods (Table 2.1).

Table 2.1   Example of correlation performance

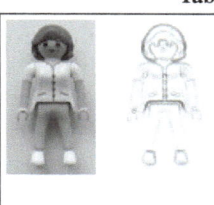  

Template image of a toy (*left*) and magnitude of its gray value gradient (*right*; high val. = black)	Scene image containing seven toys with different appearance and particularly size	Magnitude of gray value gradient of the scene image (high-gradient values are shown in black)

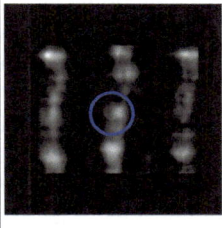 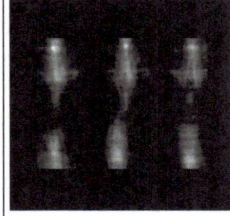

Correlation result when using raw gray values: flat maxima, low discriminative power. Observe that an areas exists where ρ is high, but where no object present (one is marked *blue*)	Correlation result when using gradient magnitudes: maxima are sharper and more distinctive compared to the correlation of intensities

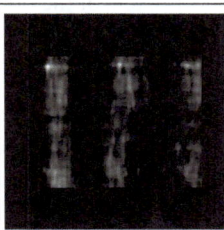 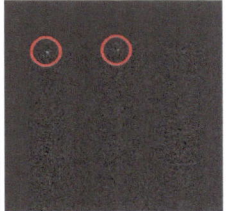

Correlation result using gradient orientation information: again, the maxima are more distinct compared to intensity or gradient magnitude correlation	Phase-only correlation; very sharp maxima (marked *red*), very distinctive: only the two upper *left* objects are similar enough to the template

2.2 Global Feature Vectors

Another possibility to model object properties are so-called *global feature vectors*. Each element of the vector describes a global characteristic of the object. Over the years many proposals which characteristics to use have been made; some examples to be mentioned are area (e.g., the number of pixels covered by the object), perimeter, circularity (perimeter^2/area), moments, mean gray value, Fourier descriptors, etc. Note however, that these vectors are suited for classifying objects, but in general not for computing accurate locations. Niblack et al. incorporated several features into the QBIC system (Query Image by Content) [11], which retrieves all images considered to be similar to a query image from a large database. After a short description of the basic proceeding, two types of features, namely moments and Fourier descriptors, are presented in more detail.

2.2.1 Main Idea

If we make a geometrical interpretation, each feature vector representing a specific object defines a point in a feature space. Each coordinate of the feature space corresponds to one element of the feature vector. In a training phase feature vectors of objects with known class label are extracted. Their corresponding points in feature space should build clusters (one cluster for each class) if the objects of the same class are similar enough. Hence, a query object can be classified by deciding to which cluster it belongs, based on its feature vector.

The selection of the features (which features should be chosen for a good object representation?) has to aim at maximizing the distinctiveness between different object classes (maximize the distance between the clusters) and minimizing the variance of the feature vectors of objects of the same class (minimize the "size" of the clusters). In other words, the feature vector has to maintain enough information (or the "right" part of it) in order to keep the ability to uniquely identify the object class, but, on the other hand, also discard information in order to become insensitive to variations between objects of the same class. Therefore the dimensionality of the feature vector is usually chosen much lower than the number of pixels of the objects, but mustn't be reduced too far.

2.2.2 Classification

During recognition classification takes place in feature space. Over the years many propositions of classification methods have been made (see e.g. Duda et al. [6] for an overview, a short introduction is also given in Appendix B). A basic and easy to implement scheme used for the classification of global feature vectors is nearest neighbor classification, where a feature vector, which was derived from an input image, is compared to feature vectors of known class type which were calculated during a training stage. The object is classified based on the class labels of the most similar training vectors (the nearest neighbors, see Appendix B).

2.2.3 Rating

Compared to correlation, classification in the feature space typically is faster. The object representation is very compact, as usually only a few feature values are calculated. Additionally, it is possible to account for some desired invariance in the design phase of the feature vector by an appropriate choice of the features, e.g., area and perimeter are invariant to rotation, the quotient thereof also to scaling.

On the other hand, this scheme typically requires a segmentation of the object from the background in a preprocessing stage. Especially in the presence of background clutter this might be impossible or at least error prone. As far as occlusion is concerned, usually it has the undesirable property of influencing every global quantity and hence all elements of the global feature vector. Furthermore, the information of only a few global features often not suffices to distinctively characterize "complex" objects exhibiting detailed surface structure.

Nevertheless, due to its speed this principle can be attractive for some industrial applications where the image acquisition process can be influenced in order to ease the task of segmentation ("good data": uniform background, proper illumination) and the objects are "simple." Additionally, feature vectors can be used for a quick pre-classification followed by a more sophisticated scheme.

2.2.4 Moments

2.2.4.1 Main Idea

Simple objects can often be characterized and classified with the help of region or gray value moments. Region moments are derived from binary images. In order to use them for object recognition, a gray value image has to be transformed to a binary image prior to moment calculation, e.g., with the help of thresholding. Its simplest form is fixed-value thresholding: all pixels with gray value equal to or above a threshold t are considered as "object" pixels, all pixels with gray value below the threshold are considered as "background."

The region moments m_{pq} of order $p + q$ are defined as

$$m_{pq} = \sum_{(x,y)\in R} x^p y^q \tag{2.6}$$

where the sum is taken over all "object pixels," which are defined by the region R. Observe that low-order moments have a physical interpretation. The moment m_{00}, for example, defines the area of the region. In order to calculate moments as characteristic features of objects independent of their size, normalized moments n_{pq} are utilized. They are given by

$$n_{pq} = \frac{1}{m_{00}} \cdot \sum_{(x,y)\in R} x^p y^q \tag{2.7}$$

The first-order normalized moments n_{10} and n_{01} define the center of gravity of the object, which can be interpreted as the position of the object. In most applications requiring a classification of objects, the moments should be independent of the object position. This can be achieved by calculating the moments relative to their center of gravity yielding the central moments μ_{pq}:

$$\mu_{pq} = \frac{1}{m_{00}} \cdot \sum_{(x,y)\in R} (x - n_{10})^p (y - n_{01})^q \tag{2.8}$$

The second-order central moments are of special interest as they help to define the dimensions and orientation of the object. In order to achieve this we approximate the object region by an ellipse featuring moments of order 1 and 2 which are identical to the moments of the object region. An ellipse is defined by five parameters which can be derived form the moments. Namely these parameters are the center of gravity defined by n_{10} and n_{01}, the major and minor axes a and b as well as the orientation ϕ. They are given by

$$a = \sqrt{2\left(\mu_{20} + \mu_{02} + \sqrt{(\mu_{20} - \mu_{02})^2 + 4\mu_{11}^2}\right)} \tag{2.9}$$

$$b = \sqrt{2\left(\mu_{20} + \mu_{02} - \sqrt{(\mu_{20} - \mu_{02})^2 + 4\mu_{11}^2}\right)} \tag{2.10}$$

$$\phi = -\frac{1}{2}\arctan\frac{2\mu_{11}}{\mu_{02} - \mu_{20}} \tag{2.11}$$

Another feature which is often used is called anisometry and is defined by a/b. The anisometry reveals the degree of elongatedness of a region.

The extension of region moments to their gray value moment counterparts is straightforward: basically, each term of the sums presented above is weighted by the gray value $I(x, y)$ of the current pixel $[x, y]$, e.g., central gray value moments μ_{00}^g are defined by

$$\mu_{00}^g = \frac{1}{m_{00}^g} \cdot \sum_{(x,y)\in R} (x - n_{10}^g)^p (y - n_{01}^g)^q \cdot I(x, y) \tag{2.12}$$

2.2.4.2 Example

Over the years, there have been many proposals for the usage of moments in object recognition (see e.g. the article of Flusser and Suk [8]). Observe that mainly low-order moments are used for recognition, as high-order moments lack of physical interpretation and are sensitive to noise. In the following, an illustrative example, where the anisometry and some low-order moments are calculated for printed characters, is given (see Table 2.2).

Table 2.2 Anisometry and low-order moments for some printed characters

Character	A	I	G	M	Y	P
Anisom.	1.09	3.21	1.05	1.24	1.27	1.40
μ_{11}	1.46	0	−20.5	−0.148	−0.176	113
μ_{20}	368	47.9	481	716	287	331
μ_{02}	444	494	507	465	460	410
μ_{22}	164,784	23,670	168,234	351,650	134,691	113,767

Some characters show their distinctive properties in some of the calculated values, for example, the anisometry of the "I" is significantly higher compared to the other characters. As far as the moment μ_{11} is concerned, the values for "P" and "G" differ from the other characters due to their lack of symmetry. On the other hand, however, some moments don't contain much information, e.g., the values of μ_{02} are similar for all objects. Classification could be done by integrating all values into a vector followed by a suitable multidimensional classification scheme. It should be noted, however, that the moments calculated in this example barely generate enough discriminative information for a robust optical character recognition (OCR) of the entire alphabet, especially if handwritten characters are to be recognized. More sophisticated approaches exist for OCR, but are beyond our scope here.

Moments can also be combined in such a way that the resulting value is invariant with respect to certain coordinate transforms like translation, rotation, or scaling, which is a very desirable property. An example of these so-called moment invariants is given later in this book (in Chapter 7).

2.2.5 Fourier Descriptors

2.2.5.1 Main Idea

Instead of using the original image representation in the spatial domain, feature values can also be derived after applying a Fourier transformation, i.e., in the spectral domain. The feature vector calculated from a data representation in the transformed domain, which is called *fourier descriptor*, is considered to be more robust with respect to noise or minor boundary modifications. This approach is widely used in literature (see, e.g., [17] for an overview) and shall be illustrated with the help of the following example.

2.2.5.2 Example

So-called fiducials of PCBs, which consist of simple geometric forms (e.g., circle, diamond, cross, double cross, or rectangle; cf. Table 2.3), are used for accurate positioning of PCBs.

Table 2.3 Examples of different fiducial shapes

The task considered here is to extract the geometry of the fiducials in an automatic manner. To this end, a classification of its shape has to be performed. This shape classification task shall be solved with Fourier descriptors; the process is visualized in detail in Fig. 2.8.

First, an image of the object, which is selected by the user and exclusively contains the fiducial to be classified, is segmented from the background. Next, the contour points of the segmented area (e.g., all pixels having a direct neighbor which is not part of the segmented object area) and their distance to the object center are determined.

When scanning the contour counterclockwise, a "distance function" consisting of the progression of the pixel distances to the object center can be built (also referred to as "centroid distance function" in literature). In order to compare structures of different size, this function is resampled to a fixed length, e.g., 128 values. Such a centroid distance function is an example of the more general class of so-called signatures, where the 2D information about the object contour is summarized in a 1D function. For each geometric form, the fixed-length distance function can be regarded as a distinctive feature vector.

In order to increase performance, this vector is transformed to Fourier space. This Fourier description of the object contour (cf., e.g., [4] or [16]) is a very

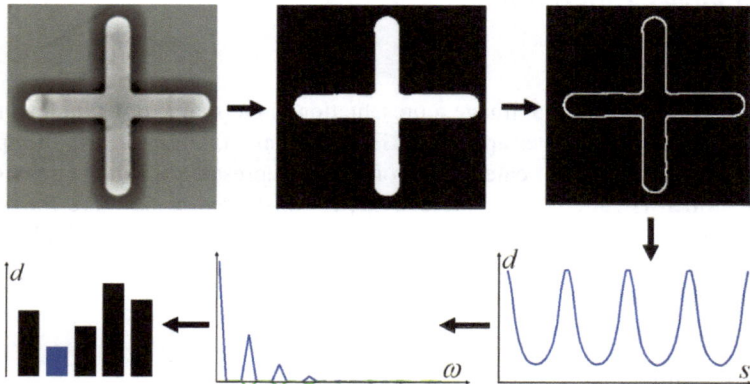

Fig. 2.8 Example of feature vector classification: locally intensity normalized image → segmented object → object boundary → centroid distance function → Fourier-transformed centroid distance function → classification vector (smallest distance marked *blue*)

compact representation of the data. Just a few Fourier coefficients are sufficient for a distinctive description if we deal with "simple" objects. Classification is done by nearest-neighbor searching in Fourier space, i.e., calculating the Euclidean distance of the Fourier-transformed feature vector of a scene object to the known Fourier-transformed feature vectors of the prototypes. Each prototype represents one geometric form (circle, cross, etc.).

2.2.5.3 Modifications

As an alternative, a wavelet representation of the object contour can also be used (e.g., [5]). Compared to Fourier descriptors, wavelet descriptors have the advantage of containing multi-resolution information in both the spatial and the frequency domain. This involves, however, that matching is extended from 1D (which is very fast) to a more time-consuming 2D matching. Fourier descriptors can be computed and matched fast and have the desirable property to incorporate global and local information. If the number of coefficients is chosen sufficiently large, Fourier descriptors can overcome the disadvantage of a rather weak discrimination ability, which is a common problem of global feature vectors such as moments.

The characterization of objects by means of Fourier descriptors is not restricted to the object boundary (as it is the case with the centroid distance function). Fourier descriptors can also be derived from the region covered by the object. A calculation based on regions is advantageous if characteristic information of the object is not restricted to the boundary. The descriptor representation is more robust to boundary variations if regional information is considered in such cases.

A straightforward approach would be to calculate the descriptors from the 2D Fourier transform of the intensity image showing an object. However, this is not recommendable as neither rotation invariance nor compactness can be achieved in that case. In order to overcome these limitations, Zhang and Lu [17] suggest the derivation of so-called "generic Fourier descriptors" from a modified polar 2D Fourier transform: to this end, a circular region of the original intensity image is sampled at polar coordinates r and θ and can be re-plotted as a rectangular image in the $[r, \theta]$-plane. The $[r, \theta]$-representation is then subject to a conventional 2D Fourier transform. Figure 2.9 illustrates the principle.

The Fourier descriptors can be derived by sampling the thus obtained Fourier spectrum (which is the amplitude derived from the real and imaginary part of the transformed signal); see [17] for details. They stated that as few as 36 elements are sufficient for a compact and distinctive representation. For speed reasons, comparison of objects is done by evaluating the so-called city block distance of descriptor vectors instead of the Euclidean distance, where simply the differences between the two values of elements with identical index are summed up.

Without going into details, let's briefly discuss the properties of the modified polar 2D Fourier transform: First, a rotation of the object in Cartesian space results in circular shift in polar space. This circular shift does not change the Fourier spectrum and hence rotation invariance of the descriptor can be achieved in a natural way. Moreover, since the gray value image is a real-valued function, its Fourier

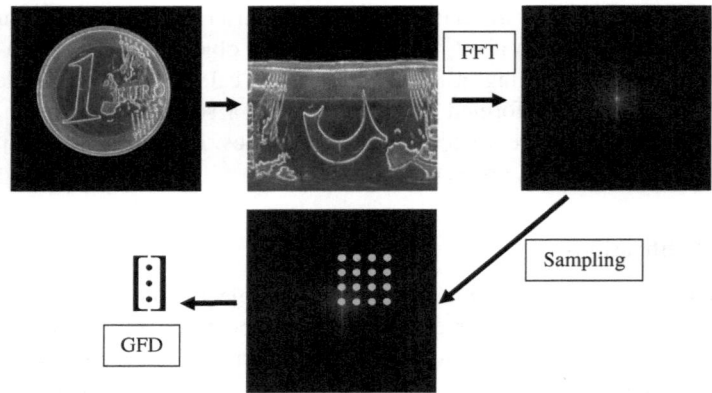

Fig. 2.9 Illustrative example for a calculation of generic Fourier descriptors with a 1 Euro coin: Original image: 1 Euro coin → Circular image region re-plotted after polar transformation → Magnitude of Fourier transformed signal of the polar image → Sampling → Descriptor Calculation

transform is circularly symmetric. Therefore, only one quarter of the spectrum function is needed to describe the object. That's the reason why the light blue sampling points in Fig. 2.9 are all located in the upper left quadrant of the spectrum.

Compared to the Fourier spectra directly calculated from an $[x, y]$-representation, it can be observed that polar Fourier spectra are more concentrated around the origin. This is a very desirable property, because for efficient object representation, the number of descriptor features which are selected to describe the object should be as small as possible. The compact representation allows a fast comparison of objects, which makes the method applicable in online retrieval applications. Despite still being a global scheme, the method can also cope with occlusion to some extent. However, a proper segmentation from the background is still necessary.

2.2.5.4 Pseudocode

```
function  classifyObjectWithGFD  (in    Image I,   in    model
descriptors dM,i, in distance threshold t, out classification
result c)

// calculate generic fourier descriptor of I
perform background subtraction, if necessary: only the object
has to be shown in the image
IP ← polar transform of I
FI ← FFT of IP // two components: real and imaginary part
AI ← √Re{FI}² + Im{FI}² // power spectrum
a ← 0
for m = 0 to M step s
   for n = 0 to N step s
```

```
                  derive GDF element d_I (a) from A_I (m, n)
                  a ← a + 1
            next
      next

      // calculation of similarity to classes of model database
      for i = 1 to number of models
            dist (i) ← city block distance between d_I and d_{M,i}
      next
      if min (dist (i)) ≤ t then
            c ← index of min
      else
            c ← -1      // none of the models is similar enough
      end if
```

2.3 Principal Component Analysis (PCA)

2.3.1 Main Idea

The principal component analysis (PCA) aims at transforming the gray value object appearance into a more advantageous representation. According to Murase and Nayar [10], the appearance of an object in an image depends on the object shape, its reflectance properties, the object pose, and the illumination conditions. While the former two are rather fixed for rigid objects, the latter two can vary considerably. One way to take account for these variances is to concentrate on rather stable features, e.g., focus on the object contour. Another strategy is to explicitly incorporate all sorts of expected appearance variations in the model. Especially if 3D objects have to be recognized in a single 2D image, the variance of object pose, e.g., due to change of camera viewpoint usually causes considerable appearance variations.

For many applications, especially if arbitrarily shaped objects are to be recognized, it is most convenient if the algorithm automatically learns the range of expected appearance variations. This is done in a training stage prior to recognition. A simple strategy would be to sample the object at different poses, different illumination settings and perhaps also from different viewpoints, and store all training images in the model. However, this is inefficient as the training images all show the same object and despite the variances almost certainly exhibit a considerable amount of redundancy.

As a consequence, a better suited representation of the sampled data is needed. To this end, the input data is transformed to another and hopefully more compact representation. In this context an image $I(x, y)$ with $W \times H$ pixels can be regarded as an $N = W \cdot H$–dimensional vector $\mathbf{x}$. Each element $i \in 1..N$ of the vector $\mathbf{x}$ represents the gray value of one pixel. A suitable transformation is based on the principal component analysis (PCA), which aims at representing the variations of the object appearance with as few dimensions as possible. It has been suggested by

Turk and Pentland [14] for face recognition, Murase and Nayar [10] presented an algorithm for recognition of more general 3D objects in a single 2D image, which were taken from a wide rage of viewpoints.

The goal is to perform a linear transformation in order to rearrange a data set of sample images such that most of its information is concentrated in as few coefficients as possible. To this end, an image $\mathbf{x}$ can be defined as the linear combination of several basis vectors $\mathbf{w}_i$ defining a basis $\mathbf{W}$:

$$\mathbf{x} = \sum_{i=1}^{N} y_i \cdot \mathbf{w}_i \qquad (2.13)$$

$$\mathbf{W} = \begin{bmatrix} \mathbf{w}_1^T \mathbf{w}_2^T \cdots \mathbf{w}_N^T \end{bmatrix} \qquad (2.14)$$

with the y_i being the transformation coefficients. We should aim for an accurate estimate $\hat{\mathbf{x}}$ of $\mathbf{x}$ while using as few coefficients as possible at the same time

$$\hat{\mathbf{x}} = \sum_{i=1}^{n} y_i \cdot \mathbf{w}_i \text{ with } n << M \qquad (2.15)$$

M defines the number of samples of the object to be recognized which are available in a training phase. Dimensionality reduction is possible because the samples should look similar and thus contain much redundancy. Therefore the $\mathbf{x}_m$ should be located close to each other in the transformed space and can be represented by using a new, low-dimensional basis. Mathematically speaking, this amounts to a projection of the original data $\mathbf{x}_m$ onto a low-dimensional subspace (see Fig. 2.10 for illustration).

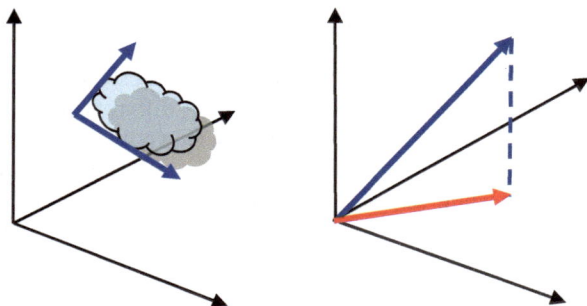

Fig. 2.10 The cloud in the *left* part illustrates the region containing the training "images" in a 3D space. Clearly, a 2D representation signalized by the *blue arrows* is better suited than the original 3D representation signalized by the *black arrows*. The effect of dimensionality reduction is illustrated in the *right* part: its geometric interpretation is a projection of a sample point (3D, *blue arrow*) onto a subspace (here a 2D plane, *red arrow*). The error made by the projection is illustrated by the dashed *blue line*

With a good choice of the projection parameters, the error E_n^2 of this estimation should be minimized. It can be defined by the expected Euclidean distance between $\hat{\mathbf{x}}$ and $\mathbf{x}$:

$$E_n^2 = E\left\{\|\hat{\mathbf{x}} - \mathbf{x}\|^2\right\} = \sum_{i=n+1}^{N} \mathbf{w}_i^T \cdot E\left\{\mathbf{x} \cdot \mathbf{x}^T\right\} \mathbf{w}_i \qquad (2.16)$$

with $E\{\cdot\}$ denoting the expectation value. The matrix $E\left\{\mathbf{x} \cdot \mathbf{x}^T\right\}$ contains the expectation values of the cross-correlations between two image pixels. It can be estimated by the sampled training images

$$E\left\{\mathbf{x} \cdot \mathbf{x}^T\right\} \approx \sum_{m=1}^{M} \mathbf{x}_m \cdot \mathbf{x}_m^T = \mathbf{S} \qquad (2.17)$$

The matrix $\mathbf{S}$ defines the so-called scattermatrix of the sample data. In other words, the transformation is optimized by exploiting statistical properties of the samples in a training phase. With the constraint of $\mathbf{W}$ defining an orthonormal basis system a component-wise minimization of E_n^2 leads to the well-known eigenvalue decomposition of $\mathbf{S}$ ($\mathbf{I}$ defines the identity matrix):

$$E_n^2 = \sum_{i=n+1}^{N} \left[\mathbf{w}_i^T \cdot \mathbf{S} \cdot \mathbf{w}_i - \lambda_i \left(\mathbf{w}_i^T \cdot \mathbf{w}_i - 1\right)\right] \qquad (2.18)$$

$$\partial E_n^2 \big/ \partial \mathbf{w}_i \equiv 0 \text{ leads to } (\mathbf{S} - \lambda_i \cdot \mathbf{I}) \cdot \mathbf{w}_i = \mathbf{0} \qquad (2.19)$$

The relation between an image $\mathbf{x}$ and its transformation $\mathbf{y}$ is defined as

$$\mathbf{y} = \mathbf{W}^T \cdot \mathbf{x} \qquad \mathbf{x} = \mathbf{W} \cdot \mathbf{y} \qquad (2.20)$$

The calculation of the eigenvalues λ_i and eigenvectors $\mathbf{w}_i$ of $\mathbf{S}$ is time-consuming, (please note that the dimensionality of $\mathbf{S}$ is defined by the number of pixels of the training images!) but can be done off-line during training. The absolute values of λ_i are a measure how much the dimension defined by $\mathbf{w}_i$ contributes to a description of the variance of the data set. Typically, only a few λ_i are necessary for covering most of the variance. Therefore, only the $\mathbf{w}_i$ belonging to the dominant λ_i are chosen for transformation, which yields an efficient dimensionality reduction of $\mathbf{y}$. In literature these $\mathbf{w}_i$ are denoted as "eigenimages" (each $\mathbf{w}_i$ can also be interpreted as an image if its data is rearranged to a $W \times H$-matrix).

If object classification has to be performed, the joint eigenspace $\mathbf{W}_J$ of samples from all object classes $k \in \{1..K\}$ of the model database is calculated. During recognition, a scene image is transformed into the eigenspace and classified, e.g., simply by assigning the class label of the nearest neighbor in transformed space. However, this involves a comparison with each of the transformed training image, which is time-consuming. In order to accelerate the classification, Murase and Nayar suggest the introduction of a so-called parametric manifold $\mathbf{g}_k\left(\theta_0,\theta_1,...,\theta_n\right)$ for each object class k which describes the distribution of the samples of object class k in feature space with the help of the parameters $\left(\theta_0,\theta_1,...,\theta_n\right)$. A classification can then be performed by evaluating the distances of the transformed input image to the hyperplanes defined by the parametric manifolds of various object classes.

If, on the other hand, the pose of a known object class has to be estimated, a specific eigenspace $\mathbf{W}_k$; $1 \leq k \leq K$ is calculated for each object class k by taking only samples from this class into account during training. Subsequently transformation of a scene image using this specific transformation reveals the object pose. Again this is done with the help of a parametric manifold $\mathbf{f}_k\left(\theta_0,\theta_1,...,\theta_n\right)$. The pose, which can be derived from the parameters $\left(\theta_0,\theta_1,...,\theta_n\right)$, can be determined by finding the parameter combination which minimizes the distance of the transformed image to the hyperplane defined by the manifold. Please note that the pose of the object in the scene image has to be "covered" during training: if the current pose is far away from each of the poses of the training samples, the method will not work. Details of the pose estimation can be found in [10].

2.3.2 Pseudocode

```
function detectObjectPosPCA (in Image I, in joint eigenspace
W_J, in object class eigenspaces W_k, parametric manifolds
g_k(θ_0,θ_1,...,θ_n)  and  f_k(θ_0,θ_1,...,θ_n),  in  distance  threshold  t,  out
classification result c, out object position p)

perform background subtraction, if necessary: only the object
has to be shown in the image
stack I into a 1-dim. vector x_I

// object classification
transform x_I into the joint eigenspace: y_J ← W_J^T · x_I
for k = 1 to number of models
    d_k ← distance of y_J to parametric manifold g_k(θ_0,θ_1,...,θ_n)
next
if min(d_k) ≤ t then
    c ← index of min
else
    c ← -1     // none of the models is similar enough
    return
end if

// object pose estimation
transform x_I into the eigenspace of class c: y_c ← W_c^T · x_I
get parameters (θ_0,θ_1,...,θ_n) which minimize the distance of y_c to
parametric manifold f_k(θ_0,θ_1,...,θ_n)
derive object pose p from (θ_0,θ_1,...,θ_n)
```

2.3.3 Rating

The PCA has the advantageous property of explicitly modeling appearance variations in an automatic manner. As a result, strong invariance with respect to these
variations is achieved. 3D object recognition can be performed from a single 2D
image if the variations caused by viewpoint change are incorporated in the model.
Moreover, the method is not restricted to objects with special properties; it works
for arbitrarily shaped objects, at least in principle.

On the other hand, a considerable number of sample images are needed for a
sufficiently accurate modeling of the variations – a fact that might cause much effort
during acquisition of the training images. Other drawbacks of PCA-based object
recognition are that the scheme is not able to detect multiple objects in a single
image, that the scene object has to be well separated from the background, and that
recognition performance degrades quite rapidly when occlusion increases.

Additionally it is more suited for a classification scheme where the position of
an object is known and/or stable, but not so much for pose estimation, because
unknown position shifts between model and scene image cause the scene image to
"move away" from the subspace in parameter space defined by the model.

2.3.4 Example

The eigenspace calculated from sample images containing shifted, rotated, and
scaled versions of a simple triangle form is shown in Table 2.4. It was calculated
from 100 sample images in total. As can easily be seen in the top part of the
table (which shows a subset of the sample images), the sample images contain a
considerable amount of redundancy.

The eigenimages depicted in the bottom part (with decreasing eigenvalue from
left to right and top to bottom; the last two rows show only a selection of eigenvectors), however, show a different behavior: the first eigenvector corresponds to
the "mean" of the training samples, whereas all following eigenimages visualize
certain variances.

As the sample triangles are essentially plain bright, their variances are located
at their borders, a fact which can easily be verified when comparing two of them
by subtraction. Accordingly, the variances shown in the eigenimages belonging to
dominant eigenvalues in the first row are clearly located at triangle borders, whereas
especially the eigenimages shown in the last two rows (a selection of the eigenvectors ranked 25–100) exhibit basically noise indicating that they contain very little or
no characteristic information of the sampled object.

Please note that the covariance matrix $\mathbf{C}$ is often calculated instead of the scattermatrix $\mathbf{S}$ in literature. $\mathbf{C}$ is strongly related to $\mathbf{S}$, the only difference is that it is
calculated from the outer product of the differences of the data samples *with respect
to their mean* $\bar{\mathbf{x}}$ instead of the data samples themselves:

$$\mathbf{C} = \sum_{m=1}^{M} (\mathbf{x}_m - \bar{\mathbf{x}}) \cdot (\mathbf{x}_m - \bar{\mathbf{x}})^T \text{ with } \bar{\mathbf{x}} = \frac{1}{M} \sum_{m=1}^{M} \mathbf{x}_m \qquad (2.21)$$

Table 2.4 Sample images and eigenspace of a simple triangle form

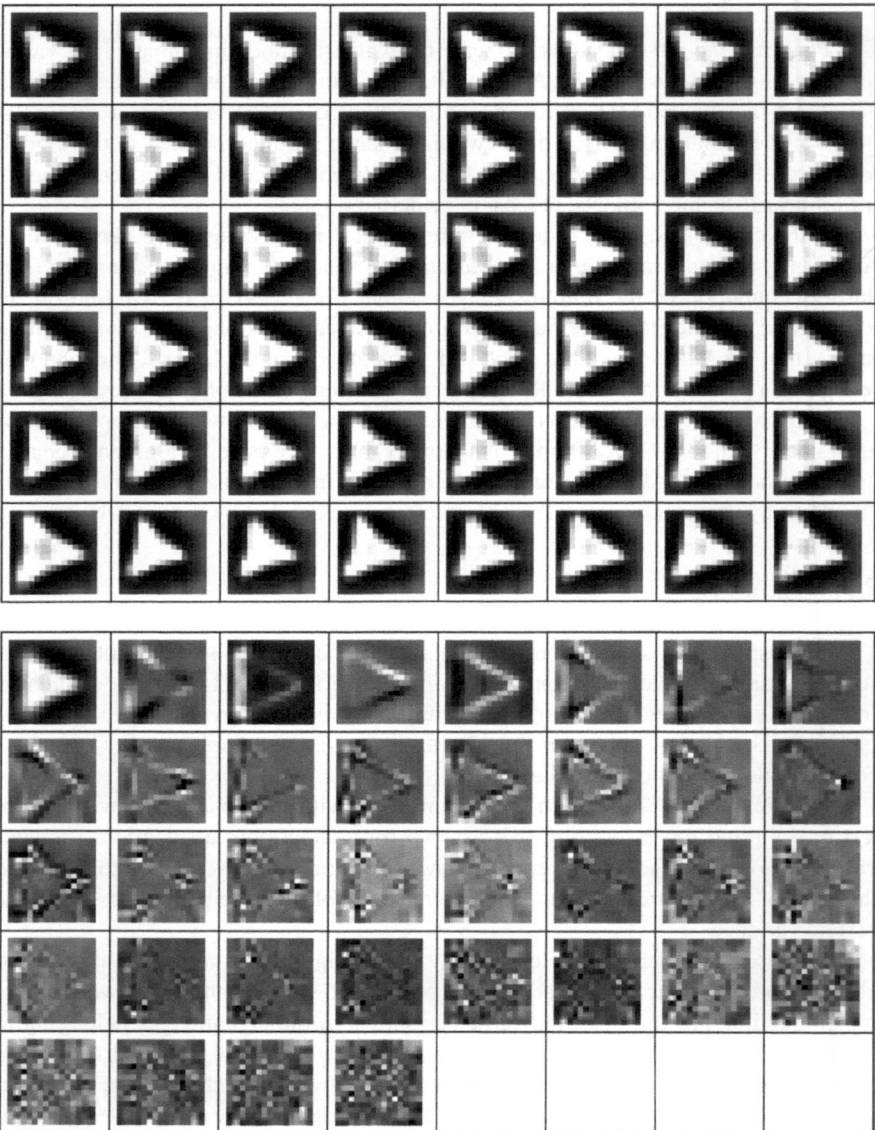

Concerning the eigenspace of **C**, its eigenvectors are the same except that the mean is missing.

The covariance matrix **C** estimated from the sample triangle images can be seen in Fig. 2.11. Bright areas indicate high-positive values and black areas high-negative values, respectively, whereas values near zero are gray. Both bright and black areas indicate strong correlation (either positive or negative) among the samples. The

Fig. 2.11 Showing the
covariance matrix of the
triangle example

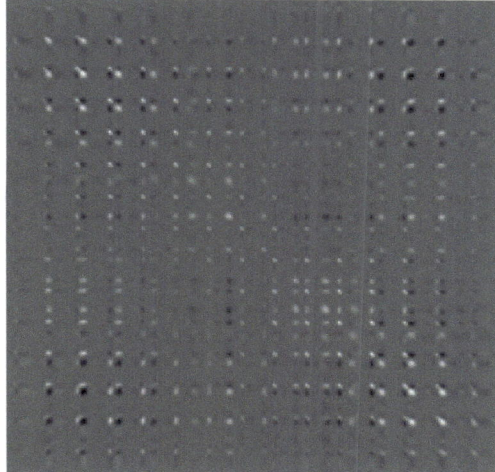

Fig. 2.12 Showing the
distribution of the eigenvalues
of the covariance matrix of
the triangle example

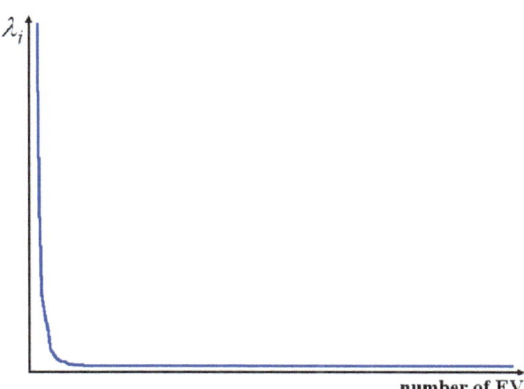

matrix – which always is symmetric – is highly structured, which means that only some areas of the samples contain characteristic information. The PCA aims at exploiting this structure.

The fact that the covariance matrix is clearly structured indicates that much of the information about the variance of the example images can be concentrated in only a few eigenvectors $\mathbf{w}_i$. Accordingly, the eigenvalues λ_i should decrease fast. Actually, this is true and can be observed in Fig. 2.12.

2.3.5 Modifications

The transformation defined by the principal component analysis – when a joint transformation for all object classes is used, e.g., for object classification –

maximizes the overall variance of the training samples. Hence, there is no mechanism which guarantees that just the inter-class variance is maximized, which would be advantageous. A modification proposed by Fisher [7] has been used by Belhumeur et al. for face recognition [2]. They point out that it is desirable to maximize the inter-class variance by the transformation, whereas intra-class variance is to be minimized at the same time. As a result, the transformed training samples should build compact clusters located far from each other in transformed space. This can be achieved by solving the generalized eigenvalue problem

$$\mathbf{S}_B \cdot \mathbf{w}_i = \lambda_i \cdot \mathbf{S}_C \cdot \mathbf{w}_i \tag{2.22}$$

with $\mathbf{S}_B$ denoting the between-class scattermatrix and $\mathbf{S}_C$ the within-class scattermatrix.

References

1. Ballard, D.H and Brown, C.M., *"Computer Vision"*, Prentice-Hall, Englewood Cliffs, N.J, 1982, **ISBN 0-131-65316-4**
2. Belhumeur P., Hespanha, J. and Kriegman, D. "Eigenfaces vs. Fisherfaces: Recognition Using Class Specific Linear Projection", *IEEE Transactions on Pattern Analysis and Machine Intelligence,* 19(7):711–720, 1997
3. Canny, J.F., "A Computational Approach to Edge Detection", *IEEE Transactions on Pattern Analysis and Machine Intelligence,* 8(6):679–698, 1986
4. Chellappa, R. and Bagdazian, R., "Optimal Fourier Coding of Image Boundaries", *IEEE Transactions on Pattern Analysis and Machine Intelligence,* 6(1):102–105, 1984
5. Chuang, G. and Kuo, C.C., "Wavelet Descriptor of Planar Curves: Theory and Applications", *IEEE Transactions on Image Processing,* 5:56–70, 1996
6. Duda, R.O., Hart, P.E. and Stork, D.G., *"Pattern Classification"*, Wiley, New York, 2000, **ISBN 0-471-05669-3**
7. Fisher, R.A., "The Use of Multiple Measures in Taxonomic Problems", *Annals of Eugenics,* 7:179–188, 1936
8. Flusser, J. and Suk, T., "Pattern Recognition by Affine Moment Invariants", *Pattern Recognition,* 26(1):167–174, 1993
9. Miyazawa, K., Ito, K., Aoki, T., Kobayashi, K. and Nakajima, N., "An Effective Approach for Iris Recognition Using Phase-Based Image Matching", *IEEE Transactions on Pattern Analysis and Machine Intelligence,* 30(10):1741–1756, 2008
10. Murase, H. and Nayar, S., "Visual Learning and Recognition of 3-D Objects from Appearance", *International Journal Computer Vision,* 14:5–24, 1995
11. Niblack, C.W., Barber, R.J., Equitz, W.R., Flickner, M.D., Glasman, D., Petkovic, D. and Yanker, P.C., "The QBIC Project: Querying Image by Content Using Color, Texture and Shape", In *Electronic Imaging: Storage and Retrieval for Image and Video Databases, Proceedings SPIE,* 1908:173–187, 1993
12. Steger, C., "Occlusion, Clutter and Illumination Invariant Object Recognition", *International Archives of Photogrammetry and Remote Sensing,* XXXIV(3A):345–350, 2002
13. Takita, K., Aoki, T., Sasaki, Y., Higuchi, T. and Kobayashi, K., "High-Accuracy Subpixel Image Registration Based on Phase-Only Correlation", *IEICE Transactions Fundamentals,* E86-A(8):1925–1934, 2003
14. Turk, M. and Pentland, A., "Face Recognition Using Eigenfaces", *Proceedings of the IEEE Conference on Computer Vision and Pattern Recognition,* Miami, USA, 586–591, 1991

15. Ulrich, M. and Steger, C., "Performance Comparison of 2D Object Recognition Techniques", *International Archives of Photogrammetry and Remote Sensing*, XXXIV(5):99–104, 2002
16. Van Otterloo, P., "*A Contour-Oriented Approach to Shape Analysis*", Prentice Hall Ltd., Englewood Cliffs, 1992
17. Zhang, D. and Lu, G., "Generic Fourier Descriptor for Shape-based Image Retrieval", *IEEE Int'l Conference on Multimedia and Expo,* 1:425–428, 2002

Chapter 3
Transformation-Search Based Methods

Abstract Another way of object representation is to utilize object models consisting of a finite set of points and their position. By the usage of point sets recognition can be performed as follows: First, a point set is extracted from a scene image. Subsequently, the parameters of a transformation which defines a mapping of the model point set to the point set derived from the scene image are estimated. To this end, the so-called transformation space, which comprises the set of all possible transform parameter combinations, is explored. By adopting this strategy occlusion (resulting in missing points in the scene image point set) and background clutter (resulting in additional points in the scene image point set) both lead to a reduction of the percentage of points that can be matched correctly between scene image and the model. Hence, occlusion and clutter can be controlled by the definition of a threshold for the portion of the point sets which has to be matched correctly. After introducing some typical transformations used in object recognition, some examples of algorithms exploring the transformation space including the so-called generalized Hough transform and the Hausdorff distance are presented.

3.1 Overview

Most of the global appearance-based methods presented so far suffer from their invariance with respect to occlusion and background clutter, because both of them can lead to a significant change in the global data representation resulting in a mismatch between model and scene image.

As far as most of the methods presented in this chapter are concerned, they utilize object models consisting of a finite set of points together with their position. In the recognition phase, a point set is extracted from a scene image first. Subsequently, transformation parameters are estimated by means of maximizing the similarity between the scene image point set and the transformed model point set (or minimizing their distance respectively). This is done by exploring the so-called transformation space, which comprises the set of all possible transform parameter combinations. Each parameter combination defines a transformation between the model data and the scene image. The aim is to find a combination which maximizes the similarity (or minimizes a distance, respectively). Finally, it can be checked whether the similarities are high enough, i.e., the searched object is actually present at the position defined by the transformation parameters.

Occlusion (leading to missing points in the scene image point set) and background clutter (leading to additional points in the scene image point set) both result in a reduction of the percentage of points that can be matched correctly between scene image and the model. Hence, the amount of occlusion and clutter which still is acceptable can be controlled by the definition of a threshold for the portion of the point sets which has to be matched correctly.

The increased robustness with respect to occlusion and clutter is also due to the fact that, with the help of point sets, *local* information can be evaluated, i.e., it can be estimated how well a single point or a small fraction of the point set located in a small neighborhood fits to a specific object pose independent of the rest of the image data (in contrast to, e.g., global feature vectors where any discrepancy between model and scene image affects the global features). Additionally, it is possible to concentrate the point set on characteristic parts of the object (in contrast to gray value correlation, for example).

After a brief discussion of some transformation classes, some methods adopting a transformation-based search strategy are discussed in more detail. The degrees of freedom in algorithm design for this class of methods are

- *Detection method for the point set* (e.g., edge detection as proposed by Canny [3], see also Appendix A). The point set must be rich enough to provide discriminative information of the object. On the other hand, however, large point sets lead to infeasible computational complexity.
- *Distance metric* for measuring the degree of similarity between the model and the content of the scene image at a particular position.
- *Matching strategy* of searching the transformation space in order to detect the minimum of the distance metric. A brute force approach which exhaustively evaluates a densely sampled search space is usually not acceptable because the algorithm runtime is too long. As a consequence a more intelligent strategy is required.
- *Class of transformations* which is evaluated, e.g., affine or similarity transforms.

3.2 Transformation Classes

Before we take a closer look at some methods which search in the transformation space we have to clarify what kind of transformation is estimated. Commonly used transformation classes are similarity transformations and affine transformations. Both of them are linear transformations, a fact that simplifies calculations and therefore reduces the computational complexity significantly compared to the usage of non-linear transformations. In reality, however, if a 3D object is moved in 3D space, the appearance change of the object in a 2D image acquired by a camera at fixed position can only be modeled exactly by a perspective transformation, which is non-linear. Fortunately, the perspective transformation can be approximated by an affine transformation with good accuracy if the "depth" of the object resulting from the third dimension is small compared to the distance to the camera and therefore the object can be regarded as *planar*. Affine transformations are given by

$$\mathbf{x}_{S,i} = \begin{bmatrix} x_{S,i} \\ y_{S,i} \end{bmatrix} = \mathbf{A} \cdot \mathbf{x}_{M,i} + \mathbf{t} = \begin{bmatrix} a_{11} \ a_{12} \\ a_{21} \ a_{22} \end{bmatrix} \cdot \begin{bmatrix} x_{M,i} \\ y_{M,i} \end{bmatrix} + \begin{bmatrix} t_x \\ t_y \end{bmatrix} \tag{3.1}$$

where $\mathbf{x}_{S,i}$ denotes the position of a point or feature (e.g. line segment) in the scene image and $\mathbf{x}_{M,i}$ its corresponding model position. The matrix $\mathbf{A}$ and a translation vector $\mathbf{t}$ parametrize the set of all allowed transformations. Altogether, affine transformations are specified by six parameters a_{11}, a_{12}, a_{21}, a_{22}, t_x, and t_y. A further simplification can be done if only movements of planar 2D objects perpendicular to the optical axis of the image acquisition system together with scaling have to be considered. In that case the affine transformation can be reduced to the similarity transform

$$\mathbf{x}_{S,i} = \begin{bmatrix} x_{S,i} \\ y_{S,i} \end{bmatrix} = \mathbf{S} \cdot \mathbf{x}_{M,i} + \mathbf{t} = s \cdot \begin{bmatrix} \cos\varphi \ -\sin\varphi \\ \sin\varphi \ \ \cos\varphi \end{bmatrix} \cdot \begin{bmatrix} x_{M,i} \\ y_{M,i} \end{bmatrix} + \begin{bmatrix} t_x \\ t_y \end{bmatrix} \tag{3.2}$$

characterized by four parameters s, φ, t_x, and t_y. s denotes a scaling factor, φ a rotation angle, and t_x and t_y a translation in the image plane. If s is explicitly set to 1, the transformation is called rigid transformation.

Some types of transformations are illustrated in Table 3.1: The rigid transform comprises translation and rotation; the similarity transform in addition contains scaling. The affine transform maps parallel lines to parallel lines again, whereas the perspective transform, which is nonlinear, maps a square to a quadrangle in the general case.

Perspective transformations can actually also be modeled linear if so-called homogeneous coordinates are used: a 2D point for example is then represented by the triple $[\lambda \cdot x, \lambda \cdot y, \lambda]$, where λ denotes a scaling factor. Points are regarded as equivalent if they have identical x and y values, regardless of the value of λ. Using homogeneous coordinates, the projective transformation of a point located in a plane to another plane can be described as

Table 3.1 Overview of some transformation classes

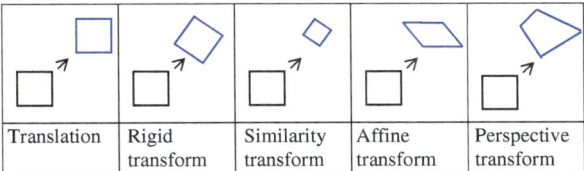

Translation	Rigid transform	Similarity transform	Affine transform	Perspective transform

$$\mathbf{x}_{S,i} = \begin{bmatrix} \lambda \cdot x_{S,i} \\ \lambda \cdot y_{S,i} \\ \lambda \end{bmatrix} = \mathbf{T} \cdot \mathbf{x}_{M,i} = \begin{bmatrix} t_{11} & t_{12} & t_{13} \\ t_{21} & t_{22} & t_{23} \\ t_{31} & t_{32} & 1 \end{bmatrix} \cdot \begin{bmatrix} x_{M,i} \\ y_{M,i} \\ 1 \end{bmatrix} \qquad (3.3)$$

Hence, eight parameters are necessary for characterization of a perspective transform.

3.3 Generalized Hough Transform

3.3.1 Main Idea

The Hough Transform was originally developed for the detection of straight lines (cf. Hough [7] or Duda and Hart [4]), but can be generalized to the detection of arbitrarily shaped objects if the object shape is known in advance.

Now let's have a look at the basic idea of the Hough transform: given a set of points $\mathbf{P}$, every pixel $p = [x, y] \in \mathbf{p}$ could possibly be part of a line. In order to detect all lines contained in $\mathbf{P}$, each p "votes" for all lines which pass through that pixel. Considering the normal form

$$r = x \cdot \cos(\alpha) + y \cdot \sin(\alpha) \qquad (3.4)$$

each of those lines can be characterized by two parameters r and α. A 2D accumulator space covering all possible $[r, \alpha]$, which is divided into cells, accounts for the votes. For a given point $[x, y]$, all parameter combinations $[r, \alpha]$ satisfying the normal form can be determined. Each of those $[r, \alpha]$ increases the corresponding accumulator cell by one. Taking all pixels of the point set into account, the local maxima of the accumulator reveal the parameters of the lines contained in the point set (if existent).

The principle of voting makes the method robust with respect to occlusion or data outliers, because even if a fraction of the line is missing, there should be enough points left for a "correct" vote. In general the Hough transform works on an edge-filtered image, e.g., all pixels with gradient magnitude above a certain threshold participate in the voting process.

For a generalization of the Hough transform   (cf. Ballard [1]) a model of the object contour has to be trained prior to recognition. The thus obtained information about the object shape is stored in a so-called R-Table. Subsequently, recognition is guided by this R-Table information. The R-Table generation proceeds as follows.

3.3.2 Training Phase

1. *Object contour point detection*: In the first step all contour points $\mathbf{x}_{T,i} = \lfloor x_{T,i}, y_{T,i} \rfloor$ of a sample image showing the object to be trained are located together with their gradient angle θ_i, e.g., with the help of the canny edge

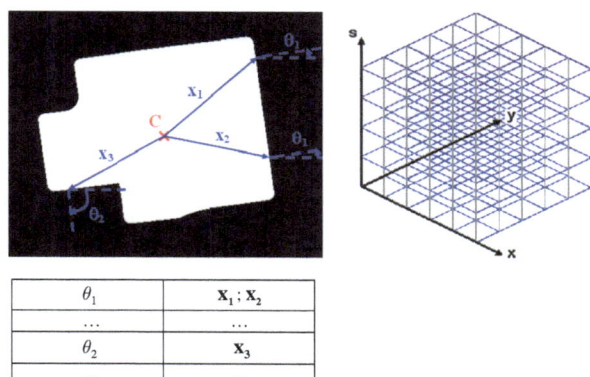

θ_1	$\mathbf{x}_1 ; \mathbf{x}_2$
...	...
θ_2	$\mathbf{x}_3$
...	...

Fig. 3.1 Illustrative example of the generalized Hough transform. *Left*: R-table generation with three example points; *Right*: 3D accumulator for translation and scale estimation of size $5 \times 5 \times 4$

detector [3] including non-maximum suppression (cf. Appendix A). The underlying assumption is that the object contour is characterized by rapid gray value changes in its neighborhood due to the fact that the background usually differs from the object in terms of gray value appearance.

2. *Center point definition*: Specification of an arbitrary point $[x_C, y_C]$.
3. *R-table calculation*: For each detected contour point, remember its gradient angle θ_i and the distance vector to the center $\lfloor x_{R,i}, y_{R,i} \rfloor = \lfloor x_{T,i} - x_C, y_{T,i} - y_C \rfloor$. This model data can be stored in form of a table (often referred to as *R-Table* in the literature) where for each θ the corresponding distance vectors to the center are stored. The space of θ (usually ranging from $-180°$ to $180°$) is quantized into equally sized intervals. If, for example, each R-table entry covers an interval of $1°$, it consists of 360 entries altogether. Note that multiple distance vectors can belong to a single gradient angle θ if multiple contour points exhibit the same θ. Figure 3.1 gives an example for three arbitrarily chosen contour points and the corresponding fraction of the R-table.

3.3.3 Recognition Phase

1. *Object contour point detection*: find all contour points $\mathbf{x}_{S,i} = \lfloor x_{S,i}, y_{S,i} \rfloor$ in a scene image and their gradient angle θ_i, in general by applying the same method as during training, e.g., the canny edge detector with non-maximum suppression.
2. *Derivation of assumed center points and voting*: For each detected contour point $\mathbf{x}_{S,i}$, assumed center points $\mathbf{x}_{CE,l} = \lfloor x_{CE,l}, y_{CE,l} \rfloor$ can be calculated considering the gradient angle θ_i and the model data:

$$\begin{bmatrix} x_{CE,l} \\ y_{CE,l} \end{bmatrix} = \begin{bmatrix} x_{S,i} \\ y_{S,i} \end{bmatrix} + s \cdot \begin{bmatrix} x_{R,l} \\ y_{R,l} \end{bmatrix} (\theta_i) \tag{3.5}$$

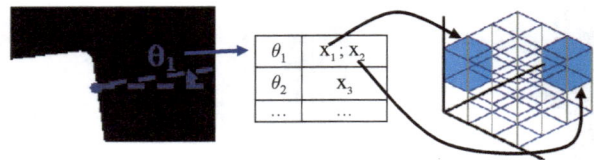

Fig. 3.2 Illustrating the voting process for one object contour point. In this example two entries can be found in the R-table for the current angle θ_1. Consequently, the content of two accumulator cells (marked *blue*) is increased

The distance vectors $\mathbf{x}_{R,l} = \lfloor x_{R,l}, y_{R,l} \rfloor (\theta)$ are obtained based on the R-table information: For each gradient angle θ a list $\mathbf{r}_\theta$ consisting of L distance vectors $\mathbf{x}_{R,l}$ with $l \in [1, ..., L]$ can be retrieved by a look-up operation in the R-table. For each distance vector a specific $\mathbf{x}_{CE,l}$ is calculated and the corresponding cell in a 2D accumulator array is increased by one (cf. Fig. 3.2). Every cell represents a certain range of x and y position values. The selection of the cell size is a trade-off between accuracy and, on the other hand, memory demand as well as algorithm runtime. s denotes a scale factor. Typically, s is varied in a certain range and with a certain step size depending on the expected scale variation of the object and the desired accuracy in scale determination. For each s another assumed center point can be calculated. Hence, for each R-table entry multiple center points are calculated and therefore multiple accumulator cells are increased. This can be done in a 2D accumulator or alternatively in a 3D accumulator where the third dimension represents the scale (see right part of Fig. 3.1). In most of the cases, also the object angle ϕ is unknown. Therefore, again multiple center points can be determined according to

$$\begin{bmatrix} x_{CE,l} \\ y_{CE,l} \end{bmatrix} = \begin{bmatrix} x_{S,i} \\ y_{S,i} \end{bmatrix} + s \cdot \begin{bmatrix} x_{R,l} \\ y_{R,l} \end{bmatrix} (\theta_i + \phi) \qquad (3.6)$$

where ϕ is varied within a certain range and with a certain step size. Please note that the distance vectors retrieved from the R-table have to be rotated by ϕ in that case. The object angle ϕ represents a fourth dimension of the accumulator.

3. *Maximum search in the accumulator*: All local maxima above a threshold t are found poses of the object.

3.3.4 Pseudocode

```
function findAllObjectLocationsGHT (in Image I, in R-Table
data R, in threshold t, out position list p)

// calculate edge point information
calculate x and y gradient of I: Ix and Iy
detect all edge points xs,i based on Ix and Iy, e.g. by
```

```
non-maximum suppression and hysteresis thresholding(Canny)
for i=1 to number of edge points
     θᵢ ← arctan (Iy/Ix) // edge point orientation
next

//voting
init 4-dimensional accumulator accu with borders
⌊xmin,xmax,xStep⌋, ⌊ymin,ymax,yStep⌋, ⌊φmin,φmax,φStep⌋, ⌊smin,smax,sStep⌋
for i=1 to number of edge points
     for φ = φmin to φmax step φStep
          retrieve list r_{φ+θᵢ} of R (entry at position φ + θᵢ)
          for l=1 to number of entries of list r_{φ+θᵢ}
               for s = smin to smax step sStep
                    x_{R,l} ← distance vector (list entry r_{φ+θᵢ,l}),
                    rotated by φ and scaled by s
                    calculate assumed object center point
                    x_{CE,l} (x_{R,l},x_{S,i},s,φ) according to Equation 3.6
                    if x_{CE,l} is inside [x,y] -pos. bounds of accu then
                         increment accu at position [x_{CE,l},y_{CE,l},φ,s]
                    end if
               next
          next
     next
next

// determine all valid object positions
find all local maxima in accu
for i=1 to number of local maxima
     if accu (xᵢ,yᵢ,φᵢ,sᵢ) ≥ t then
          append position [xᵢ,yᵢ,φᵢ,sᵢ] to p
     end if
next
```

3.3.5 Example

Table 3.2 illustrates the performance of the generalized Hough transform: as an example application, the pose of a key (x, y, scale, and rotation) has to be determined. The image shown in the left column of the top row served as training image for R-table construction in all cases.

The left column shows scene images where the key has to be detected, whereas the contour points extracted by a Canny edge detector with non-maximum suppression are depicted right to it. In the rightmost two columns two cuts through the 4D accumulator at the found position are shown; one cut revealing the $[x,y]$-subspace of the accumulator at the found $[s,\phi]$-position and another revealing the $[s,\phi]$-subspace of the accumulator at the found $[x,y]$-position.

Table 3.2 Performance of the generalized Hough transform in the case of the unaffected training image, when the object undergoes a similarity transform, in the presence of illumination change, noise, and occlusion (from top to bottom)

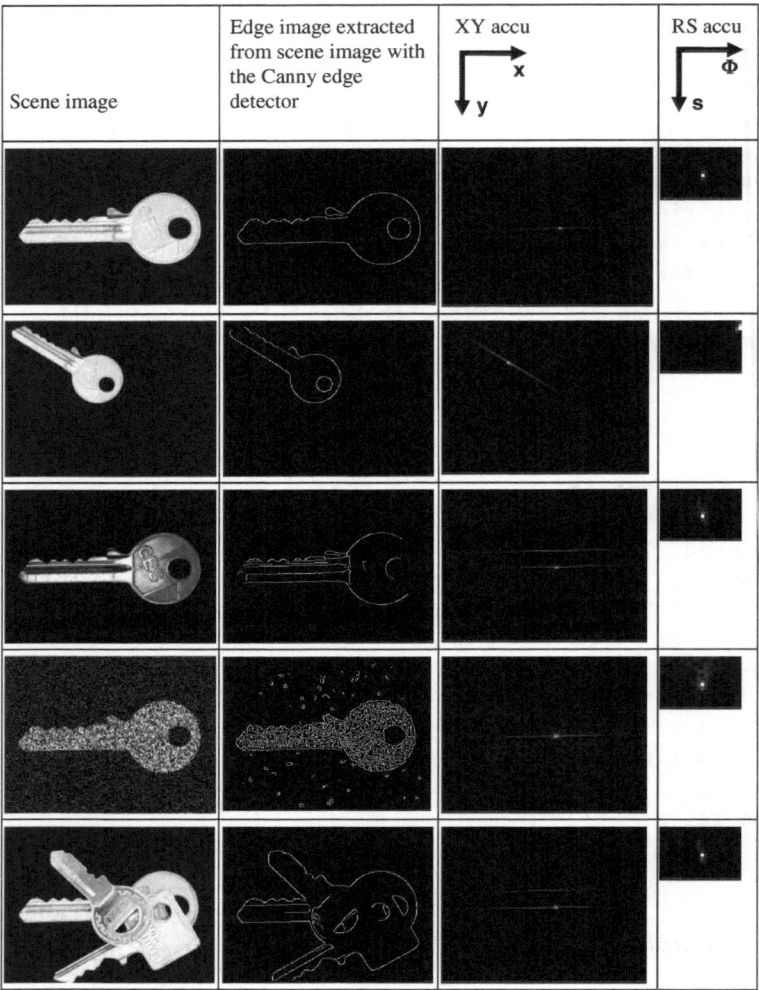

The x and y accumulator size are the image dimensions (cell size 2 pixels), the scale ranges from 0.6 to 1.4 (cell size 0.05) and the rotation from $-36°$ to $36°$ (cell size $3°$). The following examples are shown: same image for training and recognition, a similarity-transformed object, illumination change, strong noise, and finally occlusion (from top to bottom). In all examples the accumulator maximum is sharp and distinctive, which indicates good recognition reliability.

Please note that the accumulator maximum position remains stable in case of illumination change, noise, and occlusion despite a considerable appearance change of the object caused by these effects. As far as the similarity transform example is concerned, the accumulator maximum moves to the correct position (left and upward in the XY accu; to the extreme top and right position in the RS accu) and remains sharp. However, runtime of the algorithm is rather high, even for relative small images of size 300×230 pixels (in the order of 1 s on a 3.2 GHz Pentium 4).

3.3.6 Rating

The main advantage of the generalized Hough transform is that it can compensate for occlusion and data outliers (as demonstrated by the key example) as there should be enough contour pixels left which vote for the correct object pose. On the other hand, however, the accumulator size strongly depends on the dimensionality of the search space and the envisaged accuracy.

Let's consider an example with typical tolerances and resolutions: x-/y-translation tolerance 200 pixel, cell resolution 1 pixel, rotation tolerance 360°, cell resolution 1°, scale tolerance 50–200%, cell resolution 1%. As a consequence, the 4D accumulator size amounts to $200 \times 200 \times 360 \times 150 = 2.16 \times 10^9$ cells, leading to probably infeasible memory demand as well as long execution times due to the time-consuming maximum search within the accumulator. Therefore, modifications of the scheme exist which try to optimize the maximum search in the accumulator.

Another disadvantage is that the rather rigid object representation does only allow for a limited amount of local object deformations. If the deformation is restricted to minor parts of the object contour, the method is robust to these outliers, but if large parts of the shape show minor deformations the accumulator maximum might be split up into multiple maxima at similar poses. Noise can be another reason for such a split-up. This fact can be alleviated by choosing a coarse accumulator resolution. Then every accumulator cell covers a larger parameter range, and therefore a boundary point at a slightly different location often still contributes to the same accumulator cells. But keep in mind that the price we must pay is a reduction of accuracy!

There exist numerous applets in the Internet which are very suitable for experimenting with and learning more about the Hough transform, its performance, and limitations. The interested reader is encouraged to check it out.[1]

---

[1] See e.g. http://d0server1.fnal.gov/users/ngraf/Talks/UTeV/Java/Circles.html or http://homepages.inf.ed.ac.uk/rbf/HIPR2/houghdemo.htm (links active January 13th 2010)

3.3.7 Modifications

Even if the generalized Hough transform suffers from its high memory demand and complexity, due to its robustness with respect to occlusion and large outliers the usage of the Hough transform as a pre-processing step providing input for other schemes which actually determine the final pose is an interesting combination. In that case rather large accumulator cell sizes are chosen as only coarse pose estimates are necessary. This involves low or at least moderate memory and time demand as well as considerable tolerance with respect to local deformations.

A possible combination might consist of the GHT and so-called active contour models (see Chapter 6): contrary to the Hough transform, approaches aiming at compensating local deformations by finding exact object contours with the help of local information (e.g., like Snakes) only have a limited convergence area and therefore demand a reliable rough estimate of the object pose as input. Hence, advantages of both approaches can be combined (see, e.g., the method proposed by Ecabert and Thiran [5]).

In order to overcome the memory demand as well as speed limitations of the generalized Hough transform, Ulrich et al. [11] suggest a hierarchical approach utilizing image pyramids for determining the x, y and ϕ position of an object. According to their approach, the pyramids are built for the training as well as the scene image. On the top pyramid level, a conventional GHT is performed yielding coarse positions which are refined or rejected at lower levels. Therefore, a scan of the compete transformation space has only to be performed at top level, where quantization can be chosen very coarse which is beneficial in terms of memory demand. The knowledge obtained in this step helps to speed up the computation as well. It can be exploited as follows:

- *Accumulator size reduction*: as only parts of the transformation space close to the coarse positions have to be examined, the size of the accumulator can be kept small despite of the finer quantization.
- *Limitation of image region*: based on the coarse position and its estimated uncertainties, the image region for gradient orientation calculation can be restricted efficiently.
- *Accelerated voting*: as the object rotation ϕ is already approximately known, look-up in the R-table can be restricted to very few rotation steps.

Ulrich et al. implemented a strategy incorporating separate R-tables for each pyramid level and possible object rotation. This involves an increased memory demand for the model, but they showed that this is overcompensated by the reduction of accumulator size as well as runtime. Both can be reduced by several orders of magnitude compared to the standard scheme. In a comparative study Ulrich and Steger [10] showed that a GHT modified in such a way can compete with other recognition schemes which are widely used in industrial applications.

3.4 The Hausdorff Distance

3.4.1 Basic Approach

3.4.1.1 Main Idea

The Hausdorff distance H is a nonlinear metric for the proximity of the points between two point sets. When applied in object recognition, one point set M represents the model whereas the second, I, describes the content of a scene image region. H can be used as a measure of similarity between the image content in the vicinity of a given position and the model. If H is calculated for multiple positions it is possible to determine the location of an object. The absolute value of H indicates whether the object is present at all. H is defined by

$$H(M,I) = \max\left(h(M,I), h(I,M)\right) \text{ with} \tag{3.7}$$

$$h(M,I) = \max_{m \in M}\left(\min_{i \in I} \|m - i\|\right) \text{ and } h(I,M) = \max_{i \in I}\left(\min_{m \in M} \|i - m\|\right) \tag{3.8}$$

where $\|\cdot\|$ denotes some kind of distance norm between a model point m and an image point i, e.g., the Euclidean distance norm. $h(M,I)$ is called forward distance and can be determined by calculating the distance to the nearest point of I for each point of M and taking the maximum of these distances. $h(M,I)$ is small exactly when *every* point of M is located in the vicinity of *some* point of I.

$h(I,M)$ (the reverse distance) is calculated by evaluating the distance to the nearest point of M for each point of I and taking the maximum again. $h(I,M)$ is small exactly when *every* point of I is located in the vicinity of *some* point of M. Finally, H is calculated by taking the maximum of these two values.

Figure 3.3 should make things clear. The proceeding of calculating the forward distance is shown in the top row: at first, for each model point (marked green)

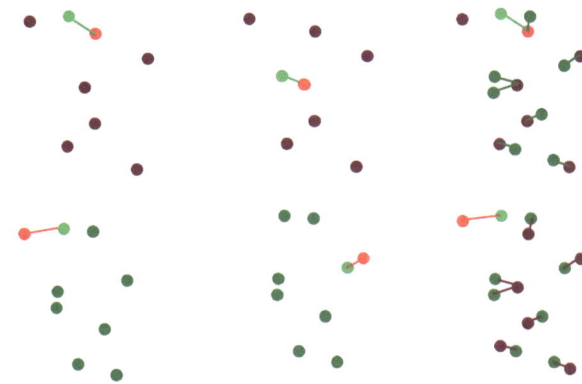

Fig. 3.3 Illustrating the process of calculating the Hausdorff distance (model points are marked *green*, image points *red*)

the nearest image point (marked red) is searched. This is explicitly shown for two model points in the two leftmost point sets (the thus established correspondences are marked by bright colors). After that, the forward distance is set to the maximum of these distances (shown in the right part; marked light green). In the bottom row the calculation of the inverse distance can be seen: for each image point the nearest model point is detected (illustrated for two example image points marked light in the leftmost two columns). Subsequently, the inverse distance is set to the maximum of these distances (marked light red). Finally, the Hausdorff distance is set to the maximum of the forward and reverse distance.

Please note that, in general, forward and inverse distance are not equal: $h(M, I) \neq h(I, M)$. In fact, this is also true for our example as one of the correspondences established during calculation of the forward distance differs from the correspondence of the reverse distance (see the upper left areas of the point sets depicted in the right part of Fig. 3.3, where correspondences are indicated by red and green lines).

The Hausdorff distance has the desirable property that the total number of model points and the total number of image points don't have to be identical, because multiple image points i can be matched to a single model point m and vice versa. Hence, a reliable calculation of the metric is still possible if the number of model points differs from the number of image points, which usually is the case in real-world applications.

For the purpose of object detection the directed Hausdorff distances have to be adjusted to the so-called partial distances $h^{f_F}(M, I)$ and $h^{f_R}(I, M)$. Imagine an image point set where one point, which is located far away form the other points, is caused by clutter. This would result in a large value of $h(I, M)$, which is obviously not intended. Respectively, an isolated point of M would produce large values of $h(M, I)$ if it is not visible in the image due to occlusion (see Table 3.3 for an illustration).

Such a behavior can be circumvented by taking the k-largest value instead of the maximum during the calculation of the directed distances $h(I, M)$ and $h(M, I)$. We can define f_F as the fraction of model points which need to have a nearest distance below the value of $h^{f_F}(M, I)$ which is finally reported. $h^{f_F}(M, I)$ is called the partial directed forward distance. If for example $f_F = 0.7$ and the model consists of 10 points, their minimum distances to the image point set can be sorted in ascending order and $h^{f_F}(M, I)$ is set to the distance value of the seventh model point. For $f_F = 1$ the partial distance $h^{f_F}(M, I)$ becomes equal to $h(M, I)$. A respective definition of f_R exists for $h^{f_R}(I, M)$.

As a consequence, it is possible to control the amount of occlusion which should be tolerated by the recognition system with the choice of f_F. The parameter f_R controls the amount of clutter to be tolerated, respectively.

3.4.1.2 Recognition Phase

Rucklidge [9] proposes to utilize the Hausdorff distance as a metric which indicates the presence of searched objects. He suggests to scan a 6D transformation space in

Table 3.3 Illustrating the problems due to occlusion and clutter which can be solved by the introduction of the partial Hausdorff distance measures

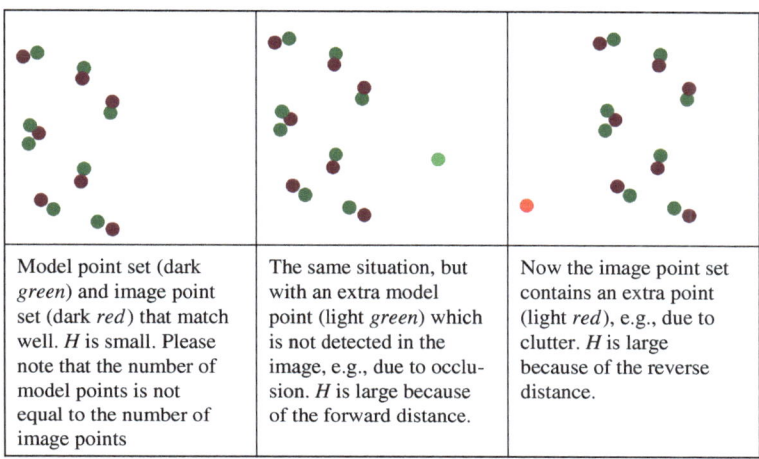

Model point set (dark *green*) and image point set (dark *red*) that match well. H is small. Please note that the number of model points is not equal to the number of image points	The same situation, but with an extra model point (light *green*) which is not detected in the image, e.g., due to occlusion. H is large because of the forward distance.	Now the image point set contains an extra point (light *red*), e.g., due to clutter. H is large because of the reverse distance.

order to determine the parameters of an affine transformation. To this end, the transformation space is sampled and for every sampled position, which consists of six specific parameter values and defines a specific transformation t, the partial forward and reverse Hausdorff distances $h_t^{f_F}(t(M), I)$ and $h_t^{f_R}(I, t(M))$ with respect to the transformed model points $t(M)$ are calculated. Valid object positions are reported for transformation parameters where the Hausdorff distance reaches local minima. Additionally, the distances have to remain below user defined thresholds τ_F and τ_R:

$$h_t^{f_F}(t(M), I) < \tau_F \wedge h_t^{f_R}(I, t(M)) < \tau_R \qquad (3.9)$$

Hence the search can be controlled with the four parameters τ_F, τ_R, f_F, and f_R.

Each dimension of the transformation space (defined by one of the six transformation parameters) is sampled equally spaced with a step size such that the resulting position difference of each transformed model point between two adjacent parameter values t_k and t_{k+1} does not exceed the size of one pixel: $|t_k(m) - t_{k+1}(m)| \leq 1$ pixel $\forall m \in M$. Additionally, for each transformation t the transformed model points $t(m)$ are rounded to integer positions for speed reasons (see below). As a result, no sub-pixel accuracy can be achieved, but a finer sampling and/or the abdication of rounding would be prohibitive in terms of runtime. However, there is still much demand for an acceleration of the search, which is until now still brute-force, in order to reduce runtime. To this end, Rucklidge [9] suggests the following modifications:

- *Size restriction of the search space*: The space of transformations which are reasonable can be restricted by applying constraints. First, all transformed model points $t(m)$ have to be located within the borders of the scene image under investigation. Additionally, in many applications a priori knowledge can be exploited, e.g., the scale and/or rotation of the object to be found have to remain within some rather narrow tolerances.

- *Box-reverse distance*: Usually, the objects to be located only cover a rather small fraction of the search image. Therefore only points located in a box $[x_{min}...x_{max}, y_{min}...y_{max}]$ have to be considered when calculating the reverse distance at a given position.
- *Optimization of calculation order*: A speedup due to rearranging the calculations can be achieved in two ways:

  - For most of the positions, the distances will not meet the threshold criteria. Therefore it is worthwhile to calculate only the forward distance at first and then to check whether its value is below τ_F. Only if this criterion is met, the reverse distance has to be calculated, because otherwise the current transformation has to be rejected anyway regardless of the reverse distance.
  - Furthermore, with a modification of the partial distance calculation it is often possible to stop the calculation with only a fraction of the points being examined. Let's consider the forward distance: instead of calculating the minimum distance to the image point set of every transformed model point $t(m)$ and then evaluating whether the distance at the f_F-quantile is below τ_F, it is better to count the number of model points which have a minimum distance to the image point set that remains below τ_F. The final check is then whether this number reaches the fraction f_F of the total number of model points. This enables us to stop the evaluation at a point where it has become clear that f_F cannot be reached any longer: this is the case when the number of model points, which are already checked and have a distance above τ_F, exceeds the fraction $1 - f_F$ with respect to the number of model points.

- *Usage of the so-called distance transform*: If the transformed model points are rounded to integer positions, it is likely that the same position results for different model points and transformations, i.e., $t_1(m_a) = t_2(m_b)$. Therefore – when evaluating the forward distance – it might be worthwhile to remember the minimum distance to the image point set at a specific position $t(m)$: provided that the already calculated distance for $t_1(m_a)$ has been stored, the distance for $t_2(m_b)$ can be set to the stored distance of $t_1(m_a)$ immediately. It can be shown that an even more efficient way is to perform a calculation of the minimum distance to the image point set for every pixel of the scene image prior to the Hausdorff distance calculation, because then information can be re-used for adjacent pixels. This is done by calculating the so-called *distance transform* $\Delta[x, y]$, which specifies the minimum distance of position $[x, y]$ to the image point set, and is defined by

$$\Delta[x, y] = \min_{i \in I} \|[x, y] - i\| \tag{3.10}$$

Fig. 3.4 Illustrating the usage of the distance transform (depicted as *grayscale* image) in order to speedup calculation of the forward distance

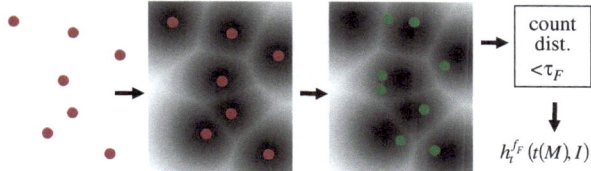

As a consequence, each $t(m)$ only probes $\Delta[x, y]$ during the calculation of $h_t^{f_F}(t(M), I)$. Figure 3.4 illustrates the proceeding: $\Delta[x, y]$ can be derived from the image point set (red points) in a pre-processing step. Dark values indicate low distances to the nearest image point. A model point set (green points) is superimposed according to the transformation t currently under investigation and the forward distance can be calculated very fast. Besides, this speedup is the reason why the forward distance is calculated first: a similar distance transform for the reverse distance would depend on the transformation t, which complicates its calculation prior to the search.

- *Recursive scan order*: Probably the most important modification is to apply a recursive coarse-to-fine approach, which allows for a significant reduction of the number of transformations that have to be checked in most cases. Roughly speaking, the transformation space is processed by dividing it recursively into equally spaced cells. In the first recursion step the cell size s is large. For each cell it is evaluated with the help of a quick check whether the cell possibly contains transformations with a Hausdorff distance below the thresholds. In that case the cell is labeled as "interesting." Only those cells are recursively split into sub-cells, which are again evaluated, and so on. The recursion stops either if the cell cannot contain Hausdorff distances meeting the criteria for a valid object location or if the cell reaches pixel-size. The quick evaluation of a cell containing many transformations is based on the observation that the distance transform $\Delta[x, y]$ decreases at most by 1 between adjacent pixels. Hence, many transformations with similar parameters can be ruled out if $\Delta[x, y]$ is large for a certain parameter setting. For details the interested reader is referred to [9].

3.4.1.3 Pseudocode

```
function findAllObjectLocationsHausdorffDist (in scene image
S, in model point set M, in thresholds fF, fR, τF, τR, out pos-
ition list p)

// calculate edge point information
detect all edge points e based on image gradients, e.g. by
non-maximum suppression and hysteresis thresholding (Canny)
set scene image point set I to locations of edge points e
```

```
// preprocessing: calculate distance transform
for y = 1 to height (S)
   for x = 1 to width (S)
      calculate Δ[x,y] (Equation 3.10)
   next
next

// scanning of transformation space
s ← s_start    // set cell size to start size (coarse level)
while s ≥ 1 do
   set the step sizes of the six transformation parameters
   such that one step causes at most s pixels position diff.
   // sampling-loop (actually six nested for-loops)
   // use step sizes just derived
   for each possible transformation cell (t's within bounds)
      if current cell of transformation space has not been
      rejected already then
         // evaluation of forward distance
         r ← 0   // initialize number of rejected points
         while unprocessed model points exist do
            m ← next unprocessed point of M
            if Δ[t(m)] > τ_F then
               r ← r + 1   // reject current point
               if r/N_M > 1 − f_F then
                  r ← N_M   // forward distance too high
                  break     // abort while-loop through all m
               end if
            end if
         end while
         if r/N_M > 1 − f_F then
            mark current cell defined by t as "rejected "
         else
            // forward-dist. ok -> evaluate reverse dist.
            calculate reverse distance h_t^{fR}(I,t(M))
            if h_t^{fR}(I,t(M)) > τ_R then
               mark current cell defined by t as "rejected"
            else if s == 1 then
               // finest sampling level-> object found
               append position defined by t to p
            end if
         end if
      end if
   next
   adjust cell size s   // e.g. multiplication with 0.5
end while
```

```
// post-processing
merge all adjacent positions in p such that only local
minima of the hausdorff distance are reported
```

3.4.1.4 Example

Two examples where the Hausdorff distance is used for object recognition are shown in Figs. 3.5 and 3.6. In each case the objects to be found have been undergone a perspective transformation. For each example the model point set is shown in part (a), followed by the scene image where the object has been undergone a projective transformation (b), the point set extracted from the scene image by edge detection (c) and, finally, all recognized instances in the scene image overlaid on the scene image point set in bold black (d). The point sets are set to edge pixels, which can be extracted, e.g., with the Canny detector including non-maximum suppression (cf. [3]).

It can be seen that all instances are recognized correctly, even in the presence of clutter and partial occlusion (second example). The computational complexity is very high, because of the rather high dimensionality of the transformation space (six dimensions, as the parameters of an affine transformation are estimated) as well as the cardinality of the sets (in the order of magnitude of 1,000 points for the model

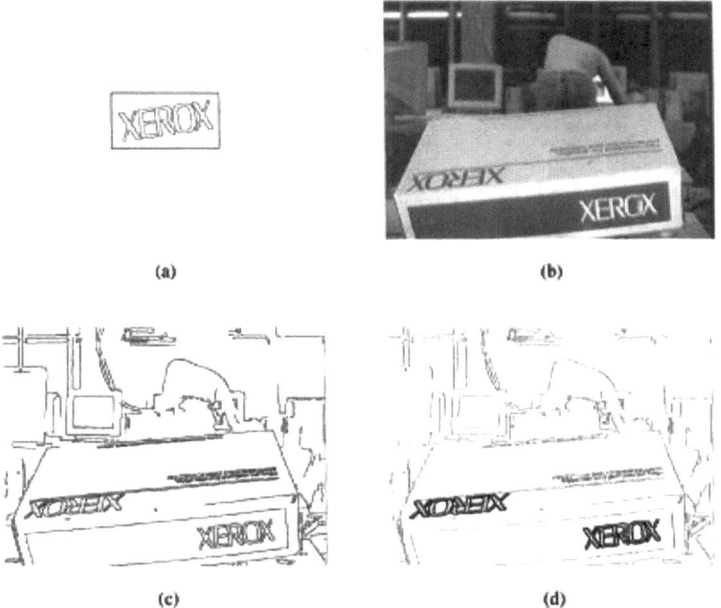

(a)   (b)

(c)   (d)

Fig. 3.5 Taken from Rucklidge [9][2] showing an example of the detection of a logo

[2] With kind permission from Springer Science+Business Media: Rucklidge [9], Fig. 1, © 1997 Springer.

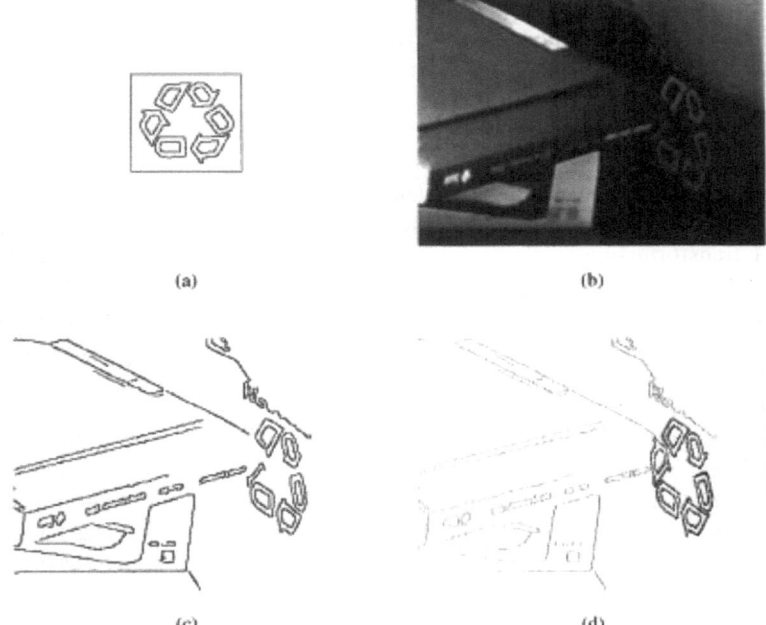

Fig. 3.6 Taken from Rucklidge [9][3] showing another example of the detection of a logo with
partial occlusion

and 10,000 points for the scene image). As a consequence, Rucklidge reported execution times in the order of several minutes for both examples. Even if the used
hardware nowadays is out of date, the method seems infeasible for industrial applications. But the method is not restricted to low-level features like edge pixels which
occur in large numbers. When high-level features like line segments are used, the
number of points in the point sets can be reduced significantly.

3.4.1.5 Rating

Due to the flexible object model consisting of an arbitrary point set a large range
of objects, including complex shaped objects, can be handled with this method.
The model generation process, which, e.g., extracts all points with gradient above
a certain threshold from a training image, imposes no a priori constraints about the
object appearance. Moreover, because of the usage of partial distances the method
is robust to occlusion and clutter.

On the other hand, the gradient threshold also implies a dependency on the illumination: if the image contrast is reduced in the scene image, some points might
be missed which are contained in the model. Additionally, the method tends to be

---

[3]With kind permission from Springer Science+Business Media: Rucklidge [9], Fig. 2, © 1997
Springer.

sensitive to erroneously detect object instances in image regions which are densely populated with pixels featuring a high gradient ("false alarms"). Therefore, Ulrich and Steger [10] reported the robustness inferior to other methods in a comparative study. In spite of the significant speedup when searching the transformation space, the scheme still is very slow. One reason is that no hierarchical search in the image domain is applied. Finally, the method doesn't achieve sub-pixel accuracy.

3.4.2 Variants

3.4.2.1 Variant 1: Generalized Hausdorff Distance

In addition to the gradient magnitude, most edge detection schemes determine gradient orientation information as well. As the object recognition scheme utilizing the Hausdorff distance discussed so far doesn't use this information, Olson and Huttenlocher [8] suggested a modification of the Hausdorff distance which is applicable to sets of edge pixels and also considers orientation information of the edge points. For example, the thus obtained generalized forward Hausdorff distance $h_a(M, I)$ is defined as

$$h_a(M, I) = \max_{m \in M} \min_{i \in I} \max \left(\left\| \begin{bmatrix} m_x - i_x \\ m_y - i_y \end{bmatrix} \right\|, \frac{|m_\varphi - i_\varphi|}{a} \right) \qquad (3.11)$$

The original $h(M, I)$ serves as a lower bound for the new measure, i.e., the gradient orientation difference $m_\varphi - i_\varphi$ between a model and an image point is considered as a second measure and the maximum of these two values is taken for the calculation of $h_a(M, I)$. The parameter a acts as a regularization term which enables us to compare location and orientation differences directly. For a robust detection the f_F-quantile instead of the maximum distance of all points $m \in M$ can also be used.

Please note that the distance transform $\Delta[x, y]$ now becomes a 3D function, with the additional dimension characterizing the distance measure evolving from orientation differences. An elegant way of considering this fact is to use separate models for each possible rotation step of the object to be found, e.g., by successively rotating the object model with a certain step size.

According to Olson and Huttenlocher [8], the additional consideration of the orientation information leads to a significantly decreased false alarm rate, especially in densely populated image regions. Interestingly enough, they also reported a considerable acceleration of the method as fewer transformations have to be checked during the search.

3.4.2.2 Variant 2: 3D Hausdorff Distance

Another suggestion made by Olson and Huttenlocher is to extend the method to a recognition scheme for 3D objects undergoing projective transformation. To this end, each object is represented by multiple models characterizing its shape from a specific viewpoint. Each model is obtained by rotating a sample of the object in 3D space with a certain step size. The recognition phase is done by calculation of the Hausdorff distance to each model.

An observation which can be exploited for accelerating the scheme is that at least a portion of the models should be very similar with respect to each other. To this end, the models are clustered hierarchically in a tree structure during the training phase. Each model is represented by a leaf at the bottom tree level. In higher levels, the most similar models/leafs (or, alternatively, nodes already containing grouped leafs) are grouped to nodes, with each node containing the portion of the edge points identical in the two sub-nodes/leafs. The congruence incorporated in this structure can be exploited in the recognition phase in a top-down approach: if the point (sub-)set assigned to a certain node suffices for a rejection of the current transformation, this holds for every leaf belonging to this node.

3.4.2.3 Variant 3: Chamfer Matching

A closely related approach, which is called "hierarchical chamfer matching", has been reported by Borgefors [2]. It utilizes the average distance of all trans-formed model points to their nearest image point as a distance measure instead of a quantile. For a rapid evaluation a distance transform is used, too. There exists a fast sequential way of calculating the distance transform of a scene image point set by passing the image only twice. Sequential distance trans-forms are known as "chamfer distances" explaining the name of the method. The search of the transformation space is not done by brute force; instead, the algo-rithm relies on reasonable initial position estimates which are refined by iterative optimization.

Speedup is achieved by employing a hierarchical search strategy, where an image pyramid of the edge image of the scene (edge pixels are used as point sets) is built. A distance transform can be computed for each level of the pyramid. As the start image is a binary image, averaging or smoothing operations for calculating the higher lev-els of the pyramid obviously don't work. Therefore a logical "OR" operation is used when adjacent pixels are summarized for higher levels.

Compared to the Hausdorff distance, chamfer matching has the property that due to averaging occluded model points still contribute to the reported distance value if a minor part of the object is not visible. Another point is the lack of a measure comparable to the reverse Hausdorff distance: this results in an increased sensitivity to false alarms in densely populated image regions which contain many edge points.

3.5 Speedup by Rectangular Filters and Integral Images

3.5.1 Main Idea

In their article "Robust Real-time Object Detection," Viola and Jones [12] proposed a transformation-search-based method which is optimized for computation speed. They showed that their scheme is capable to do real-time processing when applied to the task of detection of upright, frontal faces.

The method localizes instances of a single object class by applying a set of rectangular-structured filters to a query image instead of using a point set. The filter kernels are reminiscent of Haar wavelet filters , as they can be represented by a combination of step-functions and consist of piecewise constant intervals in 2D. The input image is convolved with a set of filters at various positions and scales. Subsequently, a decision whether an object instance is present or not can be made at each position. These decisions are based on weighted combinations of the filter outputs. In other words, the $[x, y, s]$-space is searched.

The search can be done very fast, because the specific shape of the rectangular filters allows for an extremely efficient implementation of the convolutions with the help of so-called *integral images*. Additionally, the outputs of different filters are combined in a smart way such that most of the time only a fraction of the filter set has to be calculated at a particular position. Overall, three major contributions are to be mentioned:

- *Integral images*: prior to recognition, a so-called integral image F is derived from the input image I. Roughly speaking, F contains the integrated intensities of I (details will follow). This pre-processing allows for a very rapid calculation of the filter responses, as we will see below.
- *Learning of weights*: as there are many possible instances of rectangular-shaped filter kernels, it has to be decided which ones to use and how to weight the individual outputs of the chosen filters. These questions are answered by a modified version of the AdaBoost algorithm proposed by Freund and Schapire [6], which learns the weights of the filters from a set of sample images in a training phase. The weighting favors filters that perform best if a single filter is utilized for object detection.
- *Cascaded classifying*: for speed reasons, not the complete filter set is applied to every position and scale. Instead, only a small subset of the filters searches the complete transformation space. Just promising areas, where a simple classifier based on these few filter responses reports possible object locations, are examined further by larger subsets, which are used to refine the initial estimate in those areas, and so on. This proceeding enables us to sort out large regions of I, which are very likely to be background, very quickly.

3.5.2 Filters and Integral Images

The filter kernels used by Viola and Jones [12] exhibit a rectangular structure and consist of two to four sub-rectangles. Some examples can be seen in Fig. 3.7. The filter output f_i of the convolution of an input image I with such a kernel k_i is defined by the sum of the intensities of I which are covered by the white areas minus the sum of intensities covered by the black areas.

Fig. 3.7 Examples of filter kernels utilized by Viola and Jones

Hence, the filter is well suited for rectangular-structured objects and yields high responses for object areas with a partitioning similar to the filter kernel. Different scales during search can be covered by different kernel sizes.

Overall, a great multitude of combinations of two to four sub-rectangles are possible. Note that the kernel center position, which is set arbitrarily by definition, can be shifted with respect to the actual center of the filter structure. Therefore multiple kernels with identical configurations of sub-rectangles exist.

The learning algorithm presented below has to choose the most promising filter configurations for the recognition phase. In order to make this task feasible the variety of kernels can be restricted, e.g., by considering only sub-rectangles of equal size, limiting the number of overall kernel sizes, or considering only small shifts or shifts spaced at a rather large step size.

The so-called integral image F is specified as follows: its value at position $[x, y]$ is defined by the sum of intensities of I considering all pixels located inside the rectangular area ranging from $[0, 0]$ up to and including $[x, y]$:

$$F(x, y) = \sum_{a=0}^{x} \sum_{b=0}^{y} I(a, b) \tag{3.12}$$

An example can be seen in Fig. 3.8, where the integral image is calculated for a simple cross-shaped object.

The integral image F can be calculated in a pre-processing stage prior to recognition in a recursive manner in just one pass over the original image I as follows:

$$R(x, y) = R(x, y - 1) + I(x, y) \tag{3.13a}$$

$$F(x, y) = F(x - 1, y) + R(x, y) \tag{3.13b}$$

where $R(x, y)$ denotes the cumulative row sum. R and F are initialized by $R(x, -1) = 0$ and $F(-1, y) = 0$.

By usage of F a very fast calculation of the convolution of I with one of the rectangular filter kernels is possible, because now the sum of intensities of a rectangular area ranging from $[x_0, y_0]$ to $[x_1, y_1]$ can be calculated by just considering the values

Fig. 3.8 Example of an integral image (*right*) of a cross-shaped object (*left*)

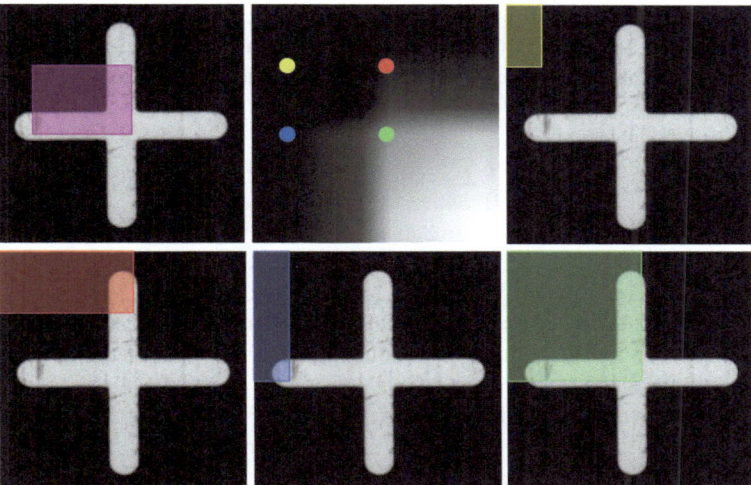

Fig. 3.9 Exemplifying the calculation of the sum of intensities in a rectangular region with the help of integral images

of F at the four corner points of the region instead of summing up the intensities of all pixels inside:

$$\sum_{a=x_0}^{x_1} \sum_{b=y_0}^{y_1} I(a, b) = F(x_1, y_1) - F(x_0, y_1) - F(x_1, y_0) + F(x_0, y_0) \qquad (3.14)$$

Figure 3.9 illustrates the proceeding: In order to calculate the intensity sum of the purple region sown in the top left image, just four values of F have to be considered (as stated in Equation 3.14). This is shown in the top middle image, where the four corner points of the region are overlaid in color upon the integral image. The value of $F(x_0, y_0)$ defines the sum of intensities of the area marked yellow (as indicated in the top right image), $F(x_1, y_0)$ the intensity sum of the red, $F(x_0, y_1)$ the intensity sum of the blue, and $F(x_1, y_1)$ the intensity sum of the green area, respectively (cf. the images in the bottom row). As a consequence, the intensity sum of any rectangular-shaped area can be calculated by considering as few as four values of F, regardless of its size. This allows for an extremely fast implementation of a convolution with one of the rectangular-shaped filter kernels describe above.

3.5.3 Classification

If multiple filter kernels are applied at a specific position, the question is how to combine their outputs in order to decide whether an instance of the object is present at this particular position or not. To this end, a so-called linear classifier cl is chosen:

its output is set to 1 (indicating that an instance is present) if a weighted combination of binarized filter outputs b_t (which is a classification in itself by thresholding the "original" filter outputs f_t) is larger than a threshold, otherwise the output is set to 0:

$$cl\,(x,y,s) = \begin{cases} 1 & \sum_{t=1}^{T} \alpha_t \cdot b_t\,(x,y,s) \geq {}^{1}\!/{}_{2} \cdot \sum_{t=1}^{T} \alpha_t \\ 0 & \text{otherwise} \end{cases} \tag{3.15}$$

where the α_t denotes the weights of the particular filters. Details of linear classification can be found in Appendix B.

Now it is also clear why shifted kernels with identical sub-rectangle configuration are used: it's because filters responding to different parts of the object should contribute to the same object position.

In order to formulate such a classifier, the two tasks of selecting the filter kernels k_t and determining their weights α_t are solved in a training step with the help of a set of positive as well as negative training samples (i.e., images where the object is not present). To this end, Viola and Jones [12] suggest an adapted version of the AdaBoost algorithm (see Freund and Schapire [6]), where so-called "weak classifiers" (which show relatively high error rates, but are simple and fast) are combined to a so-called "strong classifier" . This combination, which can be a weighted sum, enables the strong classifier to perform much better ("boost" its performance) compared to each of the weak classifiers.

The learning of the weights α_t and the selection of the kernels k_t is done in T rounds of learning. At each round $t = 1, ..., T$ one kernel k_t is selected. To this end, a classification of the training images is done for each filter kernel k_i based on its binarized output b_i. As the correct classification is known for every training image, an error rate ε_i can be calculated for each b_i. The kernel with the lowest error rate is chosen as k_t and its weight α_t is adjusted to this error rate (low ε_i lead to high α_t).

As training proceeds, the training images themselves are also weighted: if the weak classifier based on k_t misclassifies an image, its weight is increased; otherwise it is decreased. The error rates in the next round of training are calculated based on this weighting. This helps to find kernels that perform well for "critical images" in later rounds. Overall, all terms/factors which are necessary for applying the linear classifier as defined by Equation (3.15) are determined at the end of training.

Viola and Jones report good detection rates for classifiers consisting of approximately 200 filters for their example of detection of upright, frontal faces. With an implementation on a 700 MHz Pentium desktop computer processing a 384×288 image took approximately 0.7 s, which, however, is still too much for real-time processing.

In order to achieve a speedup, they altered the classification to a cascaded application of multiple classifiers. In the first stage, a classifier consisting of just a few filters is applied for the whole transformation space. Search in the scale space is implemented by changing the filter size. In the next stage, a second classifier, which is a bit more complex, is applied only at those $[x, y, s]$-positions where the first one detected an instance of the object. This proceeding goes on for a fixed number of stages, where the number of filters contained in the classifiers increases progressively. At each stage, positions, which are highly likely to be background, are sorted out. In the end, only those positions remain which are classified to contain an instance of the object to be searched.

Each classifier has to be trained separately by the boosting procedure just described. Please note that, compared to the threshold used in Equation (3.15), the decision threshold has to be set much lower as we don't want the classifier to erroneously sort out positions where an object instance is actually present. Nevertheless, much of the background can be sorted out very quickly in the first stages. Experiments by Viola and Jones revealed that a speedup of a factor of about 10 could be achieved for a 10-stage cascaded classifier with 20 filters at each stage compared to a monolithic classifier of 200 filters at comparable detection rates for the example application of face detection.

3.5.4 Pseudocode

```
function detectObjectsCascadedClassify (in Image I, in list of
linear classifiers cl, out position list p)

// calculate integral image
for y = 1 to height (I)
    for x = 1 to width (I)
        calculate F(x,y) according to Equation 3.13
    next
next

// cascaded classification
init 3D array map with 1's    // 1: obj. present; 0: no obj.
for i = 1 to number of stages
    for y = 1 to height (I) step yStep
        for x = 1 to width (I) step xStep
            for s = 1 to smax step sStep
                if map(x,y,s) == 1 then    // current pos still valid
                    for t = 1 to nbr of kernels of current stage i
                        scale kernel ki,t acc. to current scale s
                        convolve I with filter kernel ki,t, use F
                    next
                    // classification according to cli
                    if cli(ki,1,...,ki,T)==0 then
                        map(x,y,s) ← 0    // mark as background
                    end if
                end if
            next
        next
```

```
        next
next

// determine all valid object positions
for y = 1 to height(I) step y_Step
    for x = 1 to width(I) step x_Step
        for s = 1 to s_max step s_Step
            if map(x,y,s) ==1 then
                append position [x,y,s] to p
            end if
        next
    next
next
```

3.5.5 Example

Viola and Jones report experimental results for the detection of upright, frontal faces. In the training images, the faces were approximately 24×24 pixel in size. Their cascaded detector consists of 32 stages with approximately 4,300 filters used in total. As far as the detection rates are concerned, this classifier performs comparable to other state-of-the-art detectors for that task, but takes much less time.

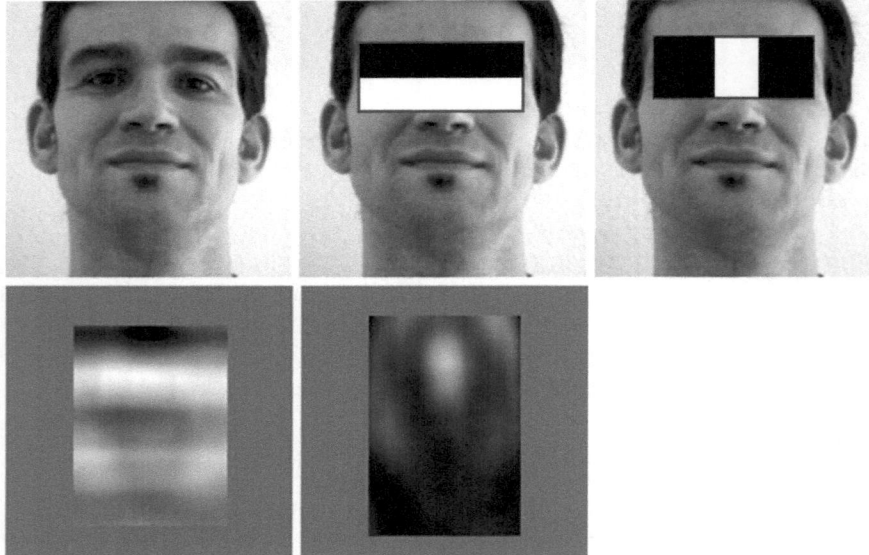

Fig. 3.10 Showing an example of the detection of an *upright*, frontal face with the filter kernels used in the first stage of the cascaded classification proposed by Viola and Jones [12]

They report processing times of about 70 ms for a 384×288 image on a 700 MHz Pentium processor.

Apparently, the combination of extremely fast filtering by integral images with the speedup through cascading works very well. In fact, the classifier used in first stage consists of as few as two filters and discards approximately 60% of the background region while almost 100% of the objects are retained at the same time.

An example can be seen in Fig. 3.10: the two filters selected by AdaBoost for the first stage relate to the facts that the eye regions typically are darker than the upper cheeks (first filter) and usually also darker than the bridge over the nose (second filter). The results of the convolution of these two filters with an example image are shown in the second row (bright areas indicate high convolution results).

3.5.6 Rating

On the positive side, in contrast to many other transformation-based schemes the method proposed by Viola and Jones is extremely fast. Real-time processing of video sequences of medium sized image frames seems possible with this method when using up-to-date hardware. Additionally, detection results for the example application of upright, frontal face recognition are comparable to state-of-the-art methods.

On the other hand, the extremely fast filtering is only possible for-rectangular-shaped filter kernels. Such a kernel structure might not be suited for some object classes. Clearly, the kernels fit best to objects showing a rectangular structure themselves. However, the authors argue that due to the extremely fast filtering a large number of filters can be applied (much larger compared to other methods using filter banks), which should contribute to alleviate such a misfitting. Another disadvantage which has to be mentioned is that the method does not explicitly account for differences of object rotation between training and recognition.

References

1. Ballard, D.H., "Generalizing the Hough Transform to Detect Arbitrary Shapes", *Pattern Recognition*, 13(2):111–122, 1981
2. Borgefors, G., "Hierarchical Chamfer Matching: A Parametric Edge Matching Algorithm", *IEEE Transactions on Pattern Analysis and Machine Intelligence*, 10(6):849–865, 1988
3. Canny, J.F., "A Computational Approach to Edge Detection", *IEEE Transactions on Pattern Analysis and Machine Intelligence*, 8(6):679–698, 1986
4. Duda, R.O. and Hart, P.E., "Use of the Hough Transform to Detect Lines and Curves in Pictures", *Communications of the ACM*, 1:11–15, 1972
5. Ecabert, O. and Thiran, J., "Adaptive Hough Transform for the Detection of Natural Shapes Under Weak Affine Transformations", *Pattern Recognition Letters*, 25(12):1411–1419, 2004
6. Freund, Y. and Schapire, R., "A Decision-Theoretic Generalization of On-Line Learning and an Application to Boosting", *Journal of Computer and System Sciences*, 55:119–139, 1997

7. Hough, P.V.C., *"Method and Means for Recognizing Complex Patterns"*, U.S. Patent No. 3069654, 1962
8. Olson, C. and Huttenlocher, D., "Automatic Target Recognition by Matching Oriented Edge Pixels". *IEEE Transactions on Signal Processing*, 6(1):103–113, 1997
9. Rucklidge, W.J., "Efficiently locating objects using the Hausdorff distance", *International Journal of Computer Vision*, 24(3):251–270, 1997
10. Ulrich, M. and Steger, C., "Performance Comparison of 2D Object Recognition Techniques", *International Archives of Photogrammetry and Remote Sensing*, XXXIV(5):99–104, 2002
11. Ulrich, M., Steger, C., Baumgartner, A. and Ebner H., "Real-Time Object Recognition Using a Modified Generalized Hough Transform", *Pattern Recognition*, 26(11):2557–2570, 2003
12. Viola, P. and Jones, M., "Robust Real-time Object Detection", *2nd International Workshop on Statistical and Computational Theories of Vision – Modelling, Learning, Computing and Sampling*, Vancouver, 1–20, 2001

Chapter 4
Geometric Correspondence-Based Approaches

Abstract Correspondence-based approaches are often used in industrial applications. Here, the geometry of the objects to be found is usually known prior to recognition, e.g., from CAD data of the object shape. Typically, these methods are feature based, meaning that the object is characterized by a limited set of primitives called features. For example, the silhouette of many industrial objects can be modeled by a set of line segments and circular arcs as features. This implies a two-stage strategy during the recognition phase: in a first step, all possible locations of features are detected. The second step tries to match the found features to the model, which leads to the pose estimation(s) of the found object(s). The search is correspondence based, i.e., one-to-one correspondences between a model feature and a scene image feature are established and evaluated during the matching step. After a short introduction of some feature types, which typically are used in correspondence-based matching, two types of algorithms are presented. The first type represents the correspondences in a graph or tree structure, where the topology is explored during matching. The second method, which is called geometric hashing, aims at speeding up the matching by the usage of hash tables.

4.1 Overview

In industrial applications the geometry of the objects to be found is usually known a priori, e.g., shape information can be supplied by CAD data or another kind of "synthetic" description of object geometry. Hence, there is no need to train it from example images, which potentially contain some kind of imperfection like noise, scratches, or minor deviations of the actual object shape compared to the ideal. Usually, this results in a more accurate representation of the object geometry. This representation, however, also involves a concentration on the geometric shape of the object; other kinds of information like gray value appearance or texture can not be included.

Typically, the object representation is feature based, i.e., the objects are characterized by a set of primitives called *features*. The silhouette of many industrial parts can be modeled by a set of line segments and circular arcs as features, for example.

During recognition, we can take advantage of this feature-based representation by applying a two-stage strategy: the first step aims at detecting all positions where features are located with high probability. Sometimes the term "feature candidates" is used in this context. In the second step we try to match the found features to the model. This matching is correspondence-based, i.e., one-to-one correspondences between model and image features are established and evaluated. Pose estimation(s) of the found object(s) can then be derived from the correspondences.

There exist several degrees of freedom as far as the design of correspondence-based algorithms is concerned, the most important are as follows:

- Selection of the feature types, e.g., line segments, corners.
- Selection of the detection method in order to find the features. Of course, this strongly relates to the types of features which are to be utilized.
- Selection of the search order for evaluating the correspondences in the matching step. The a priori knowledge of the object geometry can be exploited for the deduction of an optimized search order, e.g., salient parts of the model, which are easy to detect and/or characterize the object class very well, are detected first. This yields a hypothesis for the object pose, which can be verified with the help of other parts/features of the object.

Before some algorithms making use of geometric features for an evaluation of correspondences are presented, let's briefly review what kinds of features can be used and how they are detected.

4.2 Feature Types and Their Detection

The algorithms presented in this chapter perform object recognition by matching a set of feature positions to model data. Therefore the features have to be detected prior to the matching step. A great number of methods dealing with feature detection have been proposed over the years. As the main focus of this book lies on the matching step, a systematic introduction into feature detection shall not be given here. Let's just outline some main aspects of the field.

Most of the geometry-based algorithms presented in this book make use of two different kinds of feature types: one category intends to model the object contour (which is usually represented in the image by a curve of connected pixels featuring high intensity gradients) by a set of primitives like line segments and circular arcs. In contrast to that, some methods try to detect more or less arbitrarily shaped parts of the contour with the help of so-called geometric filters.

The main principle of both approaches shall be presented in the following. It should be mentioned, however, that – apart from the original proposition – the feature types can be used interchangeably for most of the matching methods.

4.2.1 Geometric Primitives

In the case of the usage of primitives, feature detection is composed of three steps:

1. *Edge point detection*: As the object contour should be represented by pixels with high intensity gradient, the edge pixels are detected first, e.g., with the canny operator including non-maximum suppression (cf. [2]).
2. *Edge point linking*: Subsequently, the found edge pixels are combined to curves of connected pixels. To this end, a principle called *hysteresis thresholding* can be applied: pixels with very high-gradient magnitude (i.e., when the gradient magnitude is above a certain threshold) serve as starting points ("seeds"). In a second step, they are extended by tracing adjacent pixels. A neighboring pixel is added to the current curve if its gradient remains above a second, but lower threshold. This process is repeated until the curve cannot be extended any longer. In fact, the last step of the canny operator adopts this strategy (see Appendix A for details).
3. *Feature extraction*: In the last step the thus obtained curves are approximated by a set of feature primitives. Some algorithms exclusively use line segments for this approximation, e.g., the method proposed by Ramer [8], which will be explained in more detail below. Of course, this is not sufficient if the object contour features circular parts, therefore there exist algorithms for a joint segmentation of the curve into line segments and circular arcs as well (see e.g. [3])

4.2.1.1 Polygonal Approximation

If a curve can be approximated accurate enough by line segments only, comparative studies performed by Rosin [9] revealed that one of the oldest algorithms, which was presented by Ramer [8], performed very good. The main principle of the so-called polygonal approximation of the curve is a recursive subdivision of the current approximation at positions where the distance of the approximating polygon to the curve (i.e., the approximation error) attains a maximum.

The proceeding is illustrated in Fig. 4.1. Iteration starts with a single line connecting the two end points of the curve (or, in the case of a closed curve, two arbitrarily chosen points located sufficiently far away from each other). At each iteration step i the pixel $p_{i,\max}$ of the curve with maximum distance $d_{i,\max}$ to the approximation is determined. If $d_{i,\max}$ is above a certain threshold ε, a subdivision of the line is performed, where $p_{i,\max}$ is taken as a new end point of the two sub-lines. The same procedure can be recursively applied to each of the two sub-lines, and so on. Convergence is achieved if the maximum deviation of the curve to the approximating polygon remains below ε for all curve pixels.

4.2.1.2 Approximation with Line Segments and Circular Arcs

A lot of different methods have been proposed for the segmentation of a curve into line segments and circular arcs. Roughly speaking, they can be divided into two categories:

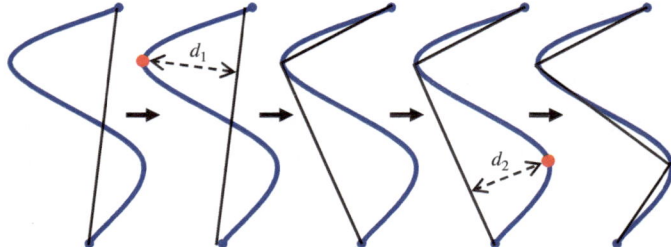

Fig. 4.1 Illustrative example of the approximation scheme proposed by Ramer [8], which consists of two iteration steps here: in the *left* part, a curve (*blue*) together with the initial approximation line (*black*) is shown. As the maximum distance d_1 between the curve and its approximation (position marked *red*) is larger than ε, the line is subdivided (*middle*). In a second step, the lower line segment is subdivided again ($d_2 > \varepsilon$); the final approximation is shown on the *right*

- Algorithms intending to identify so-called *breakpoints* on the curve (which define the starting and end points of the lines and arcs) with the help of an analysis of the curvature of the curve.
- Methods where the curve is approximated by line segments only first. A subsequent step explores if there are segments which can be combined again, e.g., to circular arcs.

A method falling into the first category (analysis of curvature) was suggested by Chen et al. [3]. In this method curvature is modeled by the change of the orientations of tangents on the curve. At each curve pixel p_i a tangent on the curve passing through p_i can be determined. In the case of high curvature, the orientations of the tangents change rapidly between adjacent curve pixels, whereas parts with low curvature are indicated by nearly constant tangent orientations. The tangent orientation $\vartheta_{i,k}$ as well as its first derivative $\delta_{i,k}$ can be calculated directly from the positions of two neighboring curve pixels as follows:

$$\vartheta_{i,k} = \tan^{-1}\left(\frac{y_i - y_{i-k}}{x_i - x_{i-k}}\right) \tag{4.1}$$

$$\delta_{i,k} = \tan^{-1}\left(\frac{y_{i+k} - y_i}{x_{i+k} - x_i}\right) - \tan^{-1}\left(\frac{y_i - y_{i-k}}{x_i - x_{i-k}}\right) \tag{4.2}$$

where $[x_i, y_i]$ determines the position of curve pixel p_i (for which the tangent orientation is calculated), i serves as an index passing through the curve pixels, and, finally, k defines the shift between the two pixels considered and thus the scope of the calculations.

Based on an evaluation of $\vartheta_{i,k}$ and $\delta_{i,k}$ Chen et al. [3] define two ways of segmenting the curve: on the one hand, corners (which usually occur at intersections between two line segments and therefore define starting- and end points of the line segments) are indicated by a discontinuity in curvature. Such discontinuities are detected by a peak search in the first derivative $\delta(i)$ of the tangent orientation function.

Please note that corners, however, are not sufficient for the detection of all end points of circular arcs. Sometimes a "smooth join" (where no discontinuity is present) can be observed at transitions between a line segment and a circular arc or two arcs. But a circular arc involves sections in the tangent orientation function $\vartheta(i)$ where the slope of $\vartheta(i)$ is constant and non-zero. Therefore it can be found by fitting a line segment with non-zero slope into $\vartheta(i)$ and taking the end points of the segment as breakpoints (see Table 4.1 for an example).

The breakpoints define the position of the starting point and end point of each primitive. The parameters of the primitives can be estimated for each primitive separately by minimization of the deviation between the positions of the curve pixels and the primitive.

A drawback of the usage of curvature, however, is its sensitivity to noise. In order to alleviate this effect the curve is smoothed prior to the calculation of the tangent orientation functions. However, smoothing also involves a considerable shift of the breakpoint locations in some cases. Therefore the breakpoint positions are refined in a second stage, which is based on the original data (for details see [3]).

Table 4.1 Example of curve segmentation into line segments and circular arcs according to [3]

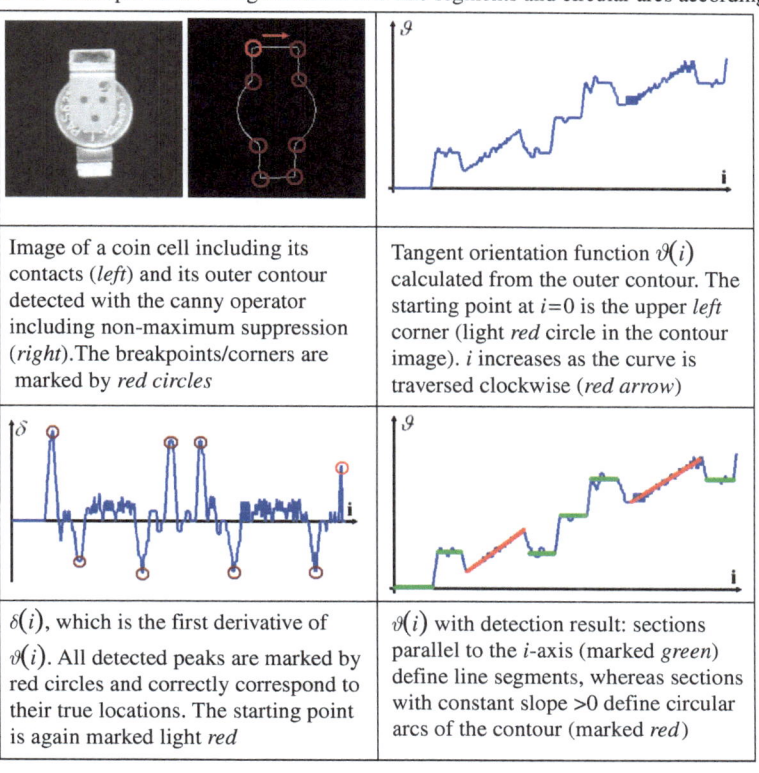

Image of a coin cell including its contacts (*left*) and its outer contour detected with the canny operator including non-maximum suppression (*right*).The breakpoints/corners are marked by *red circles*	Tangent orientation function $\vartheta(i)$ calculated from the outer contour. The starting point at $i=0$ is the upper *left* corner (light *red* circle in the contour image). i increases as the curve is traversed clockwise (*red arrow*)
$\delta(i)$, which is the first derivative of $\vartheta(i)$. All detected peaks are marked by red circles and correctly correspond to their true locations. The starting point is again marked light *red*	$\vartheta(i)$ with detection result: sections parallel to the i-axis (marked *green*) define line segments, whereas sections with constant slope >0 define circular arcs of the contour (marked *red*)

4.2.2 Geometric Filters

The technique of so-called geometric filters is not widely spread, but can be very efficient in certain cases. A geometric filter consists of a set of point pairs which are arranged along the object contour which is to be modeled. The two points of each point pair are located at different sides of the object contour: one point is located inside the object and the other one outside.

Figure 4.2 illustrates the principle for a rectangular-shaped feature: A dark rectangle is depicted upon a bright background. The black lines define the pixel grid. Altogether, the filter consists of 12 point pairs (each pair is marked by a blue ellipse), where each point pair is made up of a "+" (red) and a "−" point (green). The "+" points are located on the brighter, the "−" points on the darker side of the object boundary.

In order to decide whether a feature which corresponds well to the shape of the geometric filter is present at a specific position in a query image I, the filter can be positioned upon this specific image position – like a template image for cross coefficient calculation – and a match score can be calculated. To this end, the intensity difference of the two pixels which are covered by the two points of a single point pair is calculated for each point pair. Coming back to Fig. 4.2 helps to explain the issue: if the gray value of the "+"-pixel exceeds the gray value of the "−"-pixel by at least a certain threshold value t_{GV}, a point pair "matches" to the image content at a given position. This criterion can be written as follows:

$$I(x_+, y_+) \geq I(x_-, y_-) + t_{GV} \qquad (4.3)$$

The match score of the entire filter can then be set to the fraction of all point pairs fulfilling Equation (4.3), related to the overall number of point pairs. Hence, the match score can range between 0 (no point pair fulfills Equation (4.3)) and 1 (Equation (4.3) is fulfilled by all point pairs). If the filter is located exactly upon the object contour from which it was derived, there exist many pairs with one

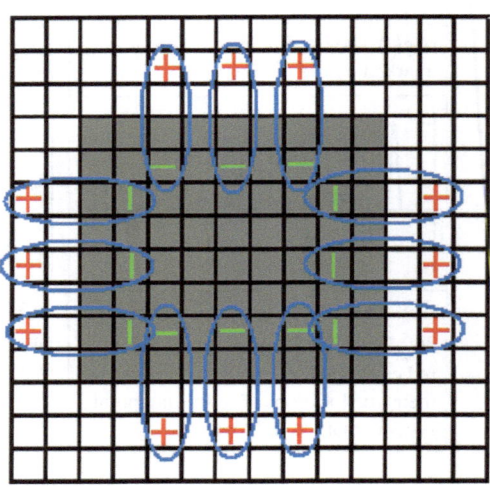

Fig. 4.2 Exemplifying the functional principle of geometrical filters

point being located outside and the other one inside the object. As a consequence, Equation (4.3) is fulfilled for many pairs, which leads to a high match score at this position.

If the filter is shifted over the image a 2D matching function can be computed. All local maxima of the matching function exceeding a threshold indicate occurrences of the feature to be searched. In fact, this proceeding relates closely to 2D correlation with a template, but in contrast to correlation only a subset of the pixels is considered. This involves a concentration on the parts with high information content (the contour) as well as faster computations. On the other hand, however, the filter is more sensitive to noise.

However, information about the shape of the features must be available in advance in order to design suitable filters. Interestingly, though, this a priori knowledge can be utilized in order to make the matching method more robust, because it is possible "suppress" certain areas and concentrate on parts of the object that are known to be stable. For example, some regions of the object to be detected could be salient in a single image (and thus would lead to many edge points), but could change significantly between two different batches of the object (e.g., inscriptions) and therefore should not be considered during recognition.

Please note also that due to the distance between the "+"- and "−"-points of each pair the filter allows for minor object deformations. If, for example, the course of the rectangle boundary depicted in Fig. 4.2 was slightly different, Equation (4.3) would still hold for all point pairs. Therefore the extent of acceptable contour deformation can be controlled by the choice of the pixel distance between the two points of a pair. As a consequence, geometric filtering also allows for minor rotation and/or scaling differences without explicitly rotating or scaling the filter.

Compared to the usage of geometric primitives, the filter-based approach has the advantage that arbitrary object contours can be modeled more exactly as we are not restricted to a set of primitives (e.g., lines and circular arcs) any longer. Moreover, the filters are quite insensitive to contour interruptions, e.g., due to noise or occlusion, at least as long as only a minor portion of the point pairs is affected. Contrary to that, a line segment can break into multiple parts if noise causes interruptions in the grouped edge pixels. On the other hand, the method becomes impractical if a large variance in rotation and/or scaling of the feature to be detected has to be considered. This stems from the fact that the match scores have to be calculated with many rotated and/or scaled versions of the filter in that case, resulting in a significant slow down.

4.3 Graph-Based Matching

4.3.1 Geometrical Graph Match

4.3.1.1 Main Idea

One approach to model the geometry of objects is to represent them as graphs : a graph $G = (N, E)$ consists of a set of nodes N as well as a set of edges E, where each edge $e(a, b)$ links the two nodes n_a and n_b. Each node represents a salient feature of the object (e.g., a characteristic part of the contour like a line, corner or circular arc); each edge represents a geometric relation between two nodes (e.g., the distance of their center points). Such a model doesn't have to be trained, it can, e.g., be derived from CAD data (which is usually available in industrial applications), thus avoiding a disturbing influence of imperfections of the training data (e.g., noise, small object deformations) during the model formation process.

The graph represents a rigid model: feature distances, for example, are an explicit part of the model. Thereby, the model doesn't allow for much intra-class variation. This property might not be suitable for the interpretation of real-world scenes, but in industrial applications it is often desirable, as the objects to be recognized must fulfill certain quality criteria, e.g., placement machines of SMT components must check that all connections are not bent in order to ensure that every connection is placed properly on the corresponding pad of the printed circuit board.

Matching between the model and scene image content is done with the help of a so-called *association graph* (cf. Ballard and Brown [1]). Each node n_q of the association graph represents a combination of a model feature $\mathbf{x}_{M,i(q)}$ and a feature candidate $\mathbf{x}_{S,k(q)}$ found in the scene image. Hence, the graph nodes represent pairings between model and scene image features. Two nodes n_a and n_b of the association graph are connected by an edge $e(a, b)$ if the distance between the model features represented by the two nodes ($\mathbf{x}_{M,i(a)}$ and $\mathbf{x}_{M,i(b)}$) is consistent with the distance between the found feature candidates $\mathbf{x}_{S,k(a)}$ and $\mathbf{x}_{S,k(b)}$. For the definition of "consistent" in this context a so-called bounded error model can be applied: a graph edge $e(a, b)$ is only built if the difference of the inter-feature distance between two features of the model and two features of the scene image doesn't exceed a fixed threshold t_d:

$$\left| \left\| \mathbf{x}_{M,i(a)} - \mathbf{x}_{M,i(b)} \right\| - \left\| \mathbf{x}_{S,k(a)} - \mathbf{x}_{S,k(b)} \right\| \right| \le t_d \qquad (4.4)$$

A match is found when enough feature correspondences are consistent with respect to each other in the above sense (details see below). Finally, the object pose can be estimated based on the found correspondences.

4.3.1.2 Recognition Phase

Object recognition using graph models can be performed in four steps (cf. Fig. 4.3):

1. *Feature detection*: at first, feature candidates are detected in a scene image and their position is estimated. This can be done with the help of an edge detection operator, followed by a linking process grouping the detected edge points to features like line segments, circle arcs as described in the previous section.
2. *Association graph creation*: The association graph is built node by node by a combinatorial evaluation of all possible 1 to 1 correspondences between the detected feature candidates and the model features. It is complete when each

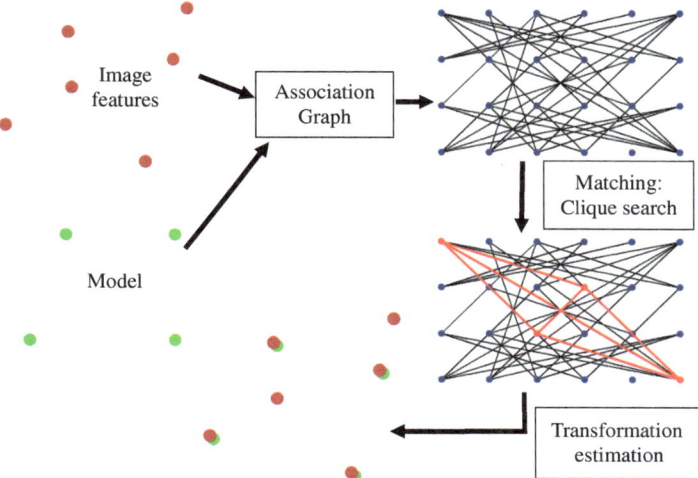

Fig. 4.3 Algorithm flow of geometrical graph matching after the initial feature extraction step

    possible feature combination is represented by a node and it has been checked whether each possible node pairing can be connected by an edge.

3. *Matching*: The next step aims at determining the correct matching between model and scene image features. For a better understanding let's have a look at the information content of the graph: Each node in the association graph can be interpreted as a matching hypothesis defining a specific transformation between model and scene image (and thus defining an object position in the scene image). Graph edges indicate whether a matching hypothesis is broadly supported by multiple nodes and thus is reliable or just is a spurious solution. Hence, the correct matching can be found by detecting the largest clique **c** of the graph, i.e., the largest sub-graph where all node pairs are exhaustively connected by an edge (An example is given in Table 4.2).

4. *Position estimation*: With the help of these correspondences, the parameters of a transformation t determining the object position in the scene image can be calculated in the last step. To this end, similarity or rigid transformations are typically used in industrial applications. Without going into detail, these parameters can be determined by setting up an error function E_c quantifying the remaining displacements between the positions of the scene image features $\mathbf{x}_{S,k}$ and the transformed positions of the model features $t(\mathbf{x}_{M,i})$. Under certain assumptions, the minimization of E leads to an over-determined linear equation system with respect to the model parameters. This equation system can be solved with a least squares approach revealing the desired parameters (cf. the digital image processing book written by Jähne [6], a more detailed theoretical overview of parameter estimation is given in [4]).

The proceeding just described allows for translation and rotation; in order to allow for considerable scaling an alternative way to build edges of the association graph can be applied: a scaling factor is estimated when the first edge of a graph clique is built; additional edges are only added to the clique if the scaled distances are consistent with this estimation.

Please note that – as only distances are checked during graph creation – the method also produces a match when a feature set is compared to its mirrored version.

4.3.1.3 Pseudocode

```
function detectObjectPosGGM (in Image I, in model feature data
[x_M, l_M],  in distance threshold  t_d,  in recognition threshold t_r,
out object position p)

detect all feature candidates in scene image I : [x_S, l_S]

// graph creation
// nodes
for i = 1 to number of model features
    for k = 1 to number of scene features
        if l_{M,i} = l_{S,k} then // features have the same label
        insert new node n(i,k) into graph
        end if
    next
next
// arcs
for a = 1 to number of nodes-1
    for b = a + 1 to number of nodes
        // distance between model features of nodes n_a and n_b
        d_M(a,b) ← ||x_{M,i(a)} − x_{M,i(b)}||
        // distance between scene features of nodes n_a and n_b
        d_S(a,b) ← ||x_{S,k(a)} − x_{S,k(b)}||
        if |d_M(a,b) − d_S(a,b)| ≤ t_d then // dist below threshold
            connect nodes n_a and n_b by an edge e(a,b)
        end if
    next
next

// detection
find largest clique c in graph G = (N,E)
n_c ← number of nodes in c
if n_c ≤ t_r then // sufficient features could be matched
    perform minimization of position deviations
    p ← arg min (E_c(p)) // minimization of position deviations
else
    p ← invalid value // object not found
end if
```

4.3.1.4 Example

Table 4.2 Geometrical graph match example: a scene image with 6 found feature candidates 1–6 is matched to a model consisting of 4 features A–D

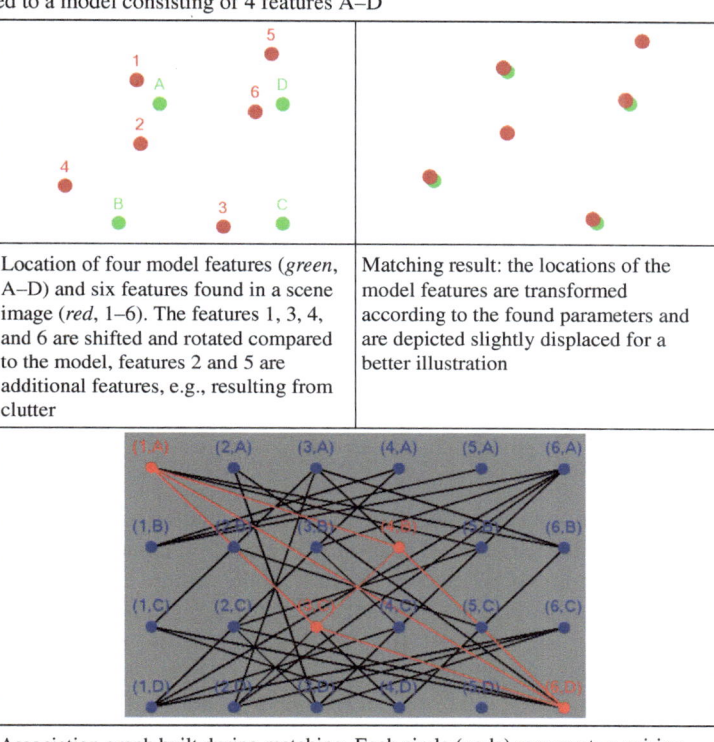

Location of four model features (*green*, A–D) and six features found in a scene image (*red*, 1–6). The features 1, 3, 4, and 6 are shifted and rotated compared to the model, features 2 and 5 are additional features, e.g., resulting from clutter	Matching result: the locations of the model features are transformed according to the found parameters and are depicted slightly displaced for a better illustration

Association graph built during matching. Each circle (node) represents a pairing between one model and one image feature. Two circles are connected by a line (edge) if the distances are consistent, e.g. (1,C) is connected to (4,D) because the distance between scene feature 1 and 4 is consistent with the distance between model feature C and D. The proper solution is the correspondences (1,A), (4,B), (3,C), and (6,D). The largest clique of the association graph, which contains exactly this solution, is shown in *red*. As easily can be seen, the nodes of the largest clique are exhaustively connected

4.3.1.5 Rating

As an advantage, geometrical graph matching can handle partial occlusion (as the remaining features still form a large clique in the association graph) as well as clutter (nodes resulting from additional image features won't be connected to many other nodes). However, because it is a combinatorial approach computational cost increases exponentially with the number of features. Therefore graph matching in this form is only practicable for rather simple objects which can be represented by a small number of features/primitives. In order to reduce the number of nodes in the association graph, labels l can be assigned to the features (e.g., "line," "circle arc"). In that case feature pairing is only done when both features have identical label assignments. A related approach trying to reduce the computational complexity is presented in the next section.

Additionally the partitioning into features during recognition can be extended in a natural way to perform inspection, which is very often required in industrial applications. The dimensional accuracy of drillings, slot holes, etc., or the overall object size can often be checked easily, e.g., because drillings or lines may have already been detected as a feature during recognition.

Another property is that due to an evaluation of inter-feature distances, graph matching employs a very rigid object model. This is suitable for industrial applications, but not in cases where the shapes of objects of the same class deviate from each other considerably.

4.3.2 Interpretation Trees

4.3.2.1 Main Idea

A significant acceleration can be achieved by replacing the combinatorial search for the largest clique in the association graph by a carefully planned search order. To this end, the 1-to-1 correspondences between a model feature and a feature candidate found in the scene image are organized in a tree (cf. the *search tree* approach proposed by Rummel and Beutel [10]). Starting from a root node, each level of the tree represents possible pairings for a specific model feature, i.e., the first level consists of the pairings containing model feature 1 (denoted as $f_{M,1}$; with position $\mathbf{x}_{M,1}$), the second level consists of the pairings containing model feature 2 (denoted as $f_{M,2}$; with position $\mathbf{x}_{M,2}$), and so on. This proceeding implies the definition of a search sequence of the model features (which feature is to be searched first, second, third, etc.?), which usually is defined prior to the recognition process. The sequence can be deduced from general considerations, e.g., features located far away from each other yield a more accurate rotation and scale estimate and therefore should be selected in early stages.

Each node $n_{q,1}$ of the first level can be seen as a hypothesis for the matching based on the correspondence between a single model and as scene image feature, which is refined with links to nodes of the next level. Based on this matching hypothesis, estimates of the transformation parameters t can be derived. A link between two nodes $n_{a,lv}$ and $n_{b,lv+1}$ can only be built between successive levels lv and $lv + 1$; it is established if the transformed position $t\left(\mathbf{x}_{M,lv+1}\right)$ of the model feature of the "candidate node" of level $lv+1$ (based on the current transform parameter estimates) is consistent with the position $\mathbf{x}_{S,k(b)}$ of the scene image feature of the candidate node. Each node of level lv can be linked to multiple nodes of level $lv + 1$. Again, a bounded error model can be applied in the consistency check: the deviation of the positions has to remain below a fixed threshold t_d:

$$\left\| \mathbf{x}_{S,k(b)} - t\left(\mathbf{x}_{M,lv+1}\right) \right\| \leq t_d \tag{4.5}$$

The structure resulting from the search is a tree structure with the number of levels being equal to the number of model features. From a node in the "bottom level" containing the leafs which define pairings for the last model feature, complete correspondence information for a consistent matching of all model features can be derived by tracking the tree back to the first level.

4.3.2.2 Recognition Phase

In the object recognition phase the tree is built iteratively. In each iteration step, a single node $n_{a,lv}$ is processed (see also example in Table 4.3): For all consistent pairings between a scene image feature $f_{S,k}$ and the model feature $f_{M,lv+1}$ new nodes $n_{b,lv+1}$ are inserted in the tree at level $lv + 1$ and linked to the current node $n_{a,lv}$. To this end, for each node candidate $n_{b,lv+1}$ (defining a correspondence between the model feature $f_{M,lv+1}$ and one feature $f_{S,k(b)}$ of the scene) a so-called cost function based on the position disparities between model and scene features is calculated. It can contain a local part (how much is the position deviation between the transformed position of the "new" model feature $t\left(\mathbf{x}_{M,lv+1}\right)$ and the corresponding scene feature position $\mathbf{x}_{S,k(b)}$, see Equation 4.5) as well as a global part (how much is the sum of all position deviations between a transformed model feature position and the corresponding scene image feature position when tracking the tree from the root node to the current node candidate). If the cost function remains below a certain threshold the node is inserted in the tree. The inverse of the cost function value of each node can be interpreted as a quality value q, which is assigned to each node.

In order to speedup computation, only a part of the tree is built (cf. Table 4.3, where only seven correspondences are evaluated compared to 24 nodes of the association graph in geometrical graph matching for the same feature configuration.). For the identification of one instance of the model object it is sufficient for the tree to contain only one "leaf-node" at bottom level. Therefore, at each iteration step, we have to elect the node from which the tree is to be expanded. It should be the node which is most likely to directly lead to a leaf node. This decision can be done with the help of a guide value g which is based on the quality value q of the node as well as the level number lv of the node:

$$g = w_q \cdot q + w_{lv} \cdot lv \tag{4.6}$$

With the help of the weighting factors w_q and w_{lv} the search can be controlled: high w_q favor the selection of nodes at low lv (where q is usually higher due to lower

Table 4.3 Tree search example showing the construction process of an interpretation tree consisting of five steps

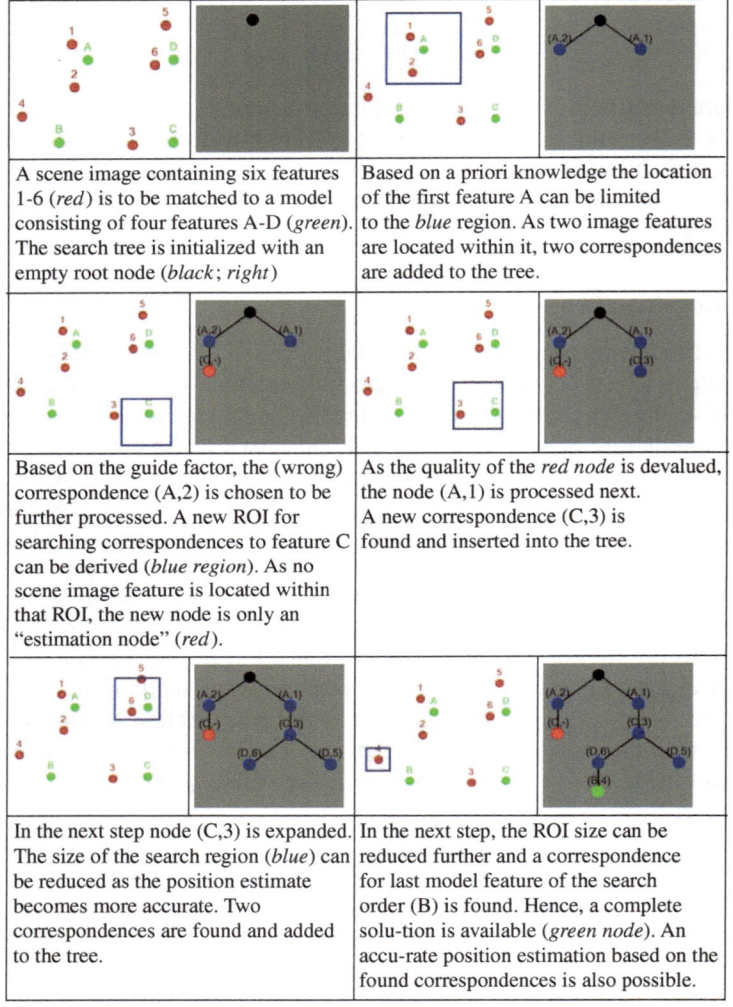

A scene image containing six features 1-6 (*red*) is to be matched to a model consisting of four features A-D (*green*). The search tree is initialized with an empty root node (*black*; *right*)	Based on a priori knowledge the location of the first feature A can be limited to the *blue* region. As two image features are located within it, two correspondences are added to the tree.
Based on the guide factor, the (wrong) correspondence (A,2) is chosen to be further processed. A new ROI for searching correspondences to feature C can be derived (*blue region*). As no scene image feature is located within that ROI, the new node is only an "estimation node" (*red*).	As the quality of the *red node* is devalued, the node (A,1) is processed next. A new correspondence (C,3) is found and inserted into the tree.
In the next step node (C,3) is expanded. The size of the search region (*blue*) can be reduced as the position estimate becomes more accurate. Two correspondences are found and added to the tree.	In the next step, the ROI size can be reduced further and a correspondence for last model feature of the search order (B) is found. Hence, a complete solu-tion is available (*green node*). An accu-rate position estimation based on the found correspondences is also possible.

global cost values) and lead to a mode complete construction of the tree, whereas high w_{lv} favor the selection of nodes at high lv and result in a rapid construction of "deep" branches.

In the case of partial occlusion no consistent pairings can be detected for the next level of some nodes. In order to compensate for this, a node $n_{e,lv+1}$ containing the estimated position based on the current transformation can be added to the tree when no correspondence could be established. Its quality q is devalued by a pre-defined value.

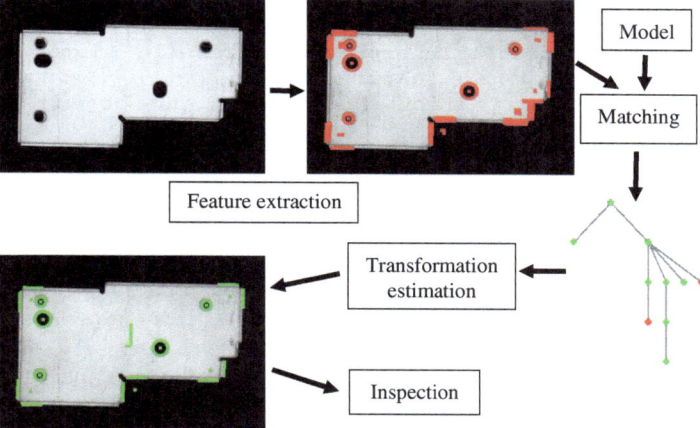

Fig. 4.4 Illustrating the proceeding of object detection with interpretation trees for a stamped sheet as a typical example for an industrial part

The overall recognition scheme in which the search tree is embedded can be characterized by four main steps (cf. Fig. 4.4, an example of a more complicated scene with some clutter is presented in Table 4.4)

1. *Feature detection*: In the first step, all features $f_{S,k} = [\mathbf{x}_{S,k}, l_{S,k}]$ in a scene image are detected and summarized in the list $\mathbf{f}_S$. Their data consists of the position $\mathbf{x}_{S,k}$ as well as a label $l_{S,k}$ indicating the feature type. One way to do this are the methods presented in Section 4.2, e.g., by a geometrical filter consisting of point pairs.
2. *Interpretation tree construction*: Based on the found feature candidates $\mathbf{f}_S$ as well as the model features $\mathbf{f}_M$ the interpretation tree is built. As a result of the tree construction, correspondences for all model features have been established. This step is very robust in cases where additional feature candidates which cannot be matched to the model are detected. This robustness justifies the usage of a "simple" and fast method for feature detection, which possibly leads to a considerable number of false positives. Additionally, for many industrial applications the initial tolerances of rotation and scaling are rather small. A consideration of this fact often leads to a significant reduction of possible correspondences, too.
3. *Transformation estimation*: The four parameters translation $[t_x, t_y]$, rotation θ and scale s are estimated with the help of the found correspondences.
4. *Inspection*: Based on the detected features it is often very easy to decide whether the quality of the part is ok. For example, it could be checked whether the position of a drilling, which can easily be represented by a specific feature, is within its tolerances, etc.

4.3.2.3 Pseudocode

```
function detectObjectPosInterpretationTree (in Image I, in
ordered list f_M of model features f_{M,i} = [x_{M,i}, l_{M,i}], in distance
threshold t_d, in recognition threshold t_r, out object position
list p)
```

detect all feature candidates $f_{S,k} = [x_{S,k}, l_{S,k}]$ in scene image I
and arrange them in list f_S

while f_S is not empty **do** // loop for multiple obj. detection
   init of tree st with empty root node n_{root} and set its quality
   value q_{root} according to maximum quality
   bFound ← FALSE
   // loop for detection of a single object instance
   while unprocessed nodes exist in st and bFound == FALSE **do**
      // expand interpretation tree
      choose next unprocessed node $n_{i,lv}$ from st which yields
      highest guide value g (Equation 4.6)
      get next model feature $f_{M,lv+1}$ to be matched according to
      level lv and search order
      calculate position estimate $t(x_{M,lv+1})$ for $f_{M,lv+1}$
      find all correspondences between elements of f_S and
      $f_{M,lv+1}$ ($f_{S,k}$ must be near $t(x_{M,lv+1})$, see Eq. 4.5) and
      arrange them in list c
      if list c is not empty **then**
         for k = 1 to number of found correspondences
            create new node $n_{k,lv+1}$ based on current c_k
            calculate quality value q_k of $n_{k,lv+1}$
            if $q_k \geq t_r$ **then**
               mark $n_{k,lv+1}$ as unprocessed
            else
               mark $n_{k,lv+1}$ as processed // expansion useless
            end if
            add $n_{k,lv+1}$ to st as child node of $n_{i,lv}$
         next
      else // no match/correspondence could be found
         create new "estimation node" $n_{e,lv+1}$
         calculate quality value q_e of $n_{e,lv+1}$
         if $q_e \geq t_r$ **then**
            mark $n_{e,lv+1}$ as unprocessed
         else
            mark $n_{e,lv+1}$ as processed // expansion useless
         end if
         add $n_{e,lv+1}$ to st as child node of $n_{i,lv}$
      end if

```
      mark node n_{i,lv} as processed
      // are all model features matched?
      if f_{M,lv+1} is last feature of search order then
          mark all "new nodes" n_{k,lv+1} as processed
          find node n_{goal} with highest qual. q_{max} among n_{k,lv+1}
          if q_{max} ≥ t_r then
              bFound ← TRUE
          end if
      end if
  end while
  if bFound = TRUE then
      // refine position estimate based on branch of st from
      n_{root} to n_{goal}
      perform minimization of position deviations
      add arg min (E_c (p)) to position list p
      remove all matched features from list f_S
  else
      return // no more object instance could be found
  end if
end while
```

4.3.2.4 Example

Table 4.4 Giving more detailed information about the detection and position measurement of stamped sheets, which are a typical example of industrial parts

 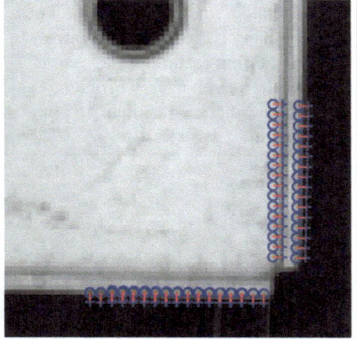

Scene image containing several stamped sheets. Due to specular reflections the brightness of the planar surface is not uniform. One object is completely visible and shown in the upper-left area	Visualization of the detection results for the lower right corner of the part. It was detected with an L-shaped point pair filter Due to ambiguities two positions are reported

Table 4.4 (continued)

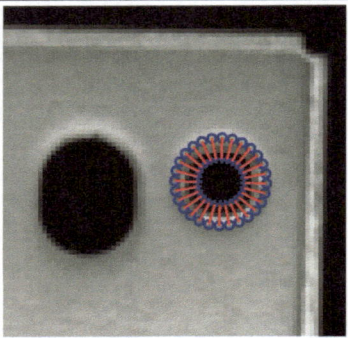

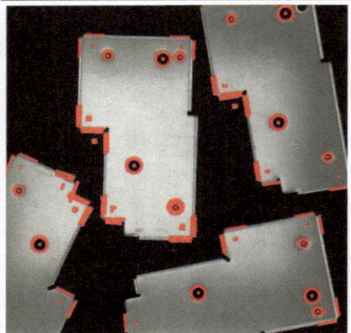

Visualization of the detection results for the stamped hole located in the *upper right* area of the part. It is detected correctly with a filter with circular arranged point pairs	View of all detected features (marked *red*). The object model consists of the holes and some corners, which are detected independently. Several additional features are detected due to clutter

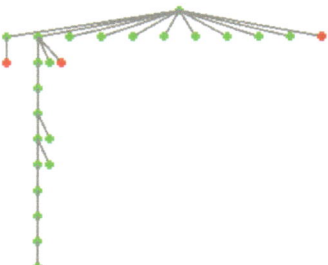

Interpretation tree: found correspondences are marked as *green*, estimated correspondences are marked as *red*. Due to clutter, many correspondences are found for the first feature of the search order, but the search is very efficient, e.g., the solution is almost unique after the third level	Matched features of the final solution of the tree (marked *green*). All correspondences are established correctly. An inspection step, e.g., for the holes, could follow

4.3.2.5 Rating

Like graph matching the interpretation tree approach also employs a very rigid object model, because the correspondences are built based on inter-feature distances. This is suitable for industrial applications, where parts very often have to meet narrow tolerances, but not for many "real-world objects" with considerable intra-class variations. In general, many statements made for the geometrical graph matching method are valid for interpretation trees, too, e.g., that the inspection is a natural extension of the feature-based approach.

Moreover, in spite of being applied to rather complex models, the method is very fast (recognition time in the order of 10–100 ms are possible), mainly because of two reasons: First, the geometric filters efficiently reduce the number of features subject to correspondence evaluation (compared to, e.g., the generalized Hough transform, where contour points are used for matching, which are typically much more numerous). Second, the number of correspondences to be evaluated is kept small due to pruning the interpretation tree efficiently.

As a consequence, however, the usage of filters involves the limitation that a priori knowledge is necessary for a proper filter design. Additionally, there exist object shapes which are not suited to the filter-based approach. Furthermore it has to be mentioned that – if symmetric components have to be measured – there exist multiple solutions due to symmetry.

Please note also that the method is much more robust with respect to clutter (when trying to expand the tree at a node that is based on a correspondence originating from clutter there is no consistent correspondence very quickly) compared to occlusion (awkward roots of the tree are possible if the first correspondences to be evaluated don't exist because of occlusion).

To sum it up, interpretation trees are well suited for industrial applications, because the method is relatively fast, an additional inspection task fits well to the method and we can concentrate on detecting characteristic details of the objects. On the other hand, the rigid object model is prohibitive for objects with considerable variations in shape.

4.4 Geometric Hashing

4.4.1 Main Idea

Another possibility to speedup the matching step is to shift computations to a pre-processing stage that can be performed off-line prior to recognition. To this end, Lamdan et al. [7] suggest building a so-called hash table based on information about geometric relations between the features. They use deep concavities and sharp convexities of the object contour as feature points (i.e., contour locations where the change of the tangent angle at successive points attains a local maximum or minimum, respectively). It should be mentioned, however, that the scheme is also applicable to other types of features.

The relationship between the positions of the model features $\mathbf{x}_{M,i}$ and scene image features $\mathbf{x}_{S,k}$ is modeled by the affine transformation $\mathbf{x}_{S,k} = \mathbf{A} \cdot \mathbf{x}_{M,i} + \mathbf{t}$. In the 2D case, this type of transformation has six degrees of freedom ($\mathbf{A}$ is a 2×2-matrix, $\mathbf{t}$ a 2D vector). Therefore, the positions of three non-collinear feature points are sufficient to determine the six transformation parameters. As a consequence, it is possible to generate a hypothesis of the object pose when as few as three non-collinear scene feature points are matched to model points.

Recognition starts by arbitrarily choosing three points. A hypothesis for the six affine transformation parameters could be generated if the 1-to-1 correspondences of the three feature points to the model features were known. The information stored in the hash table is utilized to reveal these correspondences (and thus formulate the hypothesis) with the help of the other features in a voting procedure (details see below). In case of rejection (no correspondences could be found for the chosen feature triplet), this proceeding can be repeated with a second feature triplet, and so on.

The usage of a hash table is an example of a more general technique called *indexing*: with the help of some kind of indexed access or index function (here via look-up in the hash table) it is possible to retrieve information about the object model(s) very quickly, which can be used for a rapid generation of a hypothesis of the object pose. Another example, where indexing is used for 3D object recognition, is presented later on. Now let's have a look at geometric hashing in detail.

4.4.2 Speedup by Pre-processing

In the pre-processing stage of the algorithm, hash table creation is done as follows (see also Fig. 4.5):

- Detect all features in a training image such that the object to be searched is represented by a set of features points.
- For each triplet of non-collinear feature points, do the following:

  - Compute the parameters of an affine transformation mapping the three feature point positions to coordinates (0,0), (0,1), and (1,0).
  - Transform the position of all remaining feature points using the transformation parameters just calculated.
  - Each transformed position generates an entry in the hash table. Each entry consists of information about the transformed position (the "index" of the hash table) in combination with the triplet from which it was calculated.

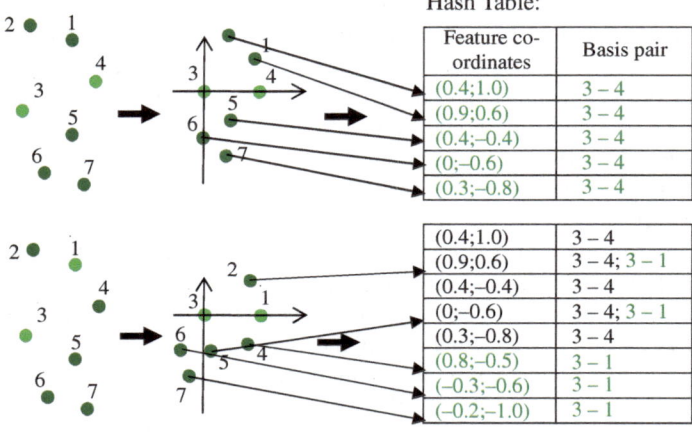

Fig. 4.5 Illustrates two steps of hash table creation in the training stage of geometric hashing (new table entries in *green*)

Two steps of this proceeding are shown in Fig. 4.5. After arbitrarily choosing features (left, marked light green), the transformation parameters are estimated and the positions of the remaining feature are transformed accordingly (middle part). Finally the hash table is extended based on the transformed positions (right). Please note that for illustrative purposes a basis consisting of only two points (which is sufficient for determining the parameters of a similarity transform) is used. Observe that a second basis pair is entered at two hash table entries in the second step even if the feature positions don't coincide exactly. This is due to the fact that each hash table bin actually covers a position range in order to allow for small deformations, noise, etc.

4.4.3 Recognition Phase

During recognition the hash table is used this way (cf. Fig. 4.6):

1. *Feature point detection*: determine all feature points in a scene image showing the object.
2. *Triplet choice*: choose a triplet of non-collinear feature points by random
3. *Parameter estimation*: Compute the parameters of an affine transformation mapping the triplet to the coordinates (0,0), (0,1), and (1,0).
4. *Transformation of feature positions*: Transform the positions of the remaining features according to these parameters
5. *Voting by indexed access*: for each transformed position, check whether there is a hash table entry containing this position. In order to allow for small variances of geometry and due to image noise, the transformed positions don't have to match the table index exactly, but their distance has to fall below a certain threshold (i.e., the hash table entries have a certain bin size, see [7] for details). If there is a suitable hash table entry, the feature triplet being stored in the entry gets a vote.
6. *Verification*: if a model triplet gets a sufficient number of votes, the matching between model and scene image is found: the features of the randomly chosen triplet belong to the model triplet with the highest number of votes. Otherwise, another triplet is chosen and voting is repeated.
7. *Transformation parameter determination*: with the help of the correspondences revealed in the last step, the affine transformation parameters mapping the model

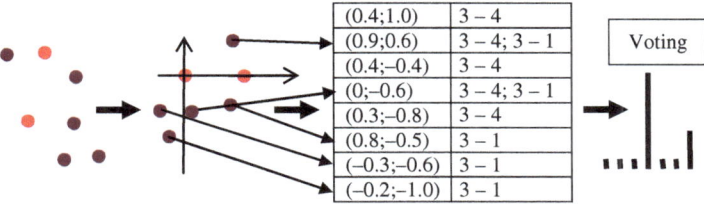

Fig. 4.6 Showing the recognition process using the indexing functionality of geometric hashing

to the scene can be calculated. Without going into detail, these parameters can be determined by setting up and minimizing an error function E_c quantifying the displacements between the positions of the scene image features $\mathbf{x}_{S,k}$ and the transformed positions of the model features $t(\mathbf{x}_{M,i})$.

This proceeding is summarized in Fig. 4.6. Again, just two arbitrarily chosen points (marked light) serve as a basis for the estimate of transform parameters. All other points are transformed according to these parameters. Their positions are used as indexes into the hash table. If a hash table entry exists for a specific index, all basis pairs stored in this entry get a vote. If a specific basis pair gets enough votes, a correct correspondence between the two arbitrarily chosen scene image points and this basis pair is found (for this example, the pair 3-1 of the above training step).

In many industrial applications the camera viewpoint is fixed and therefore the objects undergo a similarity transformation defined by the four parameters $\mathbf{t} = [t_x, t_y]$, rotation θ and scale s. Instead of using triplets feature pairs are sufficient to define the four parameters in such cases.

4.4.4 Pseudocode

```
function detectObjectPosGeometricHashing (in Image I, in hash
table H, in threshold t, out object position p)

detect all features in scene image I : x_S
v ← 0 // init of number of votes

// main loop (until threshold is reached)
while v < t ∧ untested feature triplets exist do
    choose indexes k, l and m by random
    estimate parameters t which transform x_{S,k}, x_{S,l} and x_{S,m}
    to coordinates (0,0), (0,1) and (1,0)
    init of accu
    for i = 1 to number of scene features
        if i ≠ k ∧ i ≠ l ∧ i ≠ m then
            x^t_{S,i} ← t(x_{S,i}) // transform feature position
            retrieve list h_{x^t_{S,i}} of H (hash table entry whose
            index relates to position x^t_{S,i}
            for j = 1 to number of entries of list h_{x^t_{S,i}}
                cast a vote for model triplet defined by entry j
                in accu
            next
        end if
    next
    v ← maximum of accu
end while
```

```
// position estimation
if v < t then
    return // no object instance could be found
end if
determine feature correspond. based on matching hypothesis
// perform minimization of position deviations
```
$p \leftarrow \arg\min \left(E_c \left(p\right)\right)$

4.4.5 Rating

For perfect data, the usage of a hash table accelerates the recognition stage dramatically, as only one arbitrarily chosen feature triplet suffices to calculate the matching parameters. In practice, however, additional/spurious features can be detected in the scene image that don't relate to any model feature (e.g. due to clutter). Additionally, a feature might not be visible because of occlusion or its position is significantly disturbed. For that reason, usually multiple feature triplets have to be checked. In the worst case, if the scene image doesn't contain the searched object, all possible triplet combinations have to be examined. Therefore geometric hashing is most suitable for situations with well detectable features and a high probability that the searched object is actually present, otherwise it is questionable if a significant speed advantage can be realized.

A drawback of the scheme results from the fact that the transformation parameters are estimated based upon as few as three features in the early stages of the recognition phase. Implicitly, this leads to forcing the position deviation between the scene image feature and the corresponding model feature to zero for all three features of the triplet under investigation. As a result, the quality of the parameter estimation is highly sensitive to the accuracy of the position estimation of these features. If these positions are influenced by noise, for example, this might lead to significant errors in the position calculation for the remaining features, potentially leading to a rejection of the current triplet even if the correspondences themselves are correct. This is a problem for many correspondence-based search strategies, but in geometric hashing it is particularly apparent as the algorithm tries to reduce the number of features for the initial parameter estimation as much as possible. In contrast to that, matching strategies searching the transformation space often are profiting from some kind of interpolation as they don't enforce exact position matches for a feature correspondence.

4.4.6 Modifications

The algorithm can be extended to a classification scheme if the pre-processing stage is performed for multiple object classes. In that case the object class label is additionally stored in the hash table. Each table entry now contains a (point triplet, class label) pair. Hence, during voting in the recognition stage the table entries reveal transformation as well as classification information. Please note that the fact that the model database contains multiple object classes does not necessarily lead to an increase of recognition time! In best case only one feature triplet check is still sufficient, regardless of the number of model classes. Compared to that, the straight-forward approach of repeatedly applying a recognition scheme for each model class separately results in a time increase which is linear to the number of object classes. Therefore indexing schemes are especially attractive if the model database contains a large number of object classes.

A related scheme is the alignment method proposed by Huttenlocher and Ullman [5]. The alignment method also tries to reduce the exponential complexity inherent in correspondence-based matching when all possible correspondences between two feature sets are evaluated. Similar to geometric hashing, Huttenlocher and Ullman split up the recognition process in two stages: the first stage tries to generate a matching hypothesis by aligning just the minimum number of features necessary for unique determination of the transformation coefficients, e.g., three points/features when the parameters of an affine transform have to be estimated. The subsequent second stage verifies the hypothesis by evaluating the distances between the complete point sets of query image and transformed model according to the hypothesized transformation.

During recognition all possible combinations of feature triplets are evaluated. We can then choose the hypothesis with the smallest overall error. As only triplets are considered when establishing the correspondences, the complexity has been reduced from exponential to polynomial order $O(p^3)$ (with p being the number of features).

Compared to geometric hashing, where a notable speedup is achieved by accelerating the matching step via indexing such that many hypotheses can be checked quickly, an evaluation of $O(p^3)$ correspondences still is too much. Therefore the alignment method aims at minimizing the number of feature triplets which have to be evaluated by classifying the features themselves into different types and allowing only correspondences between features of the same type. This assumes, however, that the features themselves can be classified reliably (and therefore matched quickly): only then it is possible to exclude a large number of potential model – scene feature pairings, because they belong to different feature classes.

References

1. Ballard, D.H and Brown, C.M., *"Computer Vision"* Prentice-Hall, Englewood Cliffs, N.J, 1982, ISBN 0-131-65316-4
2. Canny, J.F., "A Computational Approach to Edge Detection", *IEEE Transactions on Pattern Analysis and Machine Intelligence,* 8(6):679–698, 1986
3. Chen, J.-M., Ventura, J.A. and Wu, C.-H., "Segmentation of Planar Curves into Circular Arcs and Line Segments", *Image and Vision Computing,* 14(1):71–83, 1996
4. Horn, B., Hilden, H.M., Negahdaripour, S., "Closed-Form Solution of Absolute Orientation Using Orthonormal Matrices", *Journal of the Optical Society A,* 5(7):1127–1135, 1988
5. Huttenlocher, D. and Ullman S., "Object Recognition Using Alignment". *Proceedings of International Conference of Computer Vision,* London, 102–111, 1987
6. Jähne, B., *"Digital Image Processing"* (5th edition), Springer, Berlin, Heidelberg, New York, 2002, ISBN 3-540-67754-2

7. Lamdan, Y., Schwartz, J.T. and Wolfson, H.J., "Affine Invariant Model-Based Object Recognition", *IEEE Transactions on Robotics and Automation*, 6(5):578–589, 1990
8. Ramer, U., "An Iterative Procedure for the Polygonal Approximation of Plane Curves", *Computer Graphics and Image Processing*, 1:244–256, 1972
9. Rosin, P.L., "Assessing the Behaviour of Polygonal Approximation Algorithms", *Pattern Recognition*, 36(2):508–518, 2003
10. Rummel, P. and Beutel, W., "Workpiece recognition and inspection by a model-based scene analysis system", *Pattern Recognition*, 17(1):141–148, 1984

Chapter 5
Three-Dimensional Object Recognition

Abstract Some applications require a position estimate in 3D space (and not just in the 2D image plane), e.g., bin picking applications, where individual objects have to be gripped by a robot from an unordered set of objects. Typically, such applications utilize sensor systems which allow for the generation of 3D data and perform matching in 3D space. Another way to determine the 3D pose of an object is to estimate the projection of the object location in 3D space onto a 2D camera image. There exist methods managing to get by with just a single 2D camera image for the estimation of this 3D → 2D mapping transformation. Some of them shall be presented in this chapter. They are also examples of correspondence-based schemes, as the matching step is performed by establishing correspondences between scene image and model features. However, instead of using just single scene image and model features, correspondences between special configurations of multiple features are established here. First of all, the SCERPO system makes use of feature groupings which are perceived similar from a wide variety of viewpoints. Another method, called relational indexing, uses hash tables to speed up the search. Finally, a system called LEWIS derives so-called invariants from specific feature configurations, which are designed such that their topologies remain stable for differing viewpoints.

5.1 Overview

Before presenting the methods, let's define what is meant by "3D object recognition" here. The methods presented up to now perform matching of a 2D model to the 2D camera image plane, i.e., the estimated transformation between model and scene image describes a mapping from 2D to 2D. Of course, this is a simplification of reality where the objects to be recognized are located in a 3D coordinate system (often called *world coordinates*) and are projected onto a 2D image plane. Some of the methods intend to achieve invariance with respect to out-of-plane rotations in 3D space, e.g., by assuming that the objects to be found are nearly planar. In that case, a change of the object pose can be modeled by a 2D affine transformation. However, the mapping still is from 2D to 2D.

M. Treiber, *An Introduction to Object Recognition*, Advances in Pattern Recognition,   95
DOI 10.1007/978-1-84996-235-3_5, © Springer-Verlag London Limited 2010

In contrast to that, 3D matching describes the mapping of 3D positions to 3D positions again. In order to obtain a 3D representation of a scene, well-known methods such as triangulation or binocular stereo can be applied. Please note that many of the methods utilize so-called range images or depth maps, where information about the z-direction (e.g., z-distance to the sensor) is stored dependent on the $[x, y]$-position in the image plane. Such a data representation is not "full" 3D yet and therefore is often called $2\frac{1}{2}$ D.

Another way to determine the 3D pose of an object is to estimate the projection of the object location in 3D space onto the 2D camera image, i.e., estimate the parameters of a projective transformation mapping 3D to 2D, and that's exactly what the methods presented below are doing. The information provided by the projection can for example be utilized in bin picking applications, where individual objects have to be gripped by a robot from an unordered set of objects.

The projective transformation which maps a $[X, Y, Z]^T$ position of world coordinates onto the $[x, y]$-camera image plane is described by

$$\begin{bmatrix} a \\ b \\ c \end{bmatrix} = \mathbf{R} \cdot \begin{bmatrix} X \\ Y \\ Z \end{bmatrix} + \mathbf{t} \tag{5.1}$$

$$\begin{bmatrix} x \\ y \end{bmatrix} = \begin{bmatrix} f \cdot a/c \\ f \cdot b/c \end{bmatrix} \tag{5.2}$$

with $\mathbf{R}$ being a 3×3-rotation matrix, $\mathbf{t}$ a 3D translation vector, and f is determined by the camera focal length. Observe that in order be a rotation matrix, constraints are imposed upon $\mathbf{R}$, which makes the problem of finding the projective transformation a non-linear one, at least in the general case. Detailed solutions for the parameter estimation are not presented in this book; our focus should be the mode of operation of the matching step.

Performing 3D object recognition from a single 2D image involves matching 2D features generated from a sensed 2D scene image to a 3D object model. The methods presented here implement the matching step by establishing correspondences between scene image and model features (or, more generally, feature combinations) and are therefore also examples of correspondence-based schemes.

In terms of object representation, a complete 3D model can be derived either from 3D CAD data or from multiple 2D images acquired from different viewpoints. There exist two main strategies for model representation: an object-centered one, where the model consists of a single feature set containing features collected from all viewpoints (or the entire CAD model, respectively) or a view-centered one where nearby viewpoints are summarized to a viewpoint class and a separate feature set is derived for each viewpoint class.

Algorithms that perform 3D object recognition from a single 2D image are mostly applied in industrial applications, as industrial parts usually can be modeled by a restricted set of salient features. Additionally, the possibility to influence the

imaging conditions alleviates the difficulty involved by the fact of relying on configurations of multiple features, because usually it is very challenging to detect them
reliably. Three methods falling into this category are presented in the following.

5.2 The SCERPO System: Perceptual Grouping

5.2.1 Main Idea

The SCERPO vision system (Spatial Correspondence, Evidential Reasoning and
Perceptual Organization) developed by Lowe [3] is inspired by human recognition
abilities. It makes use of the concept of *perceptual grouping*, which defines groupings of features (e.g., lines) that are considered salient by us humans and therefore
can easily be perceived (cf. Fig. 5.1).

There is evidence that object recognition of the human vision system works in
a similar way. As there should be no assumptions about the viewpoint location
from which the image was acquired, these feature groupings should be invariant
to viewpoint changes, enabling the algorithm to detect them over a wide range of
viewpoints. Lowe describes three kinds of groupings that fulfill this criterion:

- *Parallelism*, i.e., lines which are (nearly) parallel
- *End point proximity*, i.e., lines whose end points are very close to each other
- *Collinearity*, i.e., lines whose end points are located on or nearby a single
  "master-line."

Fig. 5.1 Showing three kinds of perceptually significant line groupings: five *lines* ending at positions which are very close to each other in the *lower left* part, three *parallel lines* in the *lower right*,
and, finally, four almost *collinear lines* in the upper part of the picture

5.2.2 Recognition Phase

Based on the concept of perceptual grouping, Lowe proposes the following algorithm for recognition. Lets assume model data is available already, e.g., from CAD data. Figure 5.2 illustrates the approach: as an example, the 3D poses of multiple razors have to be found in a single scene image:

1. *Edge point detection*: at first, all edge points e have to be extracted from the image. To this end, Lowe suggests the convolution of the image with a Laplacian of Gaussian (LoG) operator. As this operation relates to the second derivative of image intensity, edge points should lie on zero-crossings of the convolution result. In order to suppress zero crossings produced by noise, pixels at zero crossing positions additionally have to exhibit sufficiently high gradient values in order to be accepted as edge pixels.
2. *Edge point grouping*: derivation of line segments l_i which approximate the edge points best (see also the previous chapter for a brief introduction).
3. *Perceptual grouping* of the found line segments considering all three kinds of grouping. In this step, a group g_n of line segments is built if at least two lines share the same type of common attribute (collinearity, parallelism or proximal end points).
4. *Matching* of the found line groups to model features taking the *viewpoint consistency constraint* into account. The viewpoint consistency constraint states that a correct match is only found if the positions of all lines of one group of the model can be fit to the positions of the scene image lines with a single common projection based on a single viewpoint. In other words, the positions of the lines have to be consistent with respect to the transformation parameters.
5. *Projection hypothesis generation*: each matching of a model line group to some scene image features can be used to derive a hypothesis of the projection parameters between a 3D object pose and the scene image.
6. *Projection hypothesis verification*: based on the hypothesis, the position of other (non-salient) features/lines in the scene image can be predicted and verified. The hypothesis is valid if enough consistent features are found.

As it might be possible to formulate many hypotheses it is desirable to do a ranking of them with respect to the probability of being a correct transformation. Most promising are groups consisting of many lines as they are supposed to be most distinctive and have the additional advantage that most likely all projection parameters can be estimated (because sufficient information is available; no underdetermination). This concept of formulating hypotheses with only a few distinctive features followed by a verification step with the help of additional features can be found quite often as it has the advantage to be insensitive to outliers (in contrast to calculating some kind of "mean").

5.2.3 *Example*

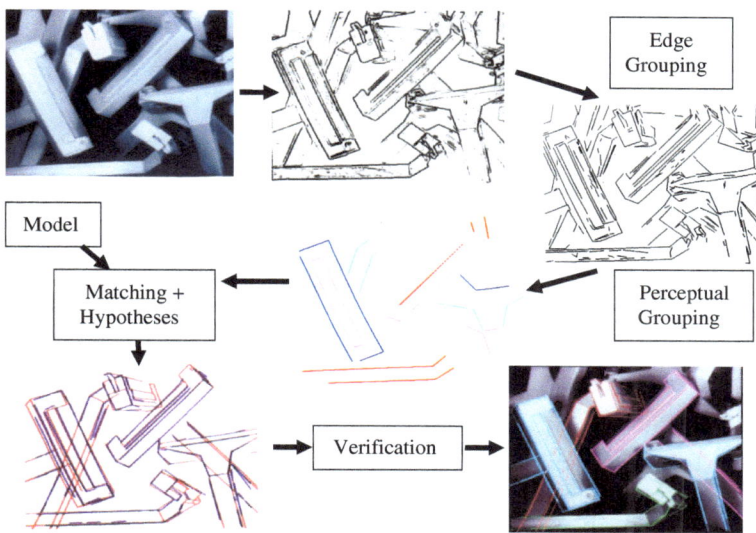

Fig. 5.2 Individual razors are detected by perceptual grouping with the SCERPO system[1]

5.2.4 *Pseudocode*

```
function detectObjectPosPerceptualGrouping (in Image I, in
list of model groups gₘ, in list of model lines Iₘ, in
distance threshold t_d, in similarity threshold t_sim, out object
position list p)
```

```
//line segment detection
Convolve I with Laplacian of Gaussian (LoG) operator
I_G ← gradient magnitude at zero crossings of convol. result
threshold I_G in order to obtain list of edge points e
group edge points e to line segments l_i, if possible
remove very short segments from line segment list I_S
```

```
// perceptual grouping
while unprocessed line segments exist in I_S do
    take next line segment l_{S,i} from list I_S
```

---

[1]Contains images reprinted from Lowe [3] (Figs. 9, 10, 11, 12, 14, and 16), © 1987, with permission from Elsevier.

```
init of group gₙ with l_{S,i}
for all line segments l_{S,k} in the vicinity of l_{S,i}
    if [endpt_prox (l_{S,k}, gₙ) ∨ collin (l_{S,k}, gₙ) ∨ parallel (l_{S,k}, gₙ)] ∧
    group type fits then
        append l_{S,k} to gₙ
        set type of group gₙ if not set already (collinear,
        endpoint prox. or parallel)
    end if
next
if number of lines of gₙ >= 2 then
    accept gₙ as perceptual group and add it to list
    of perceptual groups in scene image g_S
    remove all line segments of gₙ from list l_S
end if
end while


// matching
for i = 1 to number of model groups (elements of g_M)
    for j = 1 to number of scene groups (elements of g_S)
        if viewpoint consistency constraint is fulfilled for
        all lines of g_{M,i} and g_{S,j} then
            estimate transform parameters t // hypothesis
            //hypothesis verification
            sim ← 0
            for k = 1 to total number of line combinations
                if ‖t (l_{M,k}) − l_{S,k}‖ ≤ t_d then         // positions fit
                    increase sim
                end if
            next
            if sim ≥ t_sim then
                append t to position list p
            end if
        end if
    next
next
```

5.2.5 Rating

An advantage of this procedure is that it is a generic method which doesn't include
many specific assumptions about the objects to be detected. Furthermore, one image
is enough for 3D recognition.

In order to make the method work, however, it has to be ensured that there exist
some perceptual groups with suitable size which are detectable from all over the

expected viewpoint range. Compared to the methods presented below only lines are used, which constrains the applicability. Additionally, 3D model data has to be available, e.g., from a CAD model.

5.3 Relational Indexing

5.3.1 Main Idea

The algorithm presented by Costa and Shapiro [2], which is another example of aiming at recognizing 3D objects from a single 2D image, uses a scheme which is called *relational indexing*. In this method object matching is performed by establishing correspondences, too. However, these correspondences are not identified between single features; a pair of so-called high-level features is used instead. The features utilized by Costa and Shapiro are extracted from edge images (which, e.g., can be calculated from the original intensity image with the operator proposed by Canny [1] including non-maximum suppression) and are combinations of primitives such as lines, circular arcs, or ellipses. Therefore the method is suited best for the recognition of industrial parts like screws, wrenches, stacked cylinders. A summary of high-level features can be found in the top tow rows of Table 5.1. Most of them are combinations of two or more primitives.

For matching, two of these high-level features are combined to a pair, which can be characterized by a specific geometric relation between the two features, e.g., two features can share one common line segment or circular arc (see also the bottom two rows of Table 5.1).

The main advantage of the usage of two features and their geometric relation is that their combination is more salient and therefore produces more reliable matches compared to a single feature. This implies, however, that the object to be recognized contains enough such combinations. Additionally, these combinations have to be detected reliably, which is the more difficult the more complex the combinations are.

Object matching is performed by establishing correspondences between a pair of two high-level model features (and their geometric relation) and pairs found in a scene image. A correspondence is only valid if both pairs are composed by identical feature types and share the same geometric relation. Each of the found correspondences votes for a specific model. By counting these votes hypotheses for object classification as well as pose identification can be derived.

In order to achieve invariance with respect to viewpoint change, a view-based object model is applied. Therefore images taken at different viewpoints are processed for each object in a training phase. Images where the object has a similar appearance are summarized to a so-called *view-class*. For each view-class high-level feature pairs are derived and stored separately, i.e., the model for a specific object class consists of several lists of high-level feature pairs and their geometric relation, one list for each view class.

Table 5.1 High-level feature types (*top two rows*) and types of relations between the features (*bottom two rows*) used by relational indexing

Ellipses	Coaxials-3	Coaxials-multi	Parallel-far	Parallel-close
U-triple	Z-triple	L-Junction	Y-Junction	V-Junction

Share one arc	Share one line	Share two lines
Coaxial	Close at extremal points	Bounding box encloses/ enclosed by bounding box

The method is a further example of an indexing scheme; it can be seen as an expansion of geometric hashing, which utilizes single features, to the usage of two features and their relation for generating two indices (one based on the feature types, one based on the geometric relation) when accessing the (now 2D) look-up table. The entries of the look-up table represent view-based models which can be used directly to cast a vote for a specific model – view-class combination.

5.3.2 Teaching Phase

The teaching process, which can be repeated for different view classes, consists of the following steps:

1. *Edge image generation*: In the first step all edge pixels have to be identified. A suitable implementation for this step is the Canny edge detector with non-maximum suppression proposed in [1]. In principle one intensity image suffices for the edge image generation. Nevertheless, Costa and Shapiro [2] suggest to combine two intensity images with differently directed illumination in order to exclude edges from the model which are caused by shading.

2. *Mid-level feature extraction*: Line segments l_M, i and circular arcs $c_{M,i}$ are extracted from the edge image. As the main focus here is on the matching method, this step shall not be discussed in detail here (a short introduction to feature detection is given in the previous chapter).
3. *Mid-level feature grouping*: in order to utilize the high-level features described above (denoted by $g_{M,i}$), they have to be extracted first. This is done by grouping the mid-level features detected in the previous step.
4. *High-level feature grouping*: the high-level features just created are combined to pairs (denoted by $pg_{M,i}$) consisting of two high-level features and their geometric relation (see the two bottom rows of Table 5.1). Later on, these groups act as an index into a look-up table for the retrieval of model information.
5. *Look-up table generation*: the last training step consists of generating the look-up table just mentioned (see also Fig. 5.3). The look-up table is a 2D table, where one dimension represents the high-level feature combination (each high-level feature type is labeled with a number; for a specific feature pair, these numbers are concatenated). The other dimension incorporates the geometric relation between the two features; again each relation type is represented by a specific number. After teaching, each element of the look-up table contains a list $h_{M,ab}$ of model/view-class pairs, i.e., numbers of the object model and the class of views from which the feature group was detected in the training phase. If, for example, a pair of parallel lines and a z-triple of lines which share two lines are detected for the model "2" in a viewpoint belonging to view-class "3" during training, the information "2–3" is added to the list of the hash table entry being defined by the indexes of "parallel-far"-"z-triple" and "share two lines." Please note that, in contrast to geometric hashing or the generalized Hough transform, no quantization of the spatial position of the features is necessary here.

Figure 5.3 shows one step of the 2D hash table generation in more detail. In this example a high-level feature pair (briefly called "feature pair" in the following) consisting of parallel-far lines (e.g., defined as feature number 2) and a z-junction

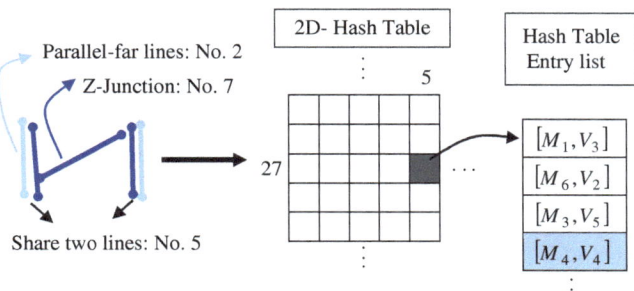

Fig. 5.3 Illustrating one step of the hash table generation

(e.g., defined as feature number 7) has been detected. Their relation is characterized by the sharing of two lines (number 5). The feature combination "27" as well
as relation "5" define the two indexes a and b of the entry $h_{M,ab}$ of the 2D hash
table which has to be adjusted: The list of this entry, where each list entry defines a
model number and view-class combination $[M_i, V_j]$, has to be extended by on entry
(marked blue). Here, the feature combination 27-5 belongs to model number 4 and
was detected in view-class number 4.

5.3.3 Recognition Phase

The beginning of the recognition process is very similar to the teaching phase. In
fact, step 1–4 are identical. At the end of step 4, all feature pairs $pg_{S,k}$ which could
be extracted from the scene image by the system are known. The rest of the method
deals with hypothesizing and verifying occurrences of objects in the scene based on
the extracted $pg_{S,k}$ and proceeds as follows:

5. *Voting*: For each high-level feature pair $pg_{S,k}$ the two indexes a and b into the
   look-up table (a is based on the two high-level features of the pair and b is based
   on their geometric relation) can be derived. The element $\mathbf{h}_{M,ab}$ of the look-up
   table that can be addressed by the two indexes consists of a list of models which
   contain a feature pair $pg_{M,i}$ with feature types as well as relation being identical
   to the ones of $pg_{S,k}$ and therefore support its occurrence in the scene image.
   Each list entry $h_{M,ab.l}$ casts a vote, i.e., a specific bin (relating to the model index
   defined in $h_{M,ab.l}$) in an accumulator array consisting of indexes for all models
   (i.e., the model database) is incremented by one.
6. *Hypothesis generation*: hypotheses for possible model occurrences in the scene
   image can be generated by searching the accumulator for values above a certain
   threshold t_R
7. *3D Pose estimation*: based on all feature pairs supporting a specific hypothesis hy
   an estimation of the 3D object pose can be derived. To this end, the matched 2D
   positions of the features in the scene image to their corresponding 3D positions
   of the 3D object model (e.g., a CAD model) are utilized. In order to estimate a
   3D pose six such 2D–3D feature matches are required. Details of the estimation
   scheme, which in general requires nonlinear estimation, but can be linearized in
   special cases, can be found in [2].
8. **Verification**: roughly speaking, a hypothesis hy is valid if enough edge points
   of the back-projected 3D model into the camera image (with the help of the
   estimated 3D pose of step 7) are located near an edge point detected in the scene
   image. To this end, the directed Hausdorff distance $h\left(t\left(m\right),I\right) = \min_{i \in I} \|m - i\|$
   to the scene image edge point set I is calculated for each back-projected model
   edge point $m \in M$. In order to consider a hypothesis as valid, two conditions must
   hold: First of all, the average of the Hausdorff distances for all back-projected
   model edge points must remain below a threshold t_{dist} and, second, the fraction
   of model pixels with actual distance below t_{dist} must be above the value t_{fr}:

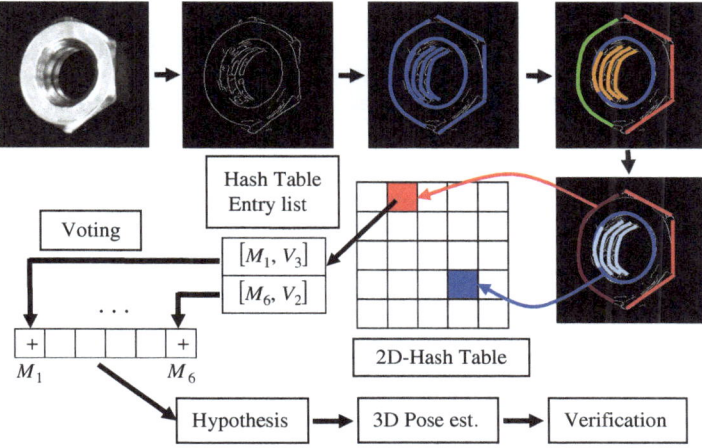

Fig. 5.4 Screw nut detection with relational indexing

$$\frac{1}{M} \sum_{m \in M} h\left(t\left(m\right), I\right) \leq t_{\text{dist}} \tag{5.3}$$

$$\frac{N\left(m \in M | h\left(t\left(m\right), I\right) \leq t_{\text{dist}}\right)}{M} \geq t_{fr} \tag{5.4}$$

where $N\left(m \in M | h\left(t\left(m\right), I\right) \leq t_{\text{dist}}\right)$ denotes the number of model points with a distance at most equal to t_{dist}. In [2] t_{dist} is set empirically to 5 pixels and t_{fr} to 0.65. Please note that t_{fr} controls the amount of occlusion which should be tolerated by the system.

The entire recognition process is illustrated in Fig. 5.4: after edge extraction and edge pixel grouping, several mid-level features (marked blue) are detected. In the next step, they're grouped to so-called high-level features (rightmost image in top row; each high-level feature is indicated by a different color). Subsequently, the high-level features are combined to pairs (e.g., the combination ellipse-coaxials combination marked blue and the u-triple-ellipse part-combination marked red). Note that other combinations are also possible, but are not considered here for better visibility. Each combination can be used as an index into the 2D hash table built during training. The hash table list entries are used during voting. Again, not all list entries are shown because of better visibility.

5.3.4 Pseudocode

```
function detectObjectPosRelIndex (in Image I, in 2D hash table
H, in model data M for each object model, in thresholds
t_R, t_dist and t_fr, out object position list p)
```

```
// detection of high-level feature pairs
detect edge pixels (e.g. Canny) and arrange them in list e
group edge points e to line segments l_{S,k} and circular arcs
c_{S,k} and add each found mid-level feature to list l_S or c_S
group mid-level features to high-level features g_{S,k}, if
possible , and build list g_S
build pairs of high-level features pg_{S,k}, if possible, and
collect them in list pg_S


// voting
Init of 1-dimensional accumulator accu
for k = 1 to number of list entries in pg_S
// derive indexes a and b for accessing the 2D hash table:
    a ← concatenation of the types of the two high-level
    features g_{S,i} and g_{S,j} which build pg_{S,k}
    b ← index of geometric relation between g_{S,i} and g_{S,j}
    retrieve model list h_{M,ab} from H(a,b)
    for l = 1 to number of model entries in h_{M,ab}
        increment accu for model defined by h_{M,ab,l}
    next
next


// hypothesis generation
for all local maxima of accu (bin index denoted by m)
    if accu(m) ≥ t_R then
        match model features to the found l_{S,k} and c_{S,k}
        estimate t based on the involved feature matches
        add hypothesis hy = [t,m] to list hy
    end if
next


// hypothesis verification
for i = 1 to number of hypotheses hy
    calculate directed hausdorff distances of back-projected
    model edge point set
    if equations 5.3 and 5.4 are fulfilled then
        append hy_i to position list p
    end if
next
```

5.3.5 *Example*

Object recognition results achieved with this method are summarized in Table 5.2 (with images taken from the original article of Costa and Shapiro [2]), where

Table 5.2   Illustrating the performance of 3D object recognition with relational indexing[2]

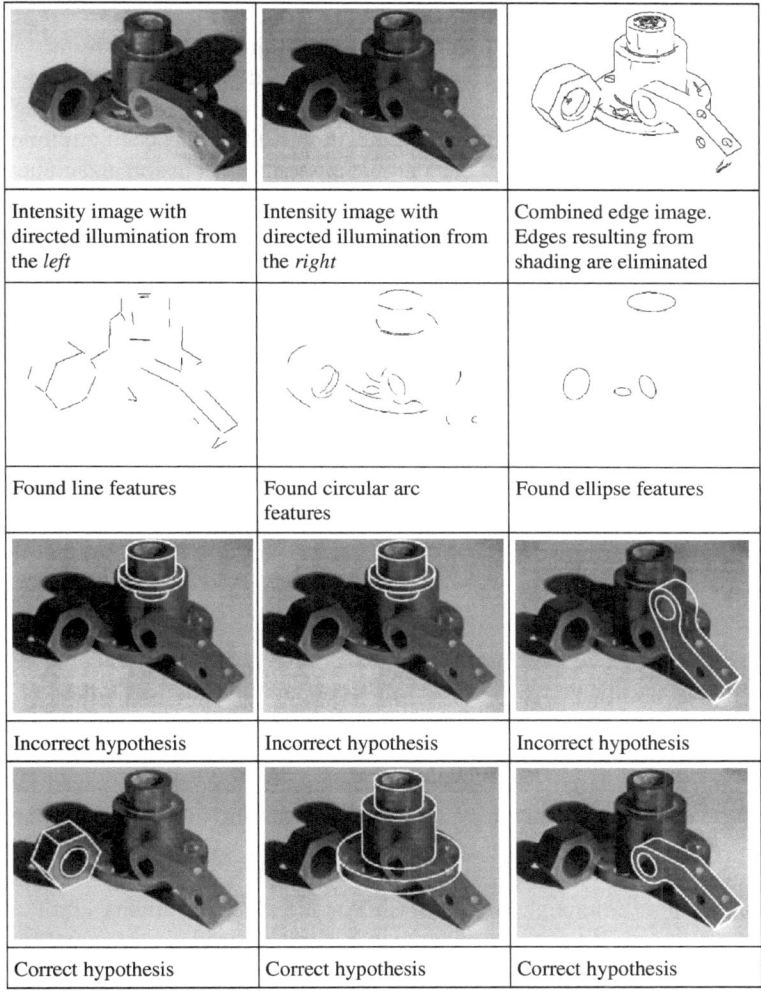

Intensity image with directed illumination from the *left*	Intensity image with directed illumination from the *right*	Combined edge image. Edges resulting from shading are eliminated
Found line features	Found circular arc features	Found ellipse features
Incorrect hypothesis	Incorrect hypothesis	Incorrect hypothesis
Correct hypothesis	Correct hypothesis	Correct hypothesis

man-made workpieces have to be detected. The first row shows the two input images (with illumination from different directions: left and right) together with the combined edge image extracted from them. The different types of mid-level features derived from the edge image are shown in the second row. The third row contains some incorrect hypotheses generated in step 6 of the recognition phase; however, all of them did not pass the verification step. All three objects of the scene were found with correct pose, as the bottom row reveals.

---

[2]Contains images reprinted from Costa and Shapiro [2] (Figs. 22, 23, and 24), © 2000, with permission from Elsevier.

5.3.6 *Rating*

Experiments performed by the authors showed quite impressive results as far as recognition performance is concerned. They reported no false detections in various test images, whereas almost all objects actually being present in the images were detected at correct position at the same time, despite the presence of multiple objects in most of the images, causing considerable amount of occlusion and clutter.

On the other hand, however, the method relies on the objects to have a "suitable" geometry, i.e., at least some of the high-level features defined in Table 5.1 have to be present. Additionally, the feature groups must be detectable in the scene image. Indeed, the major constraint of the method stems form the instability of the detection of the feature groups: sometimes a feature is missing, sometimes a feature is split because of occlusion (e.g., a long line might be detected as two separate line segments), and so on. Bear in mind that the feature group is only detected correctly if all mid-level features are found correctly as well!

5.4 LEWIS: 3D Recognition of Planar Objects

5.4.1 *Main Idea*

In order to recognize objects with arbitrary 3D pose it is desirable to derive features from the image of an object which remain constant regardless of the relative position and orientation of the object with respect to the image acquisition system. Such so-called *invariants* allow for 3D object recognition from a single 2D image of arbitrary viewpoint, because the viewpoint is allowed to change between teaching and recognition phase. The invariant value remains stable even if the object undergoes a projective transform. One example using invariants is perceptual grouping described by Lowe [3] which was already presented in a previous section. Although it can be shown that such invariants don't exist for arbitrarily shaped 3D objects, invariants can be derived for specific configurations of geometric primitives (e.g., lines or conics) or a set of linearly independent points.

The LEWIS system (*Library Entry Working through an Indexing Sequence*) developed by Rothwell et al. [4] makes use of two different types of invariants when performing recognition of planar objects (in this context "planar" means that the object is "flat," i.e., can be approximated well by a 2D plane).

Please note that, in contrast to the methods presented above, just a perspective transformation mapping a 2D model to a 2D image (with eight degrees of freedom, see Section 3.1) is estimated here. However, an extension to non-planar objects, where the estimated transformation describes a projection of the 3D object pose onto a 2D image plane, is possible and provided by the same research group [5]. The principle of invariants remains the same for both methods, and that's the reason why the LEWIS method is presented here.

Observe that the usage of invariants imposes restrictions on the objects to be recognized as they have to contain the aforementioned specific geometric configurations (examples will follow) and, additionally, the invariants have to be detected reliably in the scene images. A class of objects which meets these constraints is man-made, planar objects like spanners, lock striker plates, metal brackets (recognition examples of all of them are given in [4]), and so on.

The outline of the LEWIS method is as follows: Characteristic invariants are detected from edge images for each object to be recognized and stored in the model database in an off-line training step. During recognition, invariants of a scene image are derived with identical procedure. In order to speed up matching, indexing is applied: the value of a single invariant derived from the scene image leads to a hypothesis for the presence of an object model which contains an invariant of identical type and with similar value. In other words, if an invariant can be detected in a scene image, its value is derived and serves as an index into a hash table for retrieving a list of object classes that contain an invariant of identical type and with similar value. In a last step, the hypotheses are verified (resulting in acceptance or rejection of a hypothesis) using complete edge data.

5.4.2 Invariants

For 3D object recognition of planar objects Rothwell et al. [4] make use of two types of invariants: algebraic and canonical frame invariants. As far as algebraic invariants are concerned, they consist of a scalar value which can be derived from a specific geometric configuration of coplanar lines and/or conics. This value remains stable if the underlying feature configuration undergoes a projective transformation. Table 5.3 summarizes the geometric configurations which are utilized by the LEWIS method.

Two functionally independent projective invariants can be derived from five coplanar lines. Given five lines

$$\mathbf{l}_i = [\mu_i \sin \theta_i, -\mu_i \cos \theta_i, \mu_i d_i]^T \; ; i \in \{1, \ldots, 5\} \tag{5.5}$$

Table 5.3 Illustration of three different types of geometric configurations of *line* and *circular* features utilized by the LEWIS system in order to derive algebraic invariants

| Five lines | Two conics | One conic and two lines |

(where θ_i denotes the orientation of line i with respect to the x axis, d_i the distance of the line to the origin, and μ_i the scale factor introduced because of the usage of homogeneous coordinates) the invariants I_{L1} and I_{L2} are defined by

$$I_{L1} = \frac{|\mathbf{M}_{431}| \cdot |\mathbf{M}_{521}|}{|\mathbf{M}_{421}| \cdot |\mathbf{M}_{531}|} \tag{5.6}$$

$$I_{L2} = \frac{|\mathbf{M}_{421}| \cdot |\mathbf{M}_{532}|}{|\mathbf{M}_{432}| \cdot |\mathbf{M}_{521}|} \tag{5.7}$$

where the matrices $\mathbf{M}_{ijk}$ are built by a column-wise concatenation of the parameters of three lines $[\mathbf{l}_i, \mathbf{l}_j, \mathbf{l}_k]$. $|\mathbf{M}_{ijk}|$ denotes the determinant of $\mathbf{M}_{ijk}$.

Before we define the invariants where conics are used, let's introduce the representation of conics first. A conic is defined by the set of points $\mathbf{x}_i = [x_i, y_j, 1]$ satisfying $ax_i^2 + bx_iy_i + cy_i^2 + dx_i + ey_i + f = 0$, or equally, the quadratic form

$$\mathbf{x}_i^T \cdot \mathbf{C} \cdot \mathbf{x}_i = 0 \text{ with } \mathbf{C} = \begin{bmatrix} a & b/2 & d/2 \\ b/2 & c & e/2 \\ d/2 & e/2 & f \end{bmatrix} \tag{5.8}$$

In the presence of two conics $\mathbf{C}_1$ and $\mathbf{C}_2$, two independent invariants I_{C1} and I_{C2} can be derived:

$$I_{C1} = \frac{tr\left(\mathbf{C}_1^{-1} \cdot \mathbf{C}_2\right) \cdot |\mathbf{C}_1|^{1/3}}{|\mathbf{C}_2|^{1/3}} \tag{5.9}$$

$$I_{C2} = \frac{tr\left(\mathbf{C}_2^{-1} \cdot \mathbf{C}_1\right) \cdot |\mathbf{C}_2|^{1/3}}{|\mathbf{C}_1|^{1/3}} \tag{5.10}$$

where $tr(\cdot)$ denotes the trace of a matrix.

Two lines and one conic lead to the invariant I_{LC} which is defined by

$$I_{LC} = \frac{\left(\mathbf{l}_1^T \cdot \mathbf{C}^{-1} \cdot \mathbf{l}_2\right)^2}{\left(\mathbf{l}_1^T \cdot \mathbf{C}^{-1} \cdot \mathbf{l}_1\right) \cdot \left(\mathbf{l}_2^T \cdot \mathbf{C}^{-1} \cdot \mathbf{l}_2\right)} \tag{5.11}$$

Canonical frame invariants I_V can be applied to the more general class of planar curves. As a projective transformation is specified by eight parameters, it can be defined by four non-collinear planar points. If four non-collinear points can be uniquely identified on a planar curve, the mapping of these points onto a so-called *canonical frame*, e.g., a unit square, uniquely defines the eight parameters of a projective transformation. In this context "uniquely defines" means that the system always detects the same positions on the curve, regardless of the viewpoint from which the image was taken. To this end, four points around a concavity of the curve are utilized (see Fig. 5.5). Now the entire curve can be transformed into the canonical frame. The transformed curve remains stable regardless of the viewpoint.

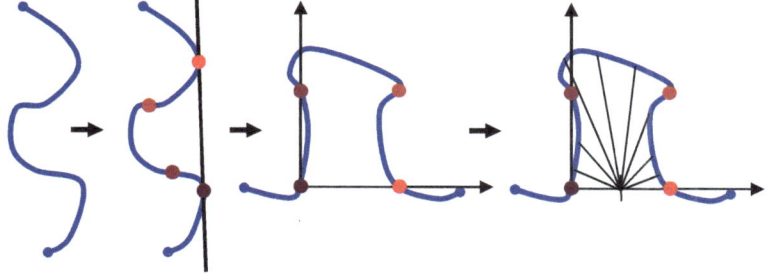

Fig. 5.5 Summarizing the derivation of canonical frame invariants as implemented in the LEWIS method, where curves of connected edge pixels which feature a concavity are exploited

For this reason a signature which is a projective invariant can be derived from the transformed curve. To this end the lengths of equally spaced rays ranging from the point $[1/2, 0]$ to the transformed curve are stacked into a vector and serve as a basis for the desired invariant I_V (details see [4]).

Figure 5.5 illustrates the proceeding: In a first step, four non-collinear points around a concavity are uniquely identified with the help of a common tangent (see [4] for details). Next, these four points are mapped onto a unit square. Subsequently, all points of the curve can be transformed to the thus defined canonical frame. The lengths of equally spaced rays (shown in black in the right part; all originating at the point $[1/2, 0]$) are the basis for the desired invariant. Observe that – compared to algebraic invariants – there are less restrictions on the shape of the object. However, the curve is not allowed to be arbitrarily shaped, as it is required to detect a common tangent passing through two distinct points of the curve.

5.4.3 Teaching Phase

The model database can be built iteratively by extracting the model data for each object class from a training image. For each model class, the data consists of a collection of edge pixels, geometric features (lines, conics and curves of connected edge pixels), and the invariant values derived from the features. The data is obtained as follows:

1. *Identification of edge pixels*: In the first step all edge pixels with rapidly changing intensity are found, e.g., with the operator proposed by Canny [1] (including non-maximum suppression). For many man-made, planar objects, the set of thus obtained edge pixels, captures most of the characteristics.
2. *Feature extraction*: Subsequently, all primitives which could potentially be part of a configuration being suitable for derivation of invariants (namely lines, conics and curves) are extracted from the edge image.

3. *Feature grouping*: Now the lines and cones are grouped to one of the three configurations from which algebraic invariant values can be derived (see Table 5.3),
   if possible.
4. *Invariant calculation*: Subsequently, several invariant values can be calculated
   and added to the object model, algebraic invariants, as well as canonical frame
   invariants.
5. *Hash Table creation*: For speed reasons, the invariant values can be used to create
   hash tables $\mathbf{H}_{L1}, \mathbf{H}_{L2}, \mathbf{H}_{LC}, \mathbf{H}_{C1}, \mathbf{H}_{C2}$, and $\mathbf{H}_V$ (one table for each functionally
   independent invariant). Each table entry consists of a list of object models which
   feature an invariant of appropriate type and with a value that falls within the hash
   table index bounds.

The data of each object model, which is available after teaching, essentially
consists of the following:

- A list $\mathbf{e}$ of edge pixels
- Lists of lines $\mathbf{l}_M$, conics $\mathbf{c}_M$ and curves $\mathbf{v}_M$ which could be extracted out of $\mathbf{e}$.
- Feature groups $\mathbf{g}_{M,L}$ (5-line configurations), $\mathbf{g}_{M,LC}$ (2-line and conic configurations), $\mathbf{g}_{M,C}$ (2-conic configurations) which serve as a basis for invariant
  calculation.
- Invariant values $I_{L1,i}, I_{L2,i}, I_{LC,j}, I_{C1,k}, I_{C2,k}$, and $I_{V,l}$ derived from the entries of
  $\mathbf{l}_M, \mathbf{c}_M$, and $\mathbf{v}_M$.

5.4.4 Recognition Phase

Recognition of the objects shown in a scene image is performed by comparing invariants. To this end, invariants have to be derived from the scene image,
too. Hence, steps 1–4 of recognition are identical to training. In the following,
classification and verification are performed as follows:

5. *Hypothesis formulation by indexing*: in order to formulate a hypothesis for the
   occurrence of a specific object based on a specific invariant value the following
   two conditions must hold:

   – An invariant of the same type (e.g., based on five lines) exists in the model
     database.
   – The value of the model database invariant is similar to the scene image
     invariant value.

   A fast hypothesis formulation can be achieved by the usage of hash tables:
   each table entry, which covers a range of invariant values, consists of a list of
   all object models containing an invariant of the same type whose value also falls
   into this range. As we have different types of functionally independent invariants,
   multiple hash tables $\mathbf{H}_{L1}, \mathbf{H}_{L2}, \mathbf{H}_{LC}, \mathbf{H}_{C1}, \mathbf{H}_{C2}$, and $\mathbf{H}_V$ are used. At this stage,

each invariant leads to a separate hypothesis. Based on the model data as well as the extracted scene image feature groups, the transformation parameters **t** can be derived.

6. *Hypothesis merging*: instead of a separate verification of each hypothesis it is advantageous to combine them if they are consistent. As a joint hypothesis is supported by more features, it is more reliable and the transformation parameters can be estimated more accurately. The merging process is based on topologic and geometric compatibility of different hypotheses, details can be found in [4].

7. *Hypothesis verification*: a (joint) hypothesis is verified if it is still broadly supported when all edge pixels and/or features (and not only the invariant values) are taken into account. Verification is performed by back-projecting the edge pixel point set as well as all extracted lines and conics of the model to the scene image. A hypothesis is accepted if more than a certain proportion of the model data is consistent with the scene image data. Two lines are regarded consistent if their orientation is similar, conics have to possess similar circumference and area and finally, edge pixels must have similar position and gradient orientation. Because back-projection of many edge pixels is expensive in terms of runtime, it is preferable to perform another verification in advance: in general, when calculating the eight parameters of the projective transform, it is possible to formulate an over-determined equation system. Over-determination should be possible, because the number of available features should exceed four non-collinear points which are necessary to determine eight transformation parameters. Consequently, if it is not possible to compute common transformation parameters where the error (due to the over-determination) remains small, the hypothesis can be rejected immediately. Otherwise the parameters just calculated can be used for the aforementioned back-projection verification.

5.4.5 Pseudocode

```
function detectObjectPosLEWIS (in Image I, in hash tables
H_{L1}, H_{L2}, H_{LC}, H_{C1}, H_{C2}, and H_V, in model data M for
each object model, in similarity threshold t_{sim}, out object
position list p)


// invariant calculation
detect all edge pixels (e.g. Canny) (summarized in e)
group edge points e to line segments l_{S,i}, cones c_{S,k} and
curves v_{S,l} and add each found feature to one of the lists
l_S, c_S or v_S
detect all 5-line configurations g_{S,L,i} and build list g_{S,L}
detect all 2-line/1-conic configs g_{S,LC,j} and build list g_{S,LC}
detect all 2-conic configurations g_{S,C,k} and build list g_{S,C}
calculate algebraic invariants I_{L1,i}, I_{L2,i}, I_{LC,j}, I_{C1,k} and
```

$I_{C2,k}$ for all elements of lists $g_{S,L}$, $g_{S,LC}$, and $g_{S,C}$
(equations 5.6 - 5.11)
calculate canonical frame invariants $I_{V,l}$ for all elems of v_S

```
// matching
// generation of hypotheses
for i = 1 to number of list entries in gS,L
    retrieve model list hM,L1 from HL1 (index specified
    by IL1,i)
    for m = 1 to number of model entries in hM,L1
        estimate t based on gS,L,i and gM,L,n
        add hypothesis hy = [t,m] to list hy // m: model index
    next
    repeat this proceeding with IL2,i
next
repeat this proceeding with gS,LC and gS,C and vS (here,
take the four non-collinear points for estimating t)
// hypothesis merging
for i = 1 to number of hypotheses hy -1
    for j = i+1 to number of hypotheses hy
        if similarity (hyi, hyj) then
            hyk = merge (hyi, hyj)
            replace hyi by hyk and delete hyj
        end if
    next
next


// hypothesis verification
for i = 1 to number of hypotheses hy
    sim ← 0
    verify lines: adjust sim based on the position similarity
    between lS,i and t (lM,i)
    repeat this for all cones and edge pixels
    if sim ≥ tsim then
        append hyi to position list p
    end if
next
```

5.4.6 Example

The following examples show object poses found and verified by the LEWIS system as white overlays on the original gray scale scene images. They demonstrate that the system is able to detect multiple objects even in the presence of heavy occlusion and/or background clutter, but also disclose some limitations of the method.

Table 5.4 Recognition examples taken from the article of Rothwell et al. [4].[3] The threshold for the edge match in the verification step was set to 50%

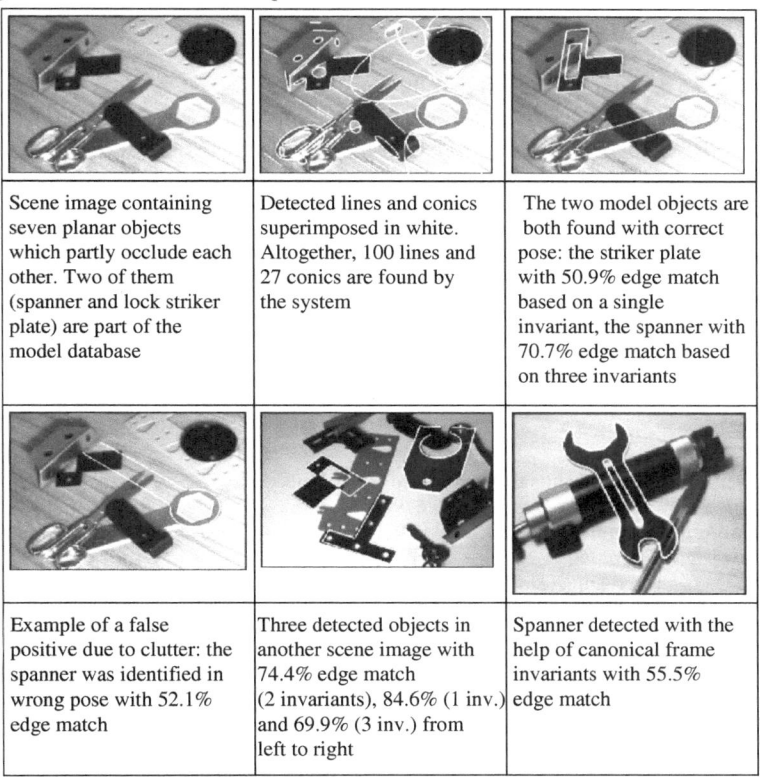

Scene image containing seven planar objects which partly occlude each other. Two of them (spanner and lock striker plate) are part of the model database	Detected lines and conics superimposed in white. Altogether, 100 lines and 27 conics are found by the system	The two model objects are both found with correct pose: the striker plate with 50.9% edge match based on a single invariant, the spanner with 70.7% edge match based on three invariants
Example of a false positive due to clutter: the spanner was identified in wrong pose with 52.1% edge match	Three detected objects in another scene image with 74.4% edge match (2 invariants), 84.6% (1 inv.) and 69.9% (3 inv.) from left to right	Spanner detected with the help of canonical frame invariants with 55.5% edge match

5.4.7 Rating

As the examples show, it is indeed possible to utilize invariants for 3D object recognition of planar objects with only a single image independent of the viewpoint from which it was acquired. Experiments performed by the authors, where objects were rotated full circle with a certain step size, revealed that algebraic as well as canonical frame invariants remained stable (the standard deviation was at approximate 1.5% of the mean value). There are numerous examples where objects were found in spite of considerable occlusion and/or clutter. Moreover, the system is also capable of identifying multiple objects in a single scene image. Compared to an alignment approach, the number of hypotheses to be tested in the verification step could be reduced dramatically (by 2–3 orders of magnitude for some example images).

---

[3]With kind permission from Springer Science+Business Media: Rothwell et. al. [4], Figs. 27, 28, 32, and 42, © 1995 Springer.

On the other hand, however, the system sometimes tends to generate false positives, especially in the presence of heavy clutter. This is due to the fact that clutter leads to a dense occurrence of features. Consequently, sometimes a spurious solution can occur when an invariant calculated from clutter can be matched to the model database (one example is shown in Table 5.4). The system doesn't consider texture or, more generally, appearance information which could contribute to alleviate this effect. Additionally, the method only works well if objects are suited, i.e., if they contain several feature primitives like lines or conics. More seriously, many features have to be detected reliably in order to make the method work. This makes the invariant calculation instable: for example, if only a single line of a five-line group is occluded by another object, it is not possible to calculate the corresponding invariant value any longer. In the meantime it is common sense that this limitation is the main drawback of methods relying on invariants.

References

1. Canny, J.F., "A Computational Approach to Edge Detection", *IEEE Transactions on Pattern Analysis and Machine Intelligence*, 8(6):679–698, 1986
2. Costa, M. and Shapiro, L., "3D Object Recognition and Pose with Relational Indexing", *Computer Vision and Image Understanding*, 79:364–407, 2000
3. Lowe, D.G., "Three-Dimensional Object Recognition from Single Two-Dimensional Images", *Artificial Intelligence*, 31(3):355–395, 1987
4. Rothwell, C.A., Zisserman, A., Forsyth, D.A. and Mundy, J.L., "Planar Object Recognition using Projective Shape Representation", *International Journal of Computer Vision*, 16:57–99, 1995
5. Zisserman, A., Forsyth, D., Mundy, J., Rothwell, C., Liu, J. and Pillow, N., "3D Object Recognition Using Invariance", *Artificial Intelligence*, 78(1–2):239–288, 1995

Chapter 6
Flexible Shape Matching

Abstract Some objects, e.g., fruits, show considerable intra-class variations of their shape. Whereas algorithms which are based on a rigid object model run into difficulties for deformable objects, specific approaches exist for such types of objects. These methods use parametric curves, which should approximate the object contour as good as possible. The parameters of the curve should offer enough degrees of freedom for accurate approximations. Two types of algorithms are presented in this chapter. Schemes belonging to the first class, like snakes or the contracting curve density algorithm, perform an optimization of the parameter vector of the curve in order to minimize the differences between the curve and the object contour. Second, there exist object classification schemes making use of parametric curves approximating an object. These methods typically calculate a similarity measure or distance metric between arbitrarily shaped curves. Turning functions or the so-called curvature scale space are examples of such measures. The metrics often follow the paradigm of perceptual similarity, i.e., they intend to behave similar to the human vision system.

6.1 Overview

In certain applications the shapes of the objects to be found exhibit considerable variations, e.g., the shape of potatoes can have substantial differences when one potato is compared to another. However, despite of these variations, most potatoes can easily be recognized and are perceived as "similar" by humans. Algorithms exploiting geometric properties like distances between characteristic features of the object or point sets are often based on a rigid object model, thus running into difficulties for deformable objects. Therefore methods have been designed which are flexible enough to cope with deformations in the object shape. Some of them intend to establish similarity measures which are inspired by the mode of operation of human visual recognition.

In this chapter, methods using parametric curves are presented. A parametric curve $\mathbf{v}(s, \varphi)$ can be written as

M. Treiber, *An Introduction to Object Recognition*, Advances in Pattern Recognition, 117
DOI 10.1007/978-1-84996-235-3_6, © Springer-Verlag London Limited 2010

$$\mathbf{v}\,(s, \varphi) = \big[x(s, \varphi), y\,(s, \varphi)\big] \tag{6.1}$$

with φ being a vector of model parameters specifying the curve and s being a scalar monotonously increasing from 0 to 1 as the curve is traversed. The course of the curve should approximate the object contour as good as possible. The parameter vector φ should offer enough degrees of freedom which enable the curve to be flexible enough for an accurate approximation of the object shape.

Two types of algorithms shall be presented in this chapter. The first class contains schemes consisting of an optimization of the parameter vector φ such that the discrepancies between the curve and the object contour are minimized. Strictly speaking, these methods are not able to classify an object shown in a scene image; instead they try to locate the exact position of a deformable object contour, e.g., find the exact borders of potatoes. Therefore they are often seen as segmentation methods. Nevertheless, they are presented here (in the first two sections of this chapter), because they offer the possibility to enhance the performance of other object recognition schemes. For example, they can be combined with a Hough transform giving a rough estimate about the object location in order to refine the object border estimation. The main motivation for such a proceeding is to combine the advantages of both schemes.

Additionally, curves which are an accurate approximation of an arbitrarily shaped object can be utilized for a subsequent classification. To this end, methods exist which calculate a similarity measure or distance metric between arbitrarily shaped curves. Some of them are presented in the second part of this chapter. Based on these measures the aforementioned classification is possible. The metrics often follow the paradigm of *perceptual similarity*, i.e., they intend to behave similar to the human vision system. Therefore they should be able to recognize objects which are perceived similar by us humans as well, even if their contour shows considerable deformations.

The usage of curves for object recognition offers the advantage of modeling arbitrarily shaped objects. Moreover, deformations can be considered in a natural way, which makes the utilization of curves suitable for flexible shape matching. However, many of the methods optimizing parametric curves rely on a stable segmentation of the object from the background, which is in itself a nontrivial task.

6.2 Active Contour Models/Snakes

6.2.1 Standard Snake

6.2.1.1 Main Idea

Snakes are parametric curves as described above and have been proposed by Kass et al. [3] as a method being able to detect contours of deformable objects. They act like an elastic band which is pulled to the contour by forces. Being an iterative scheme, eventually the course of the band converges to the object border being searched. The forces affect the snake with the help of a so-called energy functional, which is iteratively minimized.

During energy minimization by optimization of the curve model, the snakes change their location dynamically, thus showing an active behavior until they reach a stable position being conform with the object contour. Therefore they are also called *active contour models*. The "movement" of the curve during iteration reminds of snakes, which explains the name. Snakes are an example of a more general class of algorithms that match a deformable model to an image with the help of energy minimization.

According to Kass et al. [3] the energy functional E can be written as:

$$E = \int_0^1 E_{\text{int}} (\mathbf{v} (s, \varphi)) + E_{image} (\mathbf{v} (s, \varphi)) + E_{con}(\mathbf{v} (s, \varphi))ds \qquad (6.2)$$

As can be seen, the total energy consists of three components:

- E_{int} is called the *internal energy* and ensures the curve to be smooth. E_{int} depends on the first- and second-order derivatives of $\mathbf{v} (s, \varphi)$ with respect to s. Considering the first order ensures to exclude discontinuities and the second-order part helps punishing curves containing sections of high curvature. In this context, curvature can be interpreted as a measure of the energy which is necessary to bend the curve.
- E_{image} represents the *constraints imposed by the image content*. The curve should be attracted by local intensity discontinuities in the image as these gray value changes are advising of object borders. E_{image} can contain terms originating from lines, edges, or terminations. Minimizing this term of the functional achieves convergence of the curve toward the salient image features just mentioned.
- With the help of *external constraints* E_{con} it is envisaged to ensure that the snake should remain near the desired minimum during optimization. This can be achieved by user input (e.g., when E_{con} is influenced by the distance of the curve to user-selected "anchor points," which are specified as lying on the object contour by the user) or by feedback of a higher level scene interpretation in a subsequent step of the algorithm.

During optimization, the curve parameter vector φ has to be adjusted such that the energy functional E reaches a minimum. The optimization procedure is outlined in the following, details can be found in the appendix of [3].

6.2.1.2 Optimization

The internal energy is often modeled by a linear combination of the first- and second-order derivatives of $\mathbf{v} (s, \varphi)$ with respect to s:

$$E_{\text{int}} = {}^1\!/_2 \cdot \left[\alpha \, |\mathbf{v}_s (s, \varphi)|^2 + \beta \, |\mathbf{v}_{ss} (s, \varphi)|^2 \right] \qquad (6.3)$$

where the parameters α and β determine the relative influence of the first- and second-order derivatives (denoted by $\mathbf{v}_s$ and $\mathbf{v}_{ss}$) intending to punish discontinuities and high curvature parts, respectively. If β is set to 0, the curve is allowed to contain corners. It is possible to model α and β dynamically dependent on s or statically as constants.

E_{image} should take smaller values at points of interest such as edge points. Therefore the negative gradient magnitude is a natural measure for E_{image}. As object borders produce high-gradient values only within a very limited area in the surrounding of the border, this convergence area is usually very limited. It can be increased, though, by utilizing a spatially blurred version of the gradient magnitude. To this end, a convolution of the image content with a Gaussian kernel $G(x, y, \sigma)$ is applied:

$$E_{image}(x, y) = -\left| \nabla \left[G(x, y, \sigma) * I(x, y) \right] \right|^2 \tag{6.4}$$

$$\text{with } G(x, y, \sigma) = \frac{1}{\sqrt{2\pi}\sigma} \cdot e^{-(x^2 + y^2)/2\sigma^2} \tag{6.5}$$

where ∇ and $*$ denote the gradient and convolution operator, respectively.

As far as the external constraints E_{con} are concerned, they are often set to zero and therefore aren't considered any longer in this section.

A minimization of the energy functional is usually performed without explicit calculation of the model parameters φ of the curve. Instead, the curve position is optimized at N discrete positions $\mathbf{v}(s_i) = \left[x(s_i) y(s_i) \right]$ with $i \in [1..N]$ and $s_{i+1} = s_i + \Delta s$. Δs denotes a suitably chosen step size. If the internal and image constraints are modeled as described above, the snake must satisfy the Euler equation (which actually is a system of two independent equations, one in x and one in y) in order to minimize E. It is defined by

$$\sum_{i=1}^{N} \alpha \mathbf{v}_{ss}(s_i) - \beta \mathbf{v}_{ssss}(s_i) - \nabla E_{\text{image}}(s_i) = \mathbf{0} \tag{6.6}$$

with $\mathbf{v}_{ss}(s)$ being the second-order derivative and $\mathbf{v}_{ssss}(s)$ the fourth-order derivative of $\mathbf{v}$ with respect to s. A solution of this equation can be found by treating $\mathbf{v}$ as a function of time t and iteratively adjusting $\mathbf{v}(s, t)$ until convergence is achieved (see the Appendix of [3] for details).

6.2.1.3 Example

Figure 6.1 shows an example of fitting an initially circle-shaped curve to a triangle form. It was generated with the java applet available at the Computer Vision Demonstration Website of the University of Southampton.[1] The energy is minimized iteratively with the help of sample points located on the current curve

---

[1] http://users.ecs.soton.ac.uk/msn/book/new_demo/Snakes/ (link active 13 January, 2010), images printed with permission. There also exists a book written by a member of the research group [7], which gives a very good overview of snakes as well as many other image processing topics.

Fig. 6.1 Several iteration steps captured during the fitting of an initial circle-shaped curve to a triangle form are shown

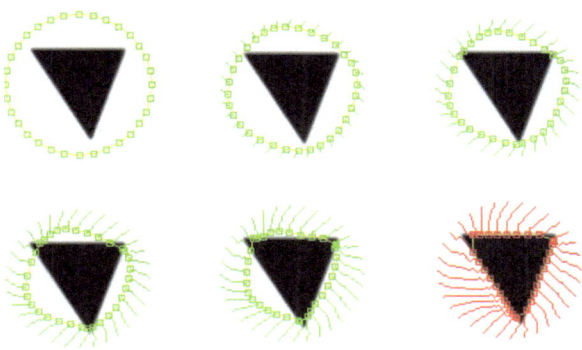

representation (green squares). The images show the location of the sample points at start, after 6, 10, 15, 20, and final iteration (from top left to bottom right). The "movement" of each sample point as iteration proceeds is also shown by a specific curve for each point (green and red curves).

6.2.1.4 Rating

With the help of snakes it is possible to detect the exact contour of deformable objects. Given a reasonable estimate, arbitrarily shaped contours can be approximated (at least in principle); the method is not restricted to a specific class of objects. In contrast to the classical approach of edge detection and edge linking, snakes as a global approach have the very desirable property of being quite insensitive to contour interruptions or local distortions. For this reason they are often used in medical applications where closed contours often are not available.

A major drawback of snakes, though, is the fact that they rely on a reasonable starting point of the curve (i.e., a rough idea where the object border could be) for ensuring convergence to the global minimum of the energy functional. If the starting point is located outside the convergence area of the global minimum the iteration will get stuck in a local minimum not being the desired solution. This is a general problem of numerical iterative optimization schemes. The convergence area is defined by the scope of the gray value gradients. This scope can be extended by increasing the σ value of Gaussian smoothing, but this is only possible at the cost of decreasing the gradient magnitude. That's the reason why σ cannot be increased too far. Another attempt to overcome this limitation is to perform several energy minimizations at different starting points. Additionally, snakes sometimes fail to penetrate into deep concavities (see next section).

In order to get an impression of the performance and limitations of the method, it is suggested to search the Internet for java applets implementing the snake algorithm[2] and experiment a bit.

---

[2]See, e.g., http://www.markschulze.net/snakes/index.html (link active 13 January, 2010).

6.2.2 Gradient Vector Flow Snake

6.2.2.1 Main Idea

Xu and Prince [10] suggested a modification aiming at extending the convergence area of the snake. Additionally, they showed that with the help of their modification, snakes were able to penetrate in deep concavities of object boundaries as well, which often isn't possible with the standard scheme. Having these two goals in mind, they replaced the part which represents the image constraints in the Euler equation (6.6), namely $-\nabla E_{\text{image}}$, by a more general force field $\mathbf{f}(x, y)$

$$\mathbf{f}(x, y) = [a(x, y), b(x, y)] \tag{6.7}$$

which they called *gradient vector flow* (GVF). A specific tuning of $\mathbf{f}(x, y)$ intends to enlarge the convergence area as well as increase the ability to model deep concavities correctly.

Figure 6.2 presents a comparison of the GVF snake (bottom row) with the standard snake method (top row) with the help of an example contour shown in the left column (in bold). It features a deep concavity. Additionally the convergence process of the snake is displayed in the left column. The iterative change of the snake approximation shows that the standard scheme isn't able to represent the concavity correctly, but the GVF snake is. In the middle, the force fields of both methods are displayed. Clearly, the GVF snake has a much larger convergence area. A close-up of the force field in the area around the concavity is shown in the right part. It reveals the reason why the standard snake doesn't penetrate into the concavity,

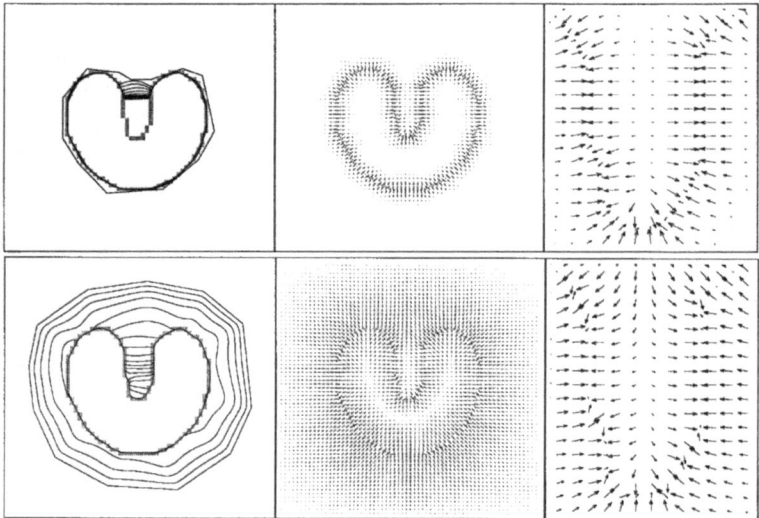

Fig. 6.2 Taken from Xu and Prince [10] (© 1998 IEEE; with permission): Comparison of the standard snake scheme (*top row*) with a GVF snake (*bottom row*)

but the GVF snake does: forces of the standard scheme inside the concavity have no portion pointing downward into the concavity, whereas the GVF forces possess such a portion.

The calculation of $\mathbf{f}(x, y)$ starts with the definition of an edge map $e(x, y)$, which should be large near gray value discontinuities. The above definition of a Gaussian-blurred intensity gradient is one example of an edge map. The GVF field is then calculated from the edge map by minimizing the energy functional

$$\varepsilon = \iint \mu \left(a_x^2 + a_y^2 + b_x^2 + b_y^2 \right) + |\nabla e|^2 \, |\mathbf{f} - \nabla e|^2 \, dxdy \qquad (6.8)$$

with $(\cdot)_n$ being the partial derivative in the n-direction. A closer look at ε reveals its desirable properties: near object boundaries, minimization of ε usually results in setting $\mathbf{f}$ very close to or even identical to ∇e and thus a behavior very similar to the standard snake. In homogenous image regions, however, $|\nabla e|$ is rather small, and therefore ε is dominated by the partial derivatives of the vector field, leading to a minimization solution which keeps the spatial change of $\mathbf{f}(x, y)$ small and hence to enlarged convergence areas. The parameter μ serves as a regularization term.

According to Xu and Prince [10], the GVF field can be calculated prior to snake optimization by separately optimizing $a(x, y)$ and $b(x, y)$. This is done by solving the two Euler equations

$$\mu \nabla^2 a - (a - e_x) \left(e_x^2 + e_y^2 \right) = 0 \qquad (6.9a)$$

$$\text{and } \mu \nabla^2 b - (b - e_y) \left(e_x^2 + e_y^2 \right) = 0 \qquad (6.9b)$$

where ∇^2 denotes the Laplacian operator (see [10] for details). The thus obtained solutions minimize ε (cf. Equation (6.8)). Once $\mathbf{f}(x, y)$ is calculated, the snake can be optimized as described in the previous section.

6.2.2.2 Pseudocode

```
function optimizeCurveGVFSnake (in Image I, in segmentation
threshold t_I, out boundary curve v(s_i))

// pre-processing
remove noise from I if necessary, e.g. with anisotropic
diffusion
init of edge map e(x, y) with Gaussian blurred intensity
gradient magnitude of I (Equation 6.4)
calculate GVF field f(x, y) by solving Equation 6.9

// init of snake: segment the object from the background and
derive the initial curve from its outer boundary
for y = 1 to height(I)
```

```
    for x = 1 to width(I)
      if I(x, y) ≤ t_I then
        add pixel [x, y] to object area o
      end if
    next
  next
next
get all boundary points b of o
sample boundary points b in order to get a discrete
representation of parametric curve v(s_i, 0)

// optimization (just outline, details see [3])
t ← 1
do
    v(s_i, t) ← solution of Euler equation 6.6// update curve
    update Euler equation 6.6 (adjust the terms of 6.6
    according to the new positions defined by v(s_i, t))
    t ← t + 1
until convergence
```

6.2.2.3 Example

GVF snakes are incorporated by Tang [8] in a lesion detection scheme for skin cancer images. Starting from a color image showing one or more lesions of the skin, which can contain clutter such as hairs or specular reflections in the lesion region, the exact boundary of the lesion(s) is extracted (cf. Fig. 6.3 and image (C) of Table 6.1).

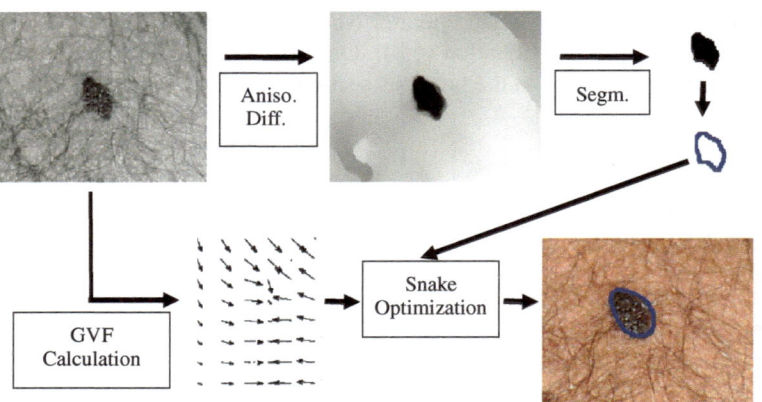

Fig. 6.3 Illustrating the boundary extraction of the lesions of skin cancer images (after the initial *gray* value conversion).[3] The proceeding is explained in the text

---

[3]Contains some images reprinted from Tang [8] (Figs. 2 and 7), © 2009, with permission from Elsevier.

Table 6.1 Illustrating the convergence problem in case of multiple objects[4]

(A) Example of convergence problems when multiple objects are present with GVF snakes (*blue* curve)	(B) Correct convergence achieved with the directional GVF snake	(C) Example of a multilesion detection

The method consists of four steps:

1. *Conversion* of the original color image to a gray value image.
2. *Noise removal* by applying a so-called *anisotropic diffusion filter*: the basic idea of anisotropic diffusion is to remove noise while preserving gradients at true object borders at the same time. To this end, the image is iteratively smoothed by application of a diffusion process where pixels with high intensity ("mountains") diffuse into neighboring pixels with lower intensity ("valleys"). This is done in an anisotropic way: diffusion does not take place in the directions of dominant gray value gradients (thereby gradient blurring is avoided!), but perpendicular to it. Details can be found in [8] and are beyond the scope of this book.
3. *Rough segmentation* with the help of simple gray value thresholding. This step serves for the determination of reasonable starting regions for the subsequent snake optimization.
4. *Fine segmentation* using a GVF snake. Compared to the GVF snake presented above, Tang [8] applied a modified version in order to make the method suitable for multi-lesion images where it should be possible to locate multiple lesions being close to each other. In those cases the snake has to be prevented to partly converge to one lesion and party to another lesion in its vicinity. This can be achieved by replacing the edge map $e(x, y)$ by a gradient that always points toward the center point of the lesion currently under investigation. The thus obtained directed gradient vector flow ensures that the whole snake converges toward the boundary of the same lesion (cf. images (A) and (B) of Table 6.1).

6.2.2.4 Rating

As shown in the example application, some restrictions of the standard snake scheme can be overcome or at least alleviated by the usage of GVF snakes. The

---

[4]Contains some images reprinted from Tang [8] (Figs. 4 and 7), © 2009, with permission from Elsevier.

additional degrees of freedom obtained by the introduction of more general force fields can be utilized to enlarge the convergence area or make the optimization more robust in situations where the scene image contains multiple objects.

On the other hand, the calculation of the force field involves a second optimization procedure during recognition which increases the computational complexity of the method. Moreover, a reasonable initial estimation of the object boundary is still necessary.

6.3 The Contracting Curve Density Algorithm (CCD)

6.3.1 Main Idea

Another algorithm falling into the class of fitting a curve model to supposed object boundaries is the contracting curve density algorithm (CCD) suggested by Hanek and Beetz [2]. It works on RGB color images and also utilizes a parametric curve model. In addition to that, a model for the probability distribution of the curve parameters is used, too. This means that the curve model is not deterministic, but instead consists of a "mean" parameter vector $\mathbf{m}_\varphi$ and a covariance matrix $\mathbf{\Sigma}_\varphi$ describing the joint probability distributions of the parameters φ of the curve model.

The algorithm consists of two iteration steps which are performed in alternation:

1. During the first step, local image statistics, e.g., the distribution of RGB values, are calculated for each of the two sides of the curve. To this end, the pixels in the vicinity of the curve are assigned probabilistically to a specific side of the curve with the help of the current curve model. Based on that assignment, the statistics can be estimated for each side separately.
2. The curve model consisting of the mean parameter vector and its covariance matrix is refined in the second step. This can be done by calculating the probability of occurrence of the actually sensed RGB values based on the assignment of each pixel to a curve side as well as the local statistics, both derived in the first step. To put it in other words: How likely are the actually acquired RGB values to occur, given the estimates of step 1? Now the curve model is updated such that it maximizes this probability. These two steps are performed iteratively until the curve model converges, i.e., the changes of $\mathbf{m}_\varphi$ and $\mathbf{\Sigma}_\varphi$ are small enough (see also Fig. 6.4).

Please note that, as the local image statistics are allowed to change as the curve is traversed and can additionally be updated in each iteration step, it is possible to use dynamically adjusted criteria for the assignment of pixels to a side of the curve. This is a considerable improvement compared to using pre-defined criteria which are applied by many conventional image segmentation schemes such as homogeneity or gradient-based information.

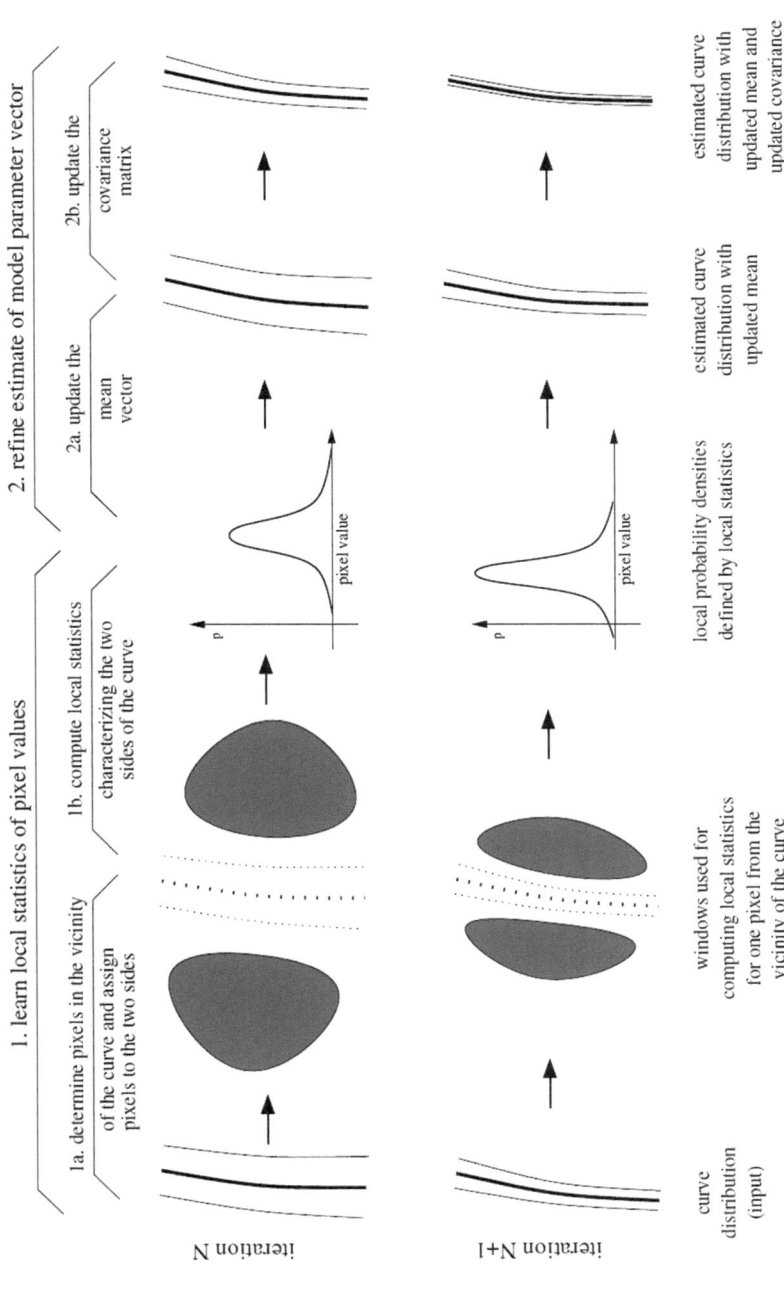

Fig. 6.4 Taken from Hanek and Beetz [2][5]: Outline of the CCD algorithm

[5]With kind permission from Springer Science+Business Media: Hanek and Beetz, [2], Figure 7, © 2004 Springer.

6.3.2 Optimization

The details of the optimization procedure involve extensive use of mathematics and are beyond our focus. Therefore just the outline of the proceeding at each iteration step i shall be presented here; the interested reader is referred to the original article of Hanek and Beetz [2] for details.

The first question that has to be answered is how to assign the pixels to side $n \in \{1, 2\}$ of the curve $\mathbf{v}$. The assignment can be done by calculating a quantity $a_{p,1}(\mathbf{m}_\varphi, \mathbf{\Sigma}_\varphi)$ for each pixel p in the vicinity v of $\mathbf{v}$ which indicates the probability of p belonging to side 1 of the curve. It depends on the location of p relative to $\mathbf{v}$ as well as the curve model parameters $\mathbf{m}_\varphi$ and $\mathbf{\Sigma}_\varphi$. Here, the term "vicinity" means that p is located close enough to $\mathbf{v}$ such that it has to be considered in the optimization procedure. The probability that p belongs to side 2 of the curve is given by $a_{p,2} = 1 - a_{p,1}$. $a_{p,1}$ consists of two parts: the probability $\tilde{a}_{p,1}$ for a given vector of model parameters φ (which corresponds to the fraction of p which is located at side 1 of the curve and is 0 or 1 in most cases) and the conditional probability $p(\varphi|\mathbf{m}_\varphi, \mathbf{\Sigma}_\varphi)$ defining the probability of occurrence of this parameter set, given the statistical properties of the model:

$$a_{p,1}(\mathbf{m}_\varphi, \mathbf{\Sigma}_\varphi) = \int \tilde{a}_{p,1}(\varphi) \cdot p(\varphi|\mathbf{m}_\varphi, \mathbf{\Sigma}_\varphi)d\varphi \qquad (6.10)$$

Second, for each pixel p in the vicinity of the curve $\mathbf{v}(s, \varphi)$ the statistics of its local neighborhoods have to be modeled. To this end, a Gaussian distribution is chosen for modeling the probability of occurrence of a specific RGB value, which is characterized by a 3D mean vector $\mathbf{m}_{p,n}$ (corresponding to the mean red, green and blue intensity) and a 3×3 covariance matrix $\mathbf{\Sigma}_{p,n}$ modeling their joint probabilities. The statistics $\mathbf{S}_{p,n} = (\mathbf{m}_{p,n}, \mathbf{\Sigma}_{p,n})$ for each pixel p are calculated separately for each of the two sides of the curve, i.e., the neighborhood is separated into two parts, one for each side of the curve. $\mathbf{m}_{p,n}$ and $\mathbf{\Sigma}_{p,n}$ can be calculated based on weighted sums of the actual RGB values of the two parts of the neighborhood. As s increases when traversing the curve, the weights are varying (only the local neighborhood of p shall be considered) and therefore the local statistics are allowed to change, which results in a suitable neighborhood representation even in challenging situations of inhomogeneous regions.

Finally, a way of updating the curve model $\mathbf{m}_\varphi$ and $\mathbf{\Sigma}_\varphi$ has to be found. To this end, a probability distribution for the occurrence of the RGB values at each pixel p (how likely is a specific value of $\mathbf{I}_p$, given the statistics $\mathbf{S}_{p,n}$?) is calculated based on the assignments $a_{p,n}$ as well as the local neighborhood statistics $\mathbf{S}_{p,n}$. Again, a Gaussian distribution is chosen. It is given by

$$\mathbf{m}_p = a_{p,1}\mathbf{m}_{p,1} + a_{p,2}\mathbf{m}_{p,2} \qquad (6.11)$$

$$\text{and} \ \ \mathbf{\Sigma}_p = a_{p,1}\mathbf{\Sigma}_{p,1} + a_{p,2}\mathbf{\Sigma}_{p,2} \qquad (6.12)$$

Given this distribution, the probability $p(\mathbf{I}_p|\mathbf{m}_p, \mathbf{\Sigma}_p)$ of the occurrence of the actual RGB value $\mathbf{I}_p$ of p can be calculated. The probability of occurrence of the sensed image data for the entire vicinity ν is characterized by the product of $p(\mathbf{I}_p|\mathbf{m}_p, \mathbf{\Sigma}_p)$ for all pixels located within ν:

$$p(\mathbf{I}_\nu|\mathbf{m}_\nu, \mathbf{\Sigma}_\nu) = \prod_{p\in\nu} p(\mathbf{I}_p|\mathbf{m}_p, \mathbf{\Sigma}_p) \tag{6.13}$$

The updated mean vector $\mathbf{m}_\varphi^{i+1}$ can be set to the parameter vector φ that maximizes the following product:

$$\mathbf{m}_\varphi^{i+1} = \arg\max\big[p\,(\mathbf{I}_\nu|\mathbf{m}_\nu, \mathbf{\Sigma}_\nu)\cdot p\big(\varphi|\mathbf{m}_\varphi^i, \mathbf{\Sigma}_\varphi^i\big)\big] \tag{6.14}$$

$\mathbf{\Sigma}_\varphi^{i+1}$ is calculated based upon a Hessian matrix derived from this product, for details see [2].

6.3.3 Example

In Fig. 6.5 the exact contour of a mug is determined: starting from the initial contour estimation shown as a red curve, the algorithm converges to the contour shown in black. Estimating the contour is a difficult task here, as both the object and the background area are highly inhomogeneous in terms of RGB values due to texture, shading, clutter, and highlights.

Fig. 6.5 Taken from Hanek and Beetz [2][6] showing the precise contour detection of a mug as a challenging example application

---

[6]With kind permission from Springer Science+Business Media: Hanek and Beetz [2], Fig. 2, © 2004 Springer.

6.3.4 Pseudocode

```
function optimizeCurveCCD (in Image I, in initial curve
estimate v(φ₀), convergence limits εₘ and ε_Σ, out refined
curve estimate v(φᵢ))
```

```
// iterative optimization
i ← -1
do
   i ← i + 1
   // step 1: estimate local statistics
   for each pixel p ∈ ν
     calculate probability aₚ,₁ that p belongs to side
     1 of the curve according to Equation 6.10
     aₚ,₂ ← 1 - aₚ,₁
   next
   for each pixel p ∈ ν
      // calculate statistics Sₚ of the neighborhood of p
      for each pixel q at side 1 and in neighborhood of p
         update mₚ,₁ and Σₚ,₁ according to q weighted by
         the distance between p and q
      next
      for each pixel q at side 2 and in neighborhood of p
         update mₚ,₂ and Σₚ,₂ according to q weighted by
         the distance between p and q
      next
      estimate mₚ and Σₚ acc. to Equation 6.11 and 6.12
   next
   // step 2: refine estimate of model params m_φ^{i+1} and Σ_φ^{i+1}
   for each pixel p ∈ ν
      calculate p(Iₚ |mₚ, Σₚ) and update p(I_ν | m_ν, Σ_ν)
      (probability that actual RGB values are observed; Equ.
      6.13)
   next
   m_φ^{i+1} ← argmax of Equation 6.14 // update mean
   update Σ_φ^{i+1} based on Hessian matrix
until ||m_φ^{i+1} - m_φ^i|| ≤ εₘ ∧||Σ_φ^{i+1} - Σ_φ^i|| ≤ ε_Σ
```

6.3.5 Rating

With the help of examples, the authors give evidence that the algorithm achieves high accuracy when detecting the object border even in very challenging situations with, e.g., severe texture, clutter, partial occlusion, shading, or illumination variance while featuring large areas of convergence at the same time (see Fig. 6.5 where the border of a mug is detected accurately despite being located in a highly inhomogeneous background; the detection result is superior to other segmentation methods for that kind of situations). This is due to the fact that the algorithm utilizes a "blurred" model (probability distribution of the curve parameters) and does not blur the image content like other algorithms do in order to enlarge convergence area.

Besides, the dynamic update of the statistical characterization of the pixel neighborhoods especially pays off in challenging situations like the mug shown in the example. If the object and/or background regions are highly inhomogeneous, a dynamic adjustment of the statistics is clearly superior to a segmentation based on any kind of pre-defined thresholds.

On the other hand, this algorithm is rather time-consuming and relies on a reasonable starting point as well.

6.4 Distance Measures for Curves

Once a curve approximating an object boundary is available, it can be compared to curves which describe the contour of known object classes and are stored in the model database. This can be done by applying a distance metric, which yields a dissimilarity measure between the curve of the query object and a model curve of the database. This measure, in turn, can be used for a classification of the object. These metrics often intend to identify curves being perceptually similar, which is an approach trying to imitate the human vision system with its impressive capabilities as far as pattern recognition is concerned.

In the following two metrics, one being derived from the curve itself (based on the so-called curvature scale space) as well as another derived from a polygonal approximation of the curve (based on a so-called turning function) are presented. Both of them showed good performance in a comparative study performed by Latecki et al. [5]).

6.4.1 Turning Functions

6.4.1.1 Main Idea

According to van Otterloo [9], a so-called *turning function* can be calculated from a polygonal approximation of the curve. In a second step, two polygons can be compared by means of a distance metric based on the discrepancies of their turning functions. For the moment, let's assume that a suitable polygonal approximation of the object contour, i.e., a polygon consisting of line segments located in the vicinity of the object boundary, is already available (see Chapter 4 how such an approximation can be obtained).

The turning function $T_p(s)$ of a polygon p defines the cumulative angle between the line segments of the polygon and the x-axis as a function of the arc length s, which increases from 0 to 1 as the polygon is traversed. Starting at an end point

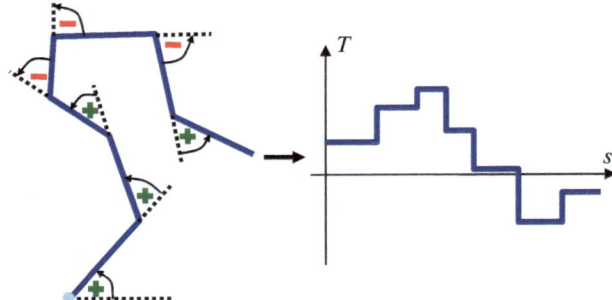

Fig. 6.6 Example for the calculation of T_p (s): The polygon is depicted in the *left* part; the deduced turning function can be seen on the *right*. The starting point is marked light *blue*

of p (or, equivalently, at $s = 0$), T is initialized by the angle between the line segment which contains the end point and the x-axis. As s increases, the value of $T_p(s)$ is changed at each vertex connecting two line segments of the polygon. $T_p(s)$ is increased by the angle between two successive line segments if the polygon turns to the left and $T_p(s)$ is decreased by the angle between two successive line segments if the polygon turns to the right (see Fig. 6.6).

Let's have a look at some properties of the turning function: First of all, it can easily be seen that T is translation invariant. As the polygons are normalized such that s ranges from 0 to 1, the turning function is scale invariant, too. A rotation θ of the polygon leads to a vertical shift of T. In the case of closed contours, a "movement" of the starting point along the contour results in a horizontal shift of T. Apart from these shifts, which can be identified easily, turning functions are suitable for a comparison of polygons featuring minor deformations due to their cumulative nature: even if the course of the polygon is different at a certain position, in cases where the polygons are perceptually similar the cumulative angle should be similar, too. This is a very desirable property for flexible model fitting.

Based on the turning function, a distance metric $d\,(a, b)$ between two polygons a and b, which integrates the differences of the cumulative angles, can be calculated as follows:

$$d(a, b) = \left(\int_0^1 |T_a(s) - T_b(s) + \theta_0|^n \, ds \right)^{1/n} \tag{6.15}$$

where $T_a(s)$ and $T_b(s)$ denote the turning functions derived from the polygons a and b. The parameter n is often chosen to $n = 2$. With the help of θ_0 a possible rotation between the two polygons can be compensated: θ_0 is chosen such that $d(a, b)$ is minimized. As a consequence, the metric is invariant to the class of similarity transformations.

An example can be seen in Fig. 6.7: Two polygons differing especially in one vertex in their upper right part are compared there. The differences of their turning

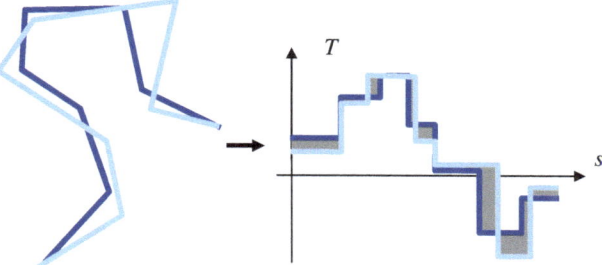

Fig. 6.7 Example of the turning-function-based distance metric

functions are indicated by gray areas in the right part of the figure. Observe that the arc lengths in T are normalized: actually, the light blue polygon is longer than the dark blue polygon. Despite considerable appearance variations between the two polygons, their turning functions are quite similar, which correlates well with the visual perception of the polygons: the basic characteristics of both polygons are usually perceived similar by human observers.

6.4.1.2 Example

Latecki and Lakämper [4] presented an object recognition scheme based on the turning function as distance measure for the comparison of curves. The method starts when the curve approximating the border of a query object has already been extracted, e.g., by a proper segmentation scheme or a snake refinement. Recognition then consists of the following steps:

1. *Polygonal approximation* of the curve: every planar curve can be represented by a series of pixels which define the locations of the curve in 2D space. This pixel representation can already be interpreted as a polygon, because any two consecutive pixels define a very short line segment. Of course, such a (initial) polygonal representation is of little use in respect of the turning function as even small amount of noise causes many turns. Hence, an iterative process called *discrete contour evolution* or discrete curve evolution (DCE) is applied. At each iteration step, the two line segments l_1 and l_2 with the least significant contribution to the curve are replaced by a single new line segment which connects the outmost two end points of l_1 and l_2 (see also Fig. 6.8) The significance of the contribution is measured by a cost function which increases with the turning angle between l_1 and l_2 as well as the length of the segments. The iteration stops if the previously defined distance metric $d(p_0, p_i)$ between the initial curve p_0 and the polygonal approximation p_i at iteration step i exceeds a certain threshold. This proceeding results in a smoothing of spurious and noisy details while the characteristic course of the curve is preserved at the same time.

2. *Distance metric calculation*: once an appropriate polygonal approximation of the object contour is available, its similarity to objects stored in a model database can

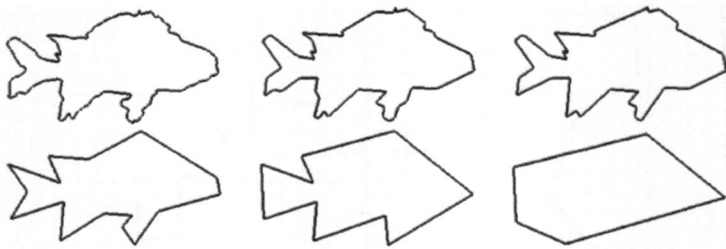

Fig. 6.8 Example of discrete curve evolution (DCE) taken from Latecki and Lakämper [4] (© 2000 IEEE; with permission). A few iteration stages of the DCE algorithm are shown when approximating the contour of a fish. The original contour is presented in the *upper left* part. At first, variations of small scale are removed. Finally, an entirely convex polygon remains (*lower right*)

be calculated with the help of the turning function-based distance metric defined by (6.15). Bear in mind, though, that a global representation of the object contour by means of a single closed polygon is sensitive to occlusion. Therefore, in order to increase robustness, the polygons are split into visual parts, and each part vp_i is compared separately to a part of a model polygon or concatenations of such parts. Details of this partitioning can be found in [4].

3. *Classification*: based on the previously computed distances to the objects of a model database, the assignment of the query object to a certain model object can be made, e.g., by nearest-neighbor classification (cf. also Appendix B).

6.4.1.3 Pseudocode

function **classifyCurveTurningFunction** (in Image I, in boundary curve $\mathbf{v}(s)$ of object in scene image, in visual parts $\mathbf{vp}_M$ of all models, in maximum polygonal approx. deviation $t_{p,\max}$, in similarity threshold t_{sim}, out model index m)

```
// DCE approximation
// set initial polygonal approximation to boundary curve
p₀ ← v(s)
i ← 0; dev ← 0
while dev ≤ tp,max do
    sigmin ← MAX_FLOAT      // init of significance minimum
    // detect the two least significant lines
    for j = 1 to number of lines of pi-1
        for k = j + 1 to number of lines of pi
            calculate significance sigj,k of lines lj and lk
            for polygon pi
            if sigj,k ≤ sigmin then
                sigmin ← sigj,k
            end if
        next
```

```
next
  replace the two lines from which sig_min was derived
  by one line connecting their outer endpoints in p_i
  dev ← d(p_0, p_i) // compare p_0 to p_i acc. to Equation 6.15
  i ← i + 1
end while
split p_i into visual parts vp_{S,i} and store them in list vp_S

// classification
for each model index m      // loop for all database models
  err_m ← 0 // cumulated turning function discrepancies
  for i = 1 to number of visual parts (elements of vp_S)
    find closest match vp_{m,k} to vp_{S,i} (Equation 6.15)
    increment err_m according to d(vp_{m,k},vp_{S,i})
  next
next
find model index m_min with smallest deviation error err_{m,min}
if err_{m,min} ≤ t_{sim} then
  // valid object class identified
  return m_min
else
  return -1    // in order to indicate an error has occurred
end if
```

6.4.1.4 Rating

The authors regard the main strength of their method to be the capability to find correct correspondences between visual salient parts of object contours. The DCE-algorithm, which can be seen as a pre-filter, effectively suppresses noise, which facilitates the matching step. The method proved to outperform many other schemes in a comparative study, where database retrieval applications were simulated [5].

However, the partitioning into parts with subsequent combinatorial matching also involves a considerable increase in computational complexity. Moreover, the scheme concentrates on classification; an estimation of the pose of the object being approximated by the polygon is not straightforward.

6.4.2 Curvature Scale Space (CSS)

6.4.2.1 Main Idea

A distance metric, which is directly based on a curve representing the border of an object, was introduced by Mokhtarian et al. [6]. It is derived from the so-called *curvature scale space*, and based on the observation that dominant characteristics of a curve remain present for a large range of scales whereas spurious characteristics soon disappear as scale increases.

Mokhtarian et al. consider locations where the curvature of the curve passes through a zero crossing as characteristic points of the curve (an interpretation which is shared by many other authors, too). A geometric interpretation is that the change of the tangent angle changes its sign at such a point, i.e., the point is located at the transition between a concave and a convex part of the curve.

After an initial segmentation step, the object boundary usually contains many curvature zero crossings, mainly due to noise and/or quantization effects. But if the curve which represents the object boundary is smoothed further and further, the spurious zero crossings will soon disappear, whereas the crossings being characteristic of the boundary remain present even in the case of strong smoothing.

An example of the evolution of zero crossings can be seen in Table 6.2, where the zero crossings of a maple leaf contour are detected at multiple smoothing levels. The original binary image is shown upper left. The blue curves represent the extracted boundaries at different levels of smoothing. All detected curvature zero crossings are marked red. It can be seen that more and more zero crossings disappear as smoothing increases. The starting point of the boundary curve is located at the top of the leaf and marked green.

Smoothing of a curve $\mathbf{v}(s) = \big[x(s), y(s)\big]$ can be realized by a separate convolution of each of the two components $x(s)$ and $y(s)$ with a 1D Gaussian function. The extent of smoothing can be controlled with the standard deviation σ of the Gaussian function. As σ increases, more and more curvature zero crossings will disappear; typically, two crossings cancel each other out at a certain scale. Finally, when σ is

Table 6.2 Evolution of a curve with increasing smoothing

Original image	Extracted boundary; $\sigma = 5$	Boundary at $\sigma = 14$
Boundary at $\sigma = 32$	Boundary at $\sigma = 72$	Boundary at $\sigma = 120$

sufficiently high, $\mathbf{v}(s)$ is entirely convex and therefore no curvature zero crossings are present any longer (cf. Table 6.2, lower right curve).

For a given smoothing level σ, it is possible to plot all positions of curvature zero crossings in terms of the arc length s at which they occur. When the plotting is repeated for various σ, the position change of the zero crossings is shown in the $[s; \sigma]$–plane, which defines the curvature scale space. The pair-wise annihilation of zero crossings is observable very well in curvature scale space. Zero crossings resulting from noise, etc., disappear at comparably low σ, whereas dominant characteristics annihilate at high σ (see Table 6.3).

The 2D pattern ("fingerprint", denoted as **fp**) of all annihilation positions (which are alternatively called "maxima", denoted as fp_i) in curvature scale space which are located at a sufficiently high σ level (e.g. above a threshold value t_σ) is considered as characteristic for a certain object boundary and should remain similar even if minor distortions occur. The positions in s-direction of the maxima should roughly correspond to locations with maximum/minimum curvature, as they are located in between two zero crossings or inflection points of the initial curve. This relates the scheme to a certain extent to the discrete curve evolution method presented in the previous section, as the polygon vertices typically are located in regions with extremal curvature, too.

The appearance of objects in CSS can be exploited for object classification by matching the 2D pattern of annihilation points of a query object to the patterns stored in a model database. The total distance between two patterns, which can be used as a measure for classification, can be set to the summation of the Euclidean distances between matched maxima of the pattern plus the vertical positions of all unmatched maxima. This ensures a proper penalization for patterns with many unmatched maxima.

Table 6.3 Curvature scale space example

Curvature scale space of the maple leaf example	All characteristic maxima (annihilation points above *red* line) are marked *red*
2D pattern of CSS maxima of the above example (*red* points), compared to a second pattern (*blue* crosses)	The comparison with a shifted version of the *blue* pattern reveals high similarity. The alignment is based on the positions of the two dominant maxima (second from *right*)

Please note that a change of the starting point (where $s = 0$) results in a horizontal shift of the whole pattern along the s-axis. As a consequence, the two patterns have to be aligned prior to matching. This can be done, for example, by aligning the "highest" maxima (annihilation points occurring at highest σ) of the two pattern (see bottom part of Table 6.3).

6.4.2.2 Pseudocode

```
function classifyCurveCSS (in Image I, in boundary curve v(s)
of object in scene image, in fingerprints of CSS maxima fp_M
of all models, in sigma threshold t_σ, in similarity threshold
t_sim, out model index m)

// CSS calculation
σ_0 ← 1.0
init of curvature scale space css
for i = 1 to n
    // smooth boundary curve
    v_i(s) ← v(s)*G(σ_i)    // convolution with Gaussian
    calculate zero crossings z of v_i(s)
    update css according to z and σ_i.
    σ_i+1 ← σ_i · k    // e.g. k = 1.2
next

// calculation of CSS pattern fp_S of scene image
fp_S ← all local maxima in css
for i = 1 to number of maxima (elements of fp_S)
    if σ(fp_S,i) ≤ t_σ then    // maximum is not dominant
        remove fp_S,i from fp_S
    end if
next

// classification
for each model index m
    align fp_m and fp_S horizontally
    err_m ← 0
    for i = 1 to number of maxima in CSS (entries in fp_S)
        find closest match fp_m,k to fp_S,i
        if no match found then
            // add sufficiently large penalty value pen
            err_m ← err_m + pen
        else
            increment err_m according to distance between
            fp_m,k and fp_S,i
        end if
```

```
    next
next
find model index mmin with smallest deviation error errm,min
if errm,min ≤ tsim then
    // valid object class identified
        return mmin
else
    return -1 // in order to indicate that no object was found
end if
```

6.4.2.3 Rating

Tests performed by the authors with various data sets showed that the CSS-metric is capable to reliably identify objects being similar to a query object, which is considered similar by human observers, too. The method, together with the turning-function based metric, proved to outperform many other schemes in a comparative study where database retrieval applications were simulated [5].

On the other hand, observe that, in contrast to polygonal approximation, a back calculation from the CSS pattern to a curve is not possible. Due to its global nature a disadvantage of this measure is that the object contour has to be present as a complete closed contour, i.e., the objects have to be segmented completely from the background, which might not be possible in some cases. Additionally, the fingerprint of CSS maxima is not scale-invariant. In order to make the method robust to changes of scale shifts have to be performed in scale direction during the matching of the 2D fingerprints. Moreover, as matching of the fingerprint has to be carried out in a 2D space (and maybe also shifts are necessary) the computational complexity is rather high.

6.4.3 Partitioning into Tokens

6.4.3.1 Main Idea

Methods relying on a closed contour of the object are very sensitive to occlusion. Partly occluded objects can be found, however, if the contour is split into parts. Then it is possible to search each part individually first. It doesn't matter if some of the parts are missing in the query image as long as the detected parts can gather enough evidence for the presence of an object.

Berretti et al. [1] adopt the strategy of breaking up an object contour into parts, which they call *tokens*. Additionally, they choose a representation of the tokens which is intended to fit well to the concept of perceptual similarity. With the help of this representation it should be possible to detect objects which show consider-able intra-class variation, but are considered similar by us humans. Moreover, they applied the principle of indexing in order to speed up the recognition process. The usage of indexing aims at a fast retrieval of the token being most similar to a query token form the model database.

Now let's have a closer look at the three contributions of the work of Berretti et al. [1] which were considered most significant by the research group:

1. *Partitioning into tokens*: There is evidence that the human vision system splits a connected contour at positions of extremal curvature, i.e., points where the contour bends most sharply. For that reason Berretti et al. [1] suggest to partition the curve at points where the curvature of the curve attains a local minimum. These points correspond to the bounding points of protrusions of the contour. If a parametric description $\mathbf{v}(s) = [x(s), y(s)], s \in [0, 1]$ of the contour is available, its curvature $c_{\mathbf{v}}(s)$ is defined by

$$c_{\mathbf{v}}(s) = \frac{x_s(s)\, y_{ss}(s) - x_{ss}(s)\, y_s(s)}{\left(x_s^2(s) + y_s^2(s)\right)^{3/2}} \qquad (6.16)$$

where $x_s(s)$, $x_{ss}(s)$, $y_s(s)$, and $y_{ss}(s)$ denote the first and second derivatives of x and y with respect to s, respectively. An example of the partitioning according to the minima of $c_{\mathbf{v}}(s)$ can be found in Fig. 6.9 (right image).

2. *Token representation*: As mentioned already, the representation of each token τ_k should reflect the concept of perceptual similarity. One feature which strongly influences perception is the "width" of a token: "narrow" tokens are considered to be dissimilar to "wide" tokens. A quantitative measure of the "width" is the maximum curvature m_k along τ_k. As the end points are defined by local minima of curvature, there also has to be a local maximum of curvature somewhere along the token. The higher m_k, the more "narrow" the token is perceived. A second characteristic measure for the token is its orientation θ_k with respect to the x-axis.

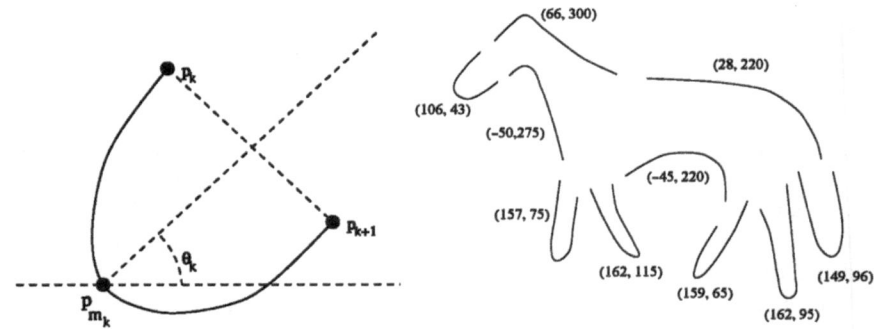

Fig. 6.9 With images taken from Berretti et al. [1] (© 2000 IEEE; with permission): In the *left part*, details of the calculation of the token orientation θ_k are shown. The *right part* depicts the partitioned contour of a horse together with the descriptor values of the tokens in the notion of (maximum curvature, orientation)

θ_k is determined by the angle between a specific line of the token and the x-axis of a reference coordinate system. The specific line connects the point of maximum curvature with the point which is located in the center of a line connecting the two end points of τ_k (see left part of Fig. 6.9). Overall, each token is characterized by its $[m_k, \theta_k]$-tuple.

3. *Indexing via M-trees*: At some stage in the matching process the token of a model database which is most similar to a given query token (detected in a query image) has to be found. In order to avoid exponential complexity which would be involved by the straightforward approach of a combinatorial evaluation of the similarity measures, the most similar model token is found by indexing. To this end, the model tokens are arranged in a tree structure. At the bottom or "leaf" level, each node n_i represents one token. Tokens with $[m_k, \theta_k]$-tuples of similar value – which form a cluster in the 2D feature space – are summarized into a new node of the tree, which is a parent of the leaf nodes. Each node is characterized by the centroid of the cluster as well as the dimension of the cluster in feature space. In higher levels of the tree several clusters can be summarized again, which yields a new node, and so on. During matching, a top-down processing of the resulting tree permits a fast determination of correspondences between query and model tokens. The term "M-Tree" results from the learning method when building the tree in a teaching stage (see [1] for details).

6.4.3.2 Example

Berretti et al. [1] applied the token-based object models in a retrieval system, where the user inputs a hand-drawn sketch and the system reports images from a database containing objects with a contour being most similar to the user sketch (cf. Fig. 6.10, which illustrates the algorithm flow). In order to retrieve the most similar objects, the user sketch is partitioned into tokens first. Images containing similar shapes are found by establishing 1-to-1 correspondences between the tokens of the sketch and

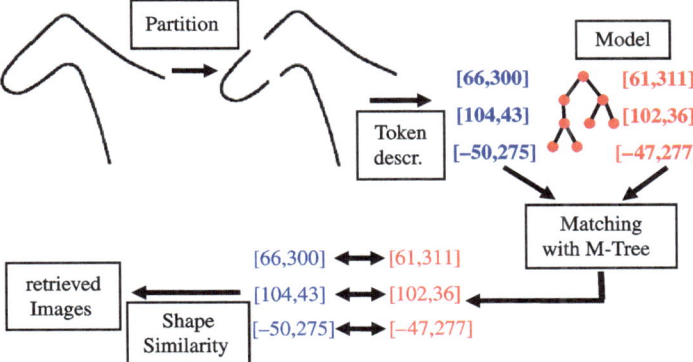

Fig. 6.10 Algorithm flow for retrieving images containing shapes which are similar to a user sketch as proposed by Berretti et al. [1], where the user sketches the outline of a head of a horse

the tokens of the database. As a measure of distance d_{ij} between two tokens $\tau_i = [m_i, \theta_i]$ and $\tau_j = [m_j, \theta_j]$ a weighted sum of curvature and orientation differences is applied:

$$d_{ij} = \alpha \cdot |m_i - m_j| + (1 - \alpha) \cdot |\theta_i - \theta_j| \qquad (6.17)$$

where α denotes a weighting factor. The search of the most similar tokens is speeded up by the tree-based organization of the model token database. The similarity measure between two shapes amounts to the sum of token differences. Geometric relations between the tokens are not considered. As a result, the images with the lowest overall dissimilarity measures (which are based upon the sum of the d_{ij}) are reported by the system.

6.4.3.3 Pseudocode

```
function retrieveSimilarObjectsToken (in boundary curve v(s)
of object in scene image, in token lists τ_M of all models, in
M-Trees of all models MT_M, in similarity threshold t_sim, out
list of indices of all similar images a)

// token partitioning of input curve
calculate curvature c_v(s) of boundary curve v(s) according
to Equation 6.16
detect all minima of c_v(s) and store them in list c_v,min
partition v(s) into tokens τ_S: each token is bounded by the
position of two successive minima c_v,min,k and c_v,min,k+1
for k = 1 to number of tokens τ_S
   calculate maximum curvature m_k in token τ_S,k
   calculate orientation θ_k of token τ_S,k
   τ_S,k  ← [m_k,θ_k] // store representation of current token
next

// matching
for a = 1 to number of models in database
   err_a ← 0
   for k = 1 to number of tokens τ_S
      // detect correspondence of current token
      i ← 1
      n_i ← root node of MT_M,a
      while n_i contains child nodes do
         find node n_i+1 representing the most similar model
         token among all child nodes of n_i (Equation 6.17)
         i ← i + 1
      end while
      τ_M,a,l ← model token defined by n_i
```

$err_a \leftarrow err_a$ + distance d_{kl} between $\tau_{S,k}$ and $\tau_{M,a,l}$
according to Equation 6.17
next
if $err_a \leq t_{sim}$ **then**
append index a to position list of similar images **a**
end if
next

6.4.3.4 Rating

In their article, Berretti et al. [1] gave evidence that their system was capable of retrieving similar images even in the presence of partial occlusion. The retrieval performance was competitive to other systems. The authors also showed that the usage of M-trees significantly accelerated the correspondence search.

However, invariance is only achieved with respect to scale, not rotation, because the token orientations θ_k were calculated with respect to an absolute coordinate system. By calculating relative angles (angle between one token with respect to another) rotation invariance can be achieved, but only at the cost of increased sensitivity to occlusion: if the "reference token" isn't present, the relative angles cannot be calculated. Additionally, the usage of curvature involves sensitivity to noise, as second derivatives are used.

References

1. Berretti, S., Del Bimbo, A. and Pala, P. "Retrieval by Shape Similarity with Perceptual Distance and Effective Indexing", *IEEE Transactions on Multimedia,* 2(4):225–239, 2000
2. Hanek, R. and Beetz, M., "The Contracting Curve Density Algorithm: Fitting Parametric Curve Models to Images Using Local Self-adapting Separation Criteria", *International Journal of Computer Vision*, 233–258, 2004
3. Kass, M., Witkin, A. and Terzopoulos, D., "Snakes: Active Contour Models", *International Journal of Computer Vision*, 321–331, 1988
4. Latecki, L.J. and Lakämper, R., "Shape Similarity Measure Based on Correspondence of Visual Parts", *IEEE Transactions on Pattern Analysis and Machine Intelligence*, 22(10):1185–1190, 2000
5. Latecki, L.J., Lakämper, R. and Eckhard, U., "Shape Descriptors for Non-rigid Shapes with a Single Closed Contour", Proceedings of the *IEEE Conference on Computer Vision and Pattern Recognition*, Hilton Head Island, USA, 424–429, 2000
6. Mokhtarian, F., Abbasi, S. and Kittler, J., "Efficient and Robust Retrieval by Shape Content through Curvature Scale Space", *Int'l. Workshop on Image Databases and Multimedia Search*, Amsterdam, Netherlands, 35–42, 1996
7. Nixon, M. and Aguado, A., "Feature Extraction and Image Processing", Academic Press, New York, 2007, ISBN 978-0-12-372538-7
8. Tang, J., "A Multi-Direction GVF Snake for the Segmentation of Skin Cancer Images", *Pattern Recognition,* 42:1172–1179, 2009
9. Van Otterloo, P., "*A Contour-Oriented Approach to Shape Analysis*", Prentice Hall Ltd., Englewood Cliffs, 1992
10. Xu, C. and Prince, J.L., "Snakes, Shapes and Gradient Vector Flow", *IEEE Transactions on Image Processing*, 7(3):359–369, 1998

Chapter 7
Interest Point Detection and Region Descriptors

Abstract Object recognition in "real-world" scenes – e.g., detect cars in a street image – often is a challenging application due to the large intra-class variety or the presence of heavy background clutter, occlusion, or varying illumination conditions, etc. These tough demands can be met by a two-stage strategy for the description of the image content: the first step consists of the detection of "interest points" considered to be characteristic. Subsequently, feature vectors also called "region descriptors" are derived, each representing the image information available in a local neighborhood around one interest point. Object recognition can then be performed by comparing the region descriptors themselves as well as their locations/spatial configuration to the model database. During the last decade, there has been extensive research on this approach to object recognition and many different alternatives for interest point detectors and region descriptors have been suggested. Some of these alternatives are presented in this chapter. It is completed by showing how region descriptors can be used in the field of scene categorization, where the scene shown in an image has to be classified as a whole, e.g., is it of type "city street," "indoor room," or "forest", etc.?

7.1 Overview

Most of the methods presented up to now use either geometrical features or point sets characterizing mainly the object contour (like the correspondence-based schemes) or the global appearance of the object (like correlation or eigenspace methods). When object recognition has to be performed in "real-world" scenes, however (e.g., detect cars in a street image), a characterization with geometric primitives like lines or circular arcs is not suitable. Another point is that the algorithm must compensate for heavy background clutter and occlusion, which is problematic for global appearance methods.

In order to cope with partial occlusion, local evaluation of image information is required. Additionally, gradient-based shape information may not be enough when dealing with a large number of similar objects or objects with smooth brightness

M. Treiber, *An Introduction to Object Recognition*, Advances in Pattern Recognition, 145
DOI 10.1007/978-1-84996-235-3_7, © Springer-Verlag London Limited 2010

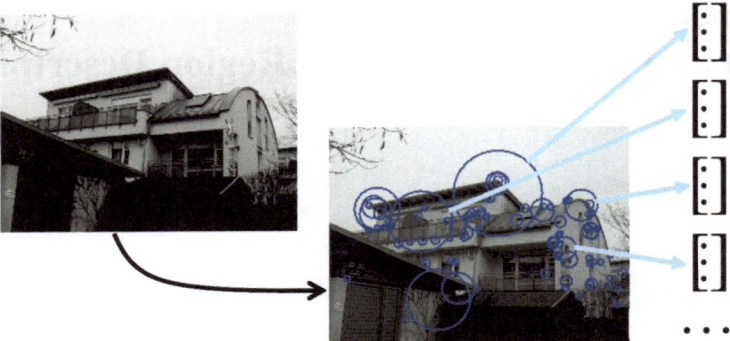

Fig. 7.1 Illustrative example of the strategy suggested by Schmid and Mohr [31]: first, interest regions are detected (*middle part*, indicated by *blue circles*). Second, a descriptor is calculated for each interest region (*right part*)

transitions. To this end, Schmid and Mohr [31] suggested a two-stage strategy for the description of the image content: the first step consists of the detection of so-called *interest points* (sometimes also called "keypoint" in literature), i.e., points exhibiting some kind of salient characteristic like a corner. Subsequently, for each interest point a feature vector called *region descriptor* is calculated. Each region descriptor characterizes the image information available in a local neighborhood around one interest point. Figure 7.1 illustrates the approach.

As far as descriptor design is concerned, the objective is to concentrate local information of the image such that the descriptor gets invariant to typical variations like viewpoint or illumination change while enough information is preserved at the same time (in order to maintain discriminative power, i.e., ability to distinguish between different object classes).

Object recognition can then be performed by comparing information of region descriptors detected in a scene image to a model database. Usually the model database is created in an automated manner during a training phase. Recognition is done by matching both the descriptor content (establishing point-to-point correspondences) and the spatial relations of the interest points.

In contrast to most of the correspondence-based matching techniques presented in the previous chapters, the number of correspondences between model and scene image descriptors can efficiently be reduced prior to spatial relation-based matching by comparing the descriptor data itself. Additionally, the information gained by using region information compared to point sets leads to increased robustness with respect to clutter and occlusion as fewer feature matches are necessary. Besides, the keypoint detection concentrates on highly characteristic image regions in an automatic manner; no assumptions about the object appearance have to be made in advance. Mainly, the descriptors are derived from appearance information, but there also exist methods making use of descriptors which are derived from shape information, e.g., the object silhouette or detected contour points.

During the last decade, there has been extensive research on this approach to object recognition and many different alternatives for interest point detection and region descriptors have been suggested (a good overview is given in [26] or [28]). Before presenting some of the alternatives for interest point detection as well as region description, a key method adopting this strategy called scale invariant feature transform (SIFT) is presented as a whole. After discussing the variations, some methods applying the local descriptor approach to shape information are presented. The chapter is completed by showing how region descriptors can be used in the field of scene categorization, where the scene shown in an image has to be classified as a whole, e.g., is it of type "city street," "indoor room," or "forest," etc.?

7.2   Scale Invariant Feature Transform (SIFT)

The SIFT descriptor method suggested by Lowe [17, 18] has received considerable attention and is representative for a whole class of algorithms performing object recognition by representing an object with the help of regional descriptors around interest points. Its principles for interest point detection and region description as well as the embedding overall object recognition strategy adopted by the SIFT method are presented in the following.

7.2.1   SIFT Interest Point Detector: The DoG Detector

7.2.1.1   Main Idea

As far as interest point detection is concerned, we have to consider that apart from the spatial position image information can be present at different scales, e.g., texture details can be visible only in fine scales whereas the outline of a large building will probably be present also at a very coarse scale. Hence, image information can be regarded to be not only a function of the spatial directions x and y but also a function of scale s, which is called the *scale space* [33].

When going from finer to coarser scales, information can only disappear and must not be introduced. A function for the calculation of image representations at different scales satisfying this constraint is the Gaussian kernel $G(x, y, \sigma)$. An image representation $I_s(x, y, \sigma)$ at a specific scale s can be calculated by the convolution of the original image $I(x, y)$ with $G(x, y, \sigma)$:

$$I_s(x, y, \sigma) = G(x, y, \sigma) * I(x, y) \tag{7.1}$$

$$\text{with } G(x, y, \sigma) = \frac{1}{\sqrt{2\pi}\sigma} \cdot e^{-(x^2+y^2)/2\sigma^2} \tag{7.2}$$

The choice of σ defines the scale s. In order to determine all "locations" containing some kind of characteristic information, interest point localization (Lowe also uses the term "keypoint") amounts to the detection of local maxima and minima in scale space. To this end, the difference $D(x, y, \sigma)$ of images at nearby scales is calculated by convolution of the image with a difference of Gaussian (DoG) function, where the σ-values of the Gaussians differ by some constant factor k (typical values of k range between 1.1 and 1.4):

$$D(x, y, \sigma) = (G(x, y, k\sigma) - G(x, y, \sigma)) * I(x, y) \qquad (7.3)$$

Here $*$ denotes the convolution operator. The scale space can be explored by variation of σ, e.g., a multiple calculation of $D(x, y, \sigma)$ with a fixed step size at which σ is increased. Local maxima and minima are detected by comparing $D(x, y, \sigma)$ at location (x, y, σ) with its eight neighbors of the same scale σ and the 3×3 regions of the two neighboring scales centered at the same x and y (see Fig. 7.2 for an example of the thus detected keypoints).

7.2.1.2 Example

An example of the regions found by the DoG detector can be found in Fig. 7.2. On the right, the image is shown with superimposed arrows based on detection results of the DoG region detector. The direction of the arrow is equal to the dominant orientation of the region, its starting point the location of the keypoint and its length corresponds to the detected scale. Altogether, 289 keypoints were found by the DoG detector. The right image was generated with the software tool available at Lowe's homepage.[1]

Fig. 7.2 Outdoor scene depicting a building with much structural information

---

[1] http://www.cs.ubc.ca/~lowe/keypoints/ (link active 13 January, 2010), images printed with permission.

7.2.2 SIFT Region Descriptor

7.2.2.1 Main Idea

The design of the descriptor is motivated by biological vision, in particular by the observation that certain neurons in the primary visual cortex respond to particular gradient orientations. In order to trigger a specific response of these neurons, the location of the gradient on the retina is allowed to exhibit a small shift in x- and y-position, an observation which is also exploited by Edelman et al. [4].

What consequences does this have for the SIFT descriptor? First, a keypoint region defined by the DoG detection results (x, y, orientation, and scale) is partitioned into 4×4 rectangular sub-regions. Subsequently, the intensity gradients are determined and their orientations are accumulated in an 8-bin histogram for each sub-region separately (see also Fig. 7.3). A weighting depending on gradient magnitude and distance to the region center is applied. The area covered by each sub-region typically is several pixels in size, which relates to the aforementioned spatial fuzziness of human vision.

This proceeding can be modified in several respects, most of them aiming at making the descriptor robust to small variations (see [18] for details). For example, if the gradient orientation of a pixel changes slightly it has to be prevented that this change makes the pixel contribute to a totally different histogram bin. To this end, each histogram entry is multiplied by the factor $1 - d$ with d being the difference of a gradient orientation to the orientation corresponding to the bin center. Thereby quantization effects are avoided, which is a primary concern of SIFT descriptor design.

The descriptor vector for one region contains $4 \times 4 \times 8 = 128$ elements altogether, a number which seems to be a good trade-off between dimensionality reduction (the region size usually is larger than 128 pixels) and information preservation.

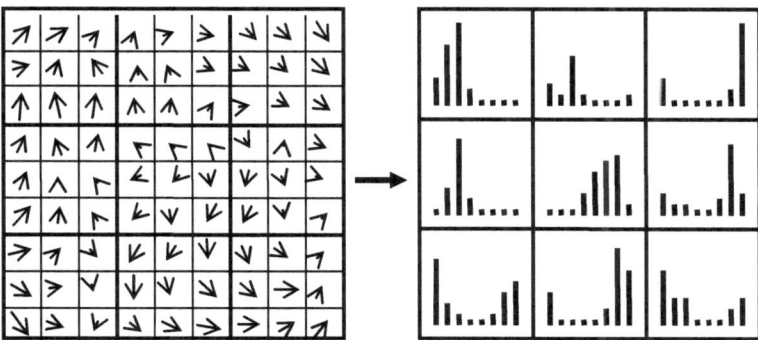

Fig. 7.3 Example of a SIFT descriptor (*right*) derived from gradient orientations of an image patch (*left*)

7.2.2.2 Example

Figure 7.3 illustrates the derivation of SIFT descriptors (right side) from image patches (left side). The arrows display the orientation and magnitude of the gradients of each pixel in a 9×9 image patch. The right part shows the SIFT descriptor for that region. For illustrative purposes, the region is divided into 3×3 sub-regions and for each sub-region an 8-bin orientation histogram is shown. Hence, the descriptor would consist of $9 \times 8 = 72$ elements.

7.2.3 Object Recognition with SIFT

In order to recognize objects, their descriptor representations have to be trained prior to the recognition phase, where descriptors are extracted from a scene image and compared to the model representations.

7.2.3.1 Training Phase

According to Lowe [18] the feature extraction process in the training phase consists of four major steps:

1. *Interest point detection* by searching in the so-called scale space of the image for extrema of the DoG detector.
2. *Exact keypoint localization* $ip_{M,l} = [x, y, \sigma]$ by refinement of the scale space positions obtained in step 1 (see "modifications").
3. *Assignment of the dominant orientation* $\theta_{ip,l}$ to each keypoint which is based on the weighted mean gradient orientation in the local neighborhood of a keypoint (see "modifications").
4. *SIFT descriptor calculation* based on gradient orientations in the region around each keypoint. The regions are defined in x, y, and scale by the maxima of the scale-space DoG function. The descriptors $\mathbf{d}_{M,l}$ consist of histograms representing the distribution of gradient orientations (relative to the assigned orientation) in the local neighborhood of the keypoints. This proceeding ensures invariance of the SIFT descriptor with respect to translation, rotation, and scale.

7.2.3.2 Recognition Phase

In order to utilize the SIFT method for object recognition, descriptors are extracted from a query image and compared to a database of feature descriptors. Calculation of the descriptors is identical to training. Additionally, the recognition stage consists of the following steps (see also Fig. 7.4 for an overview):

5. *Descriptor matching*, i.e., finding pair-wise correspondences $c = [\mathbf{d}_{S,k}, \mathbf{d}_{M,l}]$ between descriptors $\mathbf{d}_M$ of the database and descriptors $\mathbf{d}_S$ extracted form the

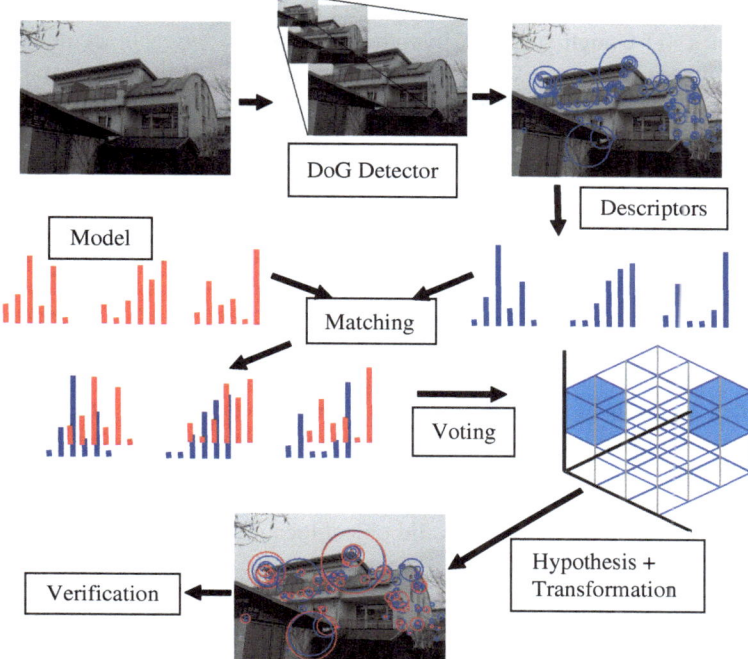

Fig. 7.4 Illustrating the algorithm flow of the SIFT method. Please note that the DoG detector is visualized with an image pyramid here, because Lowe suggested to downsample the image for large values of σ

scene image. To this end the content of the descriptors is compared. This correspondence search can, e.g., be done by nearest-neighbor search, i.e., a correspondence is established between a scene descriptor $\mathbf{d}_{S,k}$ and the database descriptor $\mathbf{d}_{M,l}$ with minimum Euclidean distance to it (in feature space, see also Appendix B). Additionally, this distance has to remain below a pre-defined threshold $t_{d,sim}$, which means that the two descriptors must exhibit enough similarity.

6. *Creation of hypotheses for object pose* by correspondence clustering with the Hough transform. Mainly due to background clutter, there is possibly a considerable amount of outliers among the correspondences (potentially over 90% of all correspondences) making it hard to find a correct object pose. Therefore in this step, a hypothesis for the object pose (x- and y-translation, rotation θ, and scale s) is created by a voting process where only a few geometrically consistent keypoint locations suffice to generate a hypothesis. The Hough transform is chosen for hypothesis generation because it has the desirable property of tolerating many outliers, as transformation estimations based on geometrically consistent correspondences should form a cluster in Hough space. From each keypoint correspondence estimations of the four pose parameters based on the locations,

orientations, and size of their regions can be derived. Each estimation casts a vote in a 4D Hough space. A hypothesis is created by each accumulator cell containing at least three votes, which means that at least three descriptor correspondences have to be geometrically consistent in order to generate a hypothesis of the object pose. In order to keep memory demand limited and tolerate for local distortions, viewpoint changes, etc., the bin size of the accumulator cells is kept rather large.

7. *Hypothesis verification*: Based on a hypothesis which consists of at least three keypoint correspondences, the six parameters of an affine transformation t between the model keypoint locations and scene keypoint locations can be estimated by taking all correspondences into account which contribute to this hypothesis. With the help of this transformation estimation it can be checked which correspondences are really consistent with it (meaning that the transformed location of a model keypoint $t\left(ip_{M,l}\right)$ has to be located nearby the corresponding scene keypoint $ip_{S,k}$), and which have to be excluded. Based on these checks, the transformation parameters can be refined, other points excluded again, until the iteration terminates. In the end, a decision can be made whether the hypothesis is accepted as a valid object location or not. One criterion might be that at least three correspondences have to remain.

7.2.3.3 Pseudocode

```
function detectObjectPosSIFT (in Image I, in model descriptors
dM, in model   interest   point   data   ipM, in descriptor
similarity threshold td,sim, out object position list p)
```

```
// interest point detection: DoG operator
```
$\sigma_0 \leftarrow 1.0$
$I_{s,0} \leftarrow I * G\left(\sigma_0\right)$
for i = 1 to n
    $\sigma_i \leftarrow \sigma_{i-1} \cdot k$ // e.g. $k = 1.4$
    $I_{s,i} \leftarrow I * G\left(\sigma_i\right)$
    $D_i \leftarrow I_{s,i} - I_{s,i-1}$
next
```
detect all local extrema in Di's; each extremum defines an
interest point
```
$ip_{S,k} = \left[x, y, \sigma\right]$
```
// refinement of interest point locations (see modifications)
```
for k = 1 to number of interest points **ip**$_S$
    refine position in scale space $\left(\left[x, y, \sigma\right]\right)$
    // calculate dominant orientation $\theta_{ip,k}$
    for each pixel p located within the region defined by $ip_{S,k}$
        calculate gradient magnitude m_p and orientation θ_p
        update histogram **h** at bin defined by θ_p, weighted

```
      by m_p
   next
   assign maximum of h to mean orientation θ_ip,k
   if multiple dominant maxima exist in h then
      add a new interest point with identical location, but
      different mean orientation for each dominant maximum
   end if
next
for k = 1 to number of interest points ip_S   // descr. calc.
   calculate descriptor d_S,k (see Fig. 7.3)
next

// matching
for k = 1 to number of descriptors d_S
   find model descriptor d_M,l being most similar to d_S,k
   if similarity (d_S,k, d_M,l) ≥ t_d,sim then // match found
      add correspondence c = [d_S,k, d_M,l] to list c
   end if
next

// generation of hypotheses
for i = 1 to number of list entries in c
   estimate transformation t based on interest point
   locations of current correspondence c_i
   cast a vote in accu according to t and model index m
next

// hypothesis verification
determine all cells of accu with at least three votes
for i = 1 to number of cells of accu with >= 3 votes
   do
      re-estimate t based on all c_k which contributed to
      current accu cell
      discard all "outliers" and remove these corresp.
   until convergence (no more discards)
   if number of remaining c_k >= 3 then
      add hypothesis hy = [t,m] to list p
   end if
next
```

7.2.3.4 Example

Figure 7.5 shows the recognition result for two objects (a frog and a toy railway engine; training images are depicted upper left) in the presence of heavy occlusion and background clutter in the scene image. It can be seen that the two instances of

Fig. 7.5 Taken from Lowe [18][2] illustrating the recognition performance in the presence of heavy occlusion and background clutter

the railway engine and one instance of the frog are recognized correctly (matched keypoint locations and region sizes are shown by red, yellow and green overlays).

7.2.3.5 Rating

The sheer fact that SIFT is used as a benchmark for many propositions of interest point detectors and region descriptors is a strong hint of its good performance, especially in situations with heavy occlusion and/or clutter (as shown in the example). A particular strength of the method is that each step is carefully designed and, additionally, all steps work hand in hand and are well coordinated.

---

[2]With kind permission from Springer Science+Business Media: Lowe [18], Fig. 12, © 2004 Springer.

However, the method only works well if a significant number of keypoints can be detected in order to generate enough descriptor information and therefore relies heavily on the keypoint detector performance. Later publications also show that overall performance can be increased if some part of the method, e.g., the descriptor design, is substituted by alternatives (see next section).

7.2.3.6 Modifications

Without going into details, Lowe [18] suggests several additional steps and checks for the selection and refinement of keypoint locations in scale space. They include accepting only extrema with an absolute value above some threshold and position refinement by fitting the scale space function to a parametric function. Furthermore, as the location of a point being part of a straight line edge is accurately defined only in the direction perpendicular to the edge, no keypoints should be located along such edges. Respective keypoints are sorted out accordingly. In contrast to that, the location of, e.g., corner points is well defined in two directions and therefore they are well suited as keypoints (see [18] for details).

In order to make the descriptors insensitive to image rotation between training and recognition the average orientations of the local neighborhoods around each keypoint are computed prior to descriptor calculation (cf. step 3 of teaching phase). The orientations used for the histogram of the descriptor can then be related to this mean orientation. To this end, the gradient orientations of all pixels located within such a neighborhood are calculated (the region size is defined by the scale of the scale-space extremum) and accumulated in an orientation histogram. Orientations are weighted by the gradient magnitude as well as the proximity to the region center with the help of a Gaussian weighting function. The assigned orientation of a keypoint corresponds to the maximum of the orientation histogram. In case there exist multiple dominant orientation maxima, multiple keypoints located at the same spatial position are generated.

In the recognition phase, many false correspondences can occur due to background clutter. In order to handle this situation, the ratio of the distance of the closest neighbor to the distance of the second closest neighbor is evaluated instead of the closest distance value alone. Correspondences are only established if this ratio is below a certain threshold. Here, the second closest neighbor distance is defined as the closest neighbor that is known to originate from a different object class than the first one. Please note that this step can become very time-consuming if some 10,000 pairs have to be evaluated. To this end, Lowe suggested an optimized algorithm called best bin first (see [18] for details).

7.3 Variants of Interest Point Detectors

Correspondences between model and scene image descriptors can only be established reliably if their interest points are detected accurate enough in both the scene and the training images. Therefore interest point detector design is an important issue if reliable object recognition is to be achieved with this kind of algorithms.

For example, the invariance properties of the detector are especially important in presence of illumination changes, object deformations, or change of camera viewpoint.

A considerable amount of alternatives to the DoG detector has been reported in literature. Basically, they can be divided in two categories:

- *Corner-based* detectors respond well to structured regions, but rely on the presence of sufficient gradient information.
- *Region-based* detectors respond well to uniform regions and are also suited to regions with smooth brightness transitions.

7.3.1 Harris and Hessian-Based Detectors

A broadly used detector falling into the first category is based on a method reported by Harris and Stephens [9]. Its main idea is that the location of an interest point is well defined if there's a considerable brightness change in two directions, e.g., at a corner point of a rectangular structure.

Imagine a small rectangular window shifted over an image. In case the window is located on top of a corner point, the intensities of some pixels located within the window change considerably if the window is shifted by a small distance, regardless of the shift direction. Points with such changes can be detected with the help of the second moment matrix $\mathbf{M}$ consisting of the partial derivatives I_x and I_y of the image intensities (i.e., gray value gradient in x- and y-direction):

$$\mathbf{M} = \begin{bmatrix} I_x^2 & I_x I_y \\ I_x I_y & I_y^2 \end{bmatrix} = \begin{bmatrix} a & b \\ b & c \end{bmatrix} \tag{7.4}$$

In order to reduce the sensitivity of the operator to noise each matrix element is usually smoothed spatially by convolution with a Gaussian kernel: For example, the spatially smoothed value of matrix element a at pixel $[x, y]$ is obtained by convolving the a's of the pixels in the vicinity of $[x, y]$ with a Gaussian kernel. Corner points are indicated if the cornerness function f_c based on the Gaussian-smoothed second moment matrix $\mathbf{M}_G$

$$f_c = \det(\mathbf{M}_G) - k \cdot tr(\mathbf{M}_G)^2 = \left(ac - b^2\right) - k \cdot (a + c)^2 \tag{7.5}$$

attains a local maximum. Here, $tr(\cdot)$ denotes the trace and $\det(\cdot)$ the determinant of matrix $\mathbf{M}_G$. k denotes a regularization constant whose value has to be chosen empirically, in literature values around 0.1 have been reported to be a good choice. The combined usage of the trace and the determinant has the advantage of making the detector insensitive to straight line edges.

Similar calculations can be done with the Hessian matrix $\mathbf{H}$ consisting of the second order derivatives of the image intensity function:

$$\mathbf{H} = \begin{bmatrix} I_{xx} & I_{xy} \\ I_{xy} & I_{yy} \end{bmatrix} \tag{7.6}$$

where the I_{xx}, I_{xy}, and I_{yy} denote the second-order derivatives in x- and y-directions. Interest points are detected at locations where the determinant of $\mathbf{H}$ reaches a local maximum. In contrast to the Harris-based detector the Hessian-based detector responds to blob- and ridge-like structures.

7.3.1.1 Rating

These two detectors have the advantage that they can be calculated rather fast, but on the other hand they do neither determine scale nor orientation. In order to overcome this disadvantage, modifications have been suggested that incorporate invariance with respect to scale (often denoted as Harris–Laplace and Hessian–Laplace detector, respectively, as they are a combination of the Harris- or Hessian-based detector with a Laplacian of Gaussian function (LoG) for scale detection, cf. [16], for example) or even affine transformations (often referred to as Harris-affine and Hessian-affine detector, respectively; see the paper of Mikolajczyk and Schmid [22] for details). The price for invariance, however, is a considerable speed loss.

7.3.2 The FAST Detector for Corners

Another detector for corner-like structures is the FAST detector (*Features from Accelerated Segment Test*) proposed by Rosten and Drummond [27]. The basic idea behind this approach is to reduce the number of calculations which are necessary at each pixel in order to decide whether a keypoint is detected at the pixel or not as much as possible. This is done by placing a circle consisting of 16 pixels centered at the pixel under investigation. For the corner test only gray value differences between each of the 16 circle pixels and the center pixel are evaluated, resulting in very fast computations (cf. Fig. 7.6).

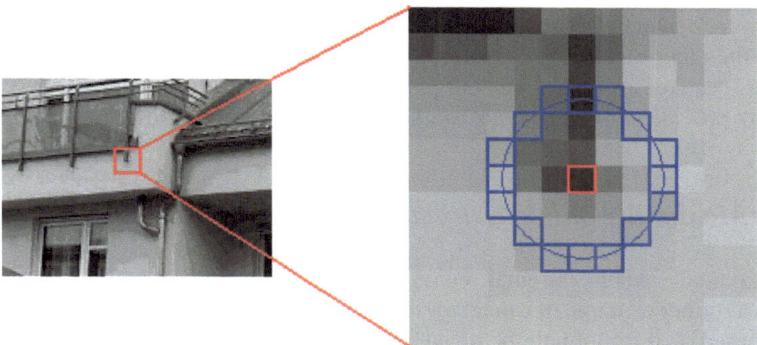

Fig. 7.6 Demonstrates the application of the FAST detector for the *dark* center point of the zoomed region shown in the *right*. A *circle* is placed around the center point (marked *red*) and consists of 16 pixels (marked *blue*). For typical values of t the cornerness criterion (Equation 7.7a) is fulfilled by all circle pixels, except for the pixel on top of the center pixel

In the first step, a center pixel p is labeled as "corner" if there exist at least n consecutive "circle pixels" c which are all either at least t gray values brighter than p or, as a second possibility, all at least t gray values darker than p:

$$I_c \geq I_p + t \ \text{for} \ n \ \text{consecutive pixels} \tag{7.7a}$$

$$\text{or} \ I_c \leq I_p - t \ \text{for} \ n \ \text{consecutive pixels} \tag{7.7b}$$

I_c denotes the gray value of pixel c and I_p the gray value of pixel p respectively. After this step, a corner usually is indicated by a connected region of pixels where this condition holds and not, as desired, by a single pixel position. Therefore, a feature is detected by non-maximum suppression in a second step. To this end, a function value v is assigned to each "corner candidate pixel" found in the first step, e.g., the maximum value of n for which p is still a corner or the maximum value t for which p is still a corner. Each pixel with at least one adjacent pixel with higher v (8-neighborhood) is removed from the corner candidates.

The initial proposition was to choose $n = 12$, because with $n = 12$ additional speedup can be achieved by testing only the top, right, bottom, and right pixel of the circle. If p is a corner the criterion defined above must hold for at least three of them. Only then all circle pixels have to be examined. It is shown in [27] that it is also possible to achieve similar speedup with other choices of n. However, n should not be chosen lower than $n = 9$, as for $n \leq 8$ the detector responds to straight line edges as well.

7.3.2.1 Rating

Compared to the other corner detectors presented above, Rosten and Drummond [27] report FAST to be significantly faster (about 20 times faster than the Harris detector and about 50 times faster than the DoG detector of the SIFT scheme). Surprisingly, tests of Rosten and Drummond with empirical data revealed that the reliability of keypoint detection of the FAST detector is equal or even superior to other corner detectors in many situations.

On the other hand, FAST is more sensitive to noise (which stems from the fact that for speed reasons the number of pixels evaluated at each position is reduced) and does not provide neither scale nor rotation information for the descriptor calculation.

7.3.3 Maximally Stable Extremal Regions (MSER)

The maximally stable extremal region (MSER) detector described by Matas et al. [20] is a further example of a detector for blob-like structures. Its algorithmic principle is based on thresholding the image with a variable brightness threshold. Imagine a binarization of a scene image depending on a gray value threshold t. All pixels with gray value below t are set to zero/black in the thresholded image, all pixels with gray value equal or above t are set to one/bright. Starting from $t = 0$ the threshold is increased successively. In the beginning the thresholded image is completely bright. As t increases, black areas will appear in the binarized image, which grow and finally merge together. Some black areas will be stable for a large range of t. These are the MSER regions, revealing a position (e.g., the center point) as well as a characteristic scale derived from region size as input data for region descriptor calculation. Altogether, all regions of the scene image are detected which are significantly darker than their surrounding. Inverting the image and repeating the same procedure with the inverted image reveals characteristic bright regions, respectively.

7.3.3.1 Rating

In contrast to many other detectors, the regions are of arbitrary shape, but can be approximated by an ellipse for descriptor calculation. The MSER detector reveals rather few regions, but their detection is very stable. Additionally, the MSER detector is invariant with respect to affine transformations, which makes it suitable for applications which have to deal with viewpoint changes.

7.3.4 Comparison of the Detectors

The well-designed SIFT method often serves as a benchmark for performance evaluation of region descriptor-based object recognition. As far as detector performance is concerned, Mikolajczyk et al. [24] reported the results of a detailed empirical evaluation of the performance of several region detectors (Mikolajczyk also maintains a website giving detailed information about his research relating to region detectors as well as region descriptors[3]). They evaluated the repeatability rate of the detectors for pairs of images, i.e., the percentage of detected interest regions which exhibit "sufficient" spatial overlap between the two images of an image pair. The repeatability rate is determined for different kinds of image modifications, e.g., JPEG compression artefacts, viewpoint or scale changes, etc., and different scene types (structured or textured scenes); see [24] for details.

As a result, there was no detector that clearly outperformed all others for all variations or scene types. In many cases, but by far not all, the MSER detector achieved best results, followed by the Hessian-affine detector. There were considerable differences between different detectors as far as the number of detected regions as well as their detected size is concerned. Furthermore, different detectors respond to different region types (e.g., highly structured or with rather uniform gray values). This gives evidence to the claim that different detectors should be used in parallel in order to achieve best performance of the overall object recognition scheme: complementary properties of different detectors increase the suitability for different object types.

---

[3]http://www.robots.ox.ac.uk/~vgg/research/affine/index.html (link active 13 January 2010).

Another aspect is invariance: some of the detectors are invariant to more kinds of transformations than others. For example, the MSER detector is invariant to affine transformations. Compared to that, the FAST detector is only rotation invariant. While the enhanced invariance of MSER offers advantages in situations where the objects to be detected actually have been undergone affine projection, it is often not advisable to use detectors featuring more invariance than actually needed.

7.4 Variants of Region Descriptors

A simple approach for characterizing a region is to describe it by its raw intensity values. Matching amounts to the calculation of the cross-correlation between two descriptors. However, this proceeding suffers from its computational complexity (as the descriptor size is equal to the number of pixels of the region) as well as the fact that it doesn't provide much invariance. Descriptor design aims at finding a balance between dimensionality reduction and maintaining discriminative power. Additionally, it should focus on converting the information of the image region such that it becomes invariant or at least robust to typical variations, e.g., non-linear illumination changes or affine transformations due to viewpoint change.

Basically, many of the descriptors found in literature belong to one of the following two categories:

- *Distribution-based descriptors* derived from the distribution of some kind of information available in the region, e.g., gradient orientation in SIFT descriptors. Commonly, the distribution is described by a histogram of some kind of "typical" information.
- *Filter-based descriptors* calculated with the help of some kind of filtering. More precisely, a bank of filters is applied to the region content. The descriptor consists of the responses of all filters. Each filter is designed to be sensitive to a specific kind of information. Commonly used filter types separate properties in the frequency domain (e.g., Gabor filters or wavelet filters) or are based on derivatives.

Some descriptors for each of the two categories are presented in the following.

7.4.1 Variants of the SIFT Descriptor

Due to its good performance, the descriptor used in the SIFT algorithm, which is based on the distribution of gradient orientations, has become very popular. During the last decade several proposals have been made trying to increase its performance even further, as far as computation speed as well as recognition rate is concerned.

Ke and Sukthankar [12] proposed a modification they called PCA-SIFT. In principle they follow the outline of the SIFT method, but instead of calculating gradient orientation histograms as descriptors they resample the interest region (its detection is identical to SIFT) into 41×41 pixels and calculate the x- and y-gradients within the resampled region yielding a descriptor consisting of $2 \times 39 \times 39 = 3,042$ elements. In the next step, they apply a PCA to the normalized gradient descriptor (cf. Chapter 2), where the eigenspace has been calculated in advance. The eigenspace is derived from normalized gradient descriptors extracted from the salient regions of a large image dataset (about 21,000 images). Usually the descriptors contain highly structured gradient information, as they are calculated around well-chosen characteristic points. Therefore, the eigenvalues decay much faster compared to randomly chosen image patches. Experiments of Ke and Sukthankar [12] showed that about 20 eigenvectors are sufficient for a proper descriptor representation.

Hence descriptor dimensionality is reduced by a factor of about 6 (it consists of 20 elements compared to 128 of standard SIFT method) resulting in a much faster matching. Additionally, Ke and Sukthankar also reported that PCA-SIFT descriptors lead to a more accurate descriptor matching compared to standard SIFT. A more extensive study by Mikolajczyk and Schmid [23], where other descriptors are compared as well, showed that accuracy of matching performance of PCA-SIFT (compared to standard SIFT) depends on the scene type; there are also scenes for which PCA-SIFT performs slightly worse than standard SIFT.

Another modification of the SIFT descriptor called gradient location orientation histogram (GLOH) is reported by Mikolajczyk and Schmid [23] and is based on an idea very similar to the log-polar choice of the histogram bins for shape contexts, which are presented in a subsequent section. Contrary to the SIFT descriptor, where the region is separated into a 4×4 rectangular grid, the descriptor is calculated for a log-polar location grid consisting of three bins in radial direction, the outer two radial bins are further separated into eight sectors (see Fig. 7.7).

Hence the region is separated into 17 location bins altogether. For each spatial bin a 16-bin histogram of gradient orientation is calculated, yielding a 272 bin histogram altogether. The log-polar choice enhances the descriptors robustness as the relatively large outer location bins are more insensitive to deformations. Descriptor dimensionality is reduced to 128 again by applying a PCA based on the eigenvectors of a covariance matrix which is estimated from 47,000 descriptors collected from various images. With the help of the PCA, distinctiveness is increased compared to standard SIFT although descriptor dimensionality remains the same. Extensive studies reported in [23] show that GLOH slightly outperforms SIFT for most image data.

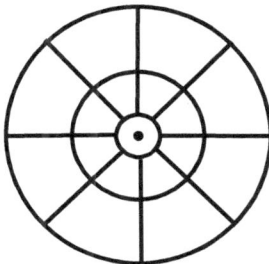

Fig. 7.7 Depicts the spatial partitioning of the descriptor region in the GLOH method

Fig. 7.8 Showing an
example of a CCH descriptor.
For illustration purposes, the
region is just separated into
two radial and four angular
sub-regions (four radial and
eight angular bins are used in
the original descriptor)

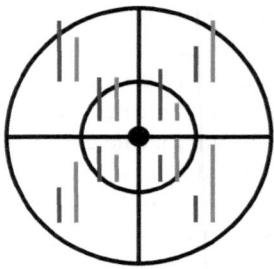

Contrast context histograms (CCH), which were proposed recently by Huang
et al. [10] aim at a speedup during descriptor calculation. Instead of calculating the
local gradient at all pixels of the region, the intensity difference of each region pixel
to the center pixel of the region is calculated, which yields a contrast value for each
region pixel. Similar to the GLOH method, the region is separated into spatial bins
with the help of a log-polar grid. For each spatial bin, all positive contrast values
as well as all negative contrast values are added separately, resulting in a two-bin
contrast histogram for each spatial bin (see Fig. 7.8 for an example: at each sub-
region, the separate addition of all positive and negative contrast values yields the
blue and green histogram bins, respectively.).

In empirical studies performed by the authors, a 64-bin descriptor (32 spatial bins, two contrast value for each spatial bin) achieved comparable accuracy
compared to the standard SIFT descriptor, whereas the descriptor calculation was
accelerated by a factor of 5 (approximately) and the matching stage by a factor of 2.

7.4.2 Differential-Based Filters

Biological visual systems give motivation for another approach to model the content of a region around an interest point. Koenderink and Van Doorn [13] reported
the idea to model the response of specific neurons of a visual system with blurred
partial derivatives of local image intensities. This amounts to the calculation of a
convolution of the partial derivative of a Gaussian kernel with a local image patch.
For example the first partial derivative with respect to the x-direction yields:

$$d_{R,x} = \partial G\left(x, y, \sigma\right) / \partial x * I_R\left(x, y\right) \tag{7.8}$$

where $*$ denotes the convolution operator. As the size of the Gaussian deriva-
tive $\partial G / \partial x$ equals the size of the region R, the convolution result is a scalar $d_{R,x}$.
Multiple convolution results with derivatives in different directions and of different
order can be combined to a vector $\mathbf{d}_R$, the so-called local jet, giving a distinctive,
low-dimensional representation of the content of an image region. Compared to
distribution-based descriptors the dimensionality is usually considerably lower here.
For example, partial derivatives in x- and y-direction (Table 7.1) up to fourth order
yield a 14D descriptor.

Table 7.1 Showing the 14 derivatives of a Gaussian kernel G (Size 41×41 pixel, $\sigma = 6.7$) in x- and y-direction up to fourth order (*top row* from *left* to *right*: G_x, G_y, G_{xx}, G_{xy}, G_{yy}; *middle row* from *left* to *right*: G_{xxx}, G_{xxy}, G_{xyy}, G_{yyy}, G_{xxxx}; *bottom row* from *left* to *right*: G_{xxxy}, G_{xxyy}, G_{xyyy}, G_{yyyy})

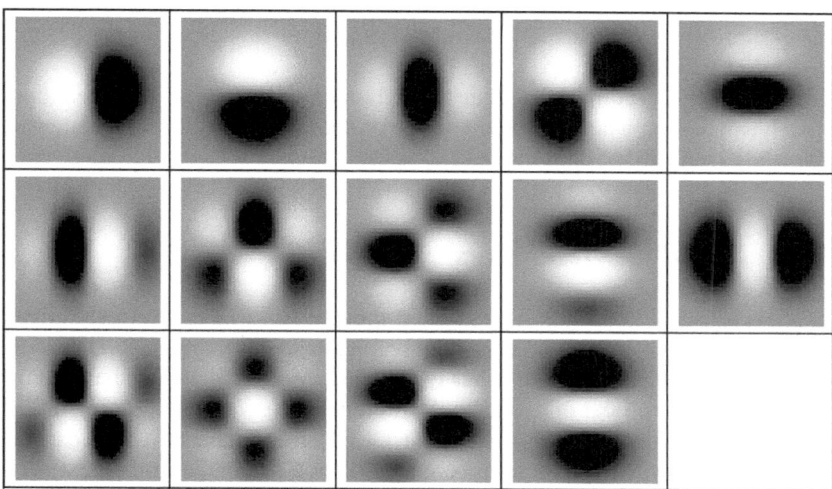

In order to achieve rotational invariance, the directions of the partial derivatives of the Gaussian kernels have to be adjusted such that they are in accord with the dominant gradient orientation of the region. This can be either done by rotating the image region content itself or with the usage of so-called steerable filters developed by Freeman and Adelson [7]: they developed a theory enabling to steer the derivatives, which are already calculated in x- and y-direction, to a particular direction and hence making the local jet invariant to rotation.

Florack et al. [5] developed so-called "differential invariants": they consist of specific combinations of the components of the local jet. These combinations make the descriptor invariant to rotation, too.

7.4.3 Moment Invariants

Moment invariants are low-dimensional region descriptors proposed by Van Gool et al. [32]. Each element of the descriptor represents a combination of moments M_{pq}^a of order $p + q$ and degree a. The moments are calculated for the derivatives of the image intensities $I_d(x, y)$ with respect to direction d. All pixels located within an image region of size s are considered. The M_{pq}^a can be defined as

$$M_{pq}^a = 1/s \sum_x \sum_y x^p y^q \cdot I_d(x, y)^a \tag{7.9}$$

Flusser and Suk [6] have shown for binary images that specific polynomial combinations of moments are invariant to affine transformations. In other words, the value of a moment invariant should remain constant if the region from which it was derived has undergone an affine transformation. Hence, the usage of these invariants is a way of achieving descriptor invariance with respect to viewpoint change. Several invariants can be concatenated in a vector yielding a low-dimensional descriptor with the desired invariance properties.

Note that in [32] moment invariants based on color images are reported, but the approach can be easily adjusted to the usage of derivatives of gray value intensities, which leads to the above definition.

7.4.4 Rating of the Descriptors

Mikolajczyk and Schmid [23] investigated moment invariants with derivatives in x- and y-directions up to second order and second degree (yielding a 20D descriptor without usage of M_{00}^a) as well as other types of descriptors in an extensive comparative study with empirical image data of different scene types undergoing different kinds of modifications. They showed that GLOH performed best in most cases, closely followed by SIFT. The shape context method presented in the next section also performs well, but is less reliable in scenes that lack of clear gradient information. Gradient moments and steerable filters (of Gaussian derivatives) perform worse, but consist of only very few elements. Hence, their dimensionality is considerably lower compared to distribution-based descriptors. These two methods are found to be the best-performing low-dimensional descriptors.

7.5 Descriptors Based on Local Shape Information

7.5.1 Shape Contexts

7.5.1.1 Main Idea

Descriptors can also be derived from the shape information of an image region. Belongie et al. [2] proposed a descriptor with focus on the capability of classifying objects that are subject to considerable local deformation. At the core of the method is the concept of so-called shape contexts : Let's assume that the object is represented by a set of contour points ("landmark points"), located at positions with rapid local changes of intensity. At each landmark point, a shape context can be calculated: it defines a histogram of the spatial distribution of all other landmark points relative to the current one (see also Fig. 7.9). These histograms provide a distinctive characterization for each landmark point, which can be used as a descriptor. Correspondences between model landmark points and their counterparts detected in a scene image can be established if their descriptors show a sufficient degree of similarity.

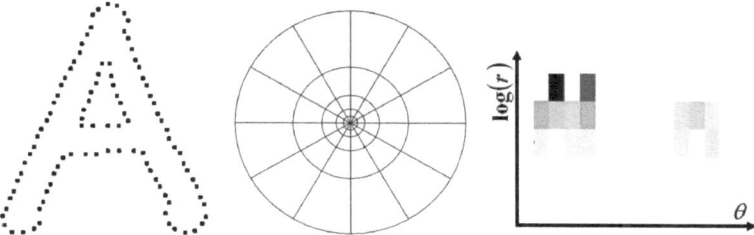

Fig. 7.9 With images taken from Belongie et al. [2] (© 2002 IEEE; with permission) exemplifying shape context calculation

Shape contexts are pretty insensitive to local distortions of the objects, as each histogram bin covers an area of pixels. In case the exact location of the shape varies, a contour point still contributes to the same bin if its position deviation does not exceed a certain threshold defined by the bin size. Thus, large bins allow for more deformation than small bins. That's the reason for the choice of a log-polar scale for bin partitioning: contour points located very close to the landmark point for which the shape context shall be calculated are expected to be less affected by deformation than points located rather far away. Accordingly, bin size is small near the region center and large in the outer areas.

A shape context example is depicted in Fig. 7.9: In the left part, sampled contour points of a handwritten character "A" are shown. At the location of each of them, the local neighborhood is partitioned into bins according to the log-polar grid shown in the middle. For each bin, the number of contour points located within that bin is calculated. The result is a 2D histogram of the spatial distribution of neighboring contour points: the shape context. One randomly chosen example of these histograms is shown on the right (dark regions indicate a high number of points).

7.5.1.2 Recognition Phase

The recognition stage consists of four steps (see also Fig. 7.10 for an overview):

1. *Calculation of descriptors called "shape contexts"* at contour points located upon inner or outer contours of the object shown in a scene image.
2. *Establishment of correspondences* between the shape contexts of the scene image and those of a stored model based on their similarity.
3. *Estimation of the parameters of an aligning transform* trying to match the location of each contour point of the scene image to the location of the corresponding model point as exactly as possible.
4. *Computation of the distance between scene image shape and model shape* (e.g., the sum of matching errors between corresponding points). Based on this distance a classification of the scene image can be done if the distance is calculated for multiple models.

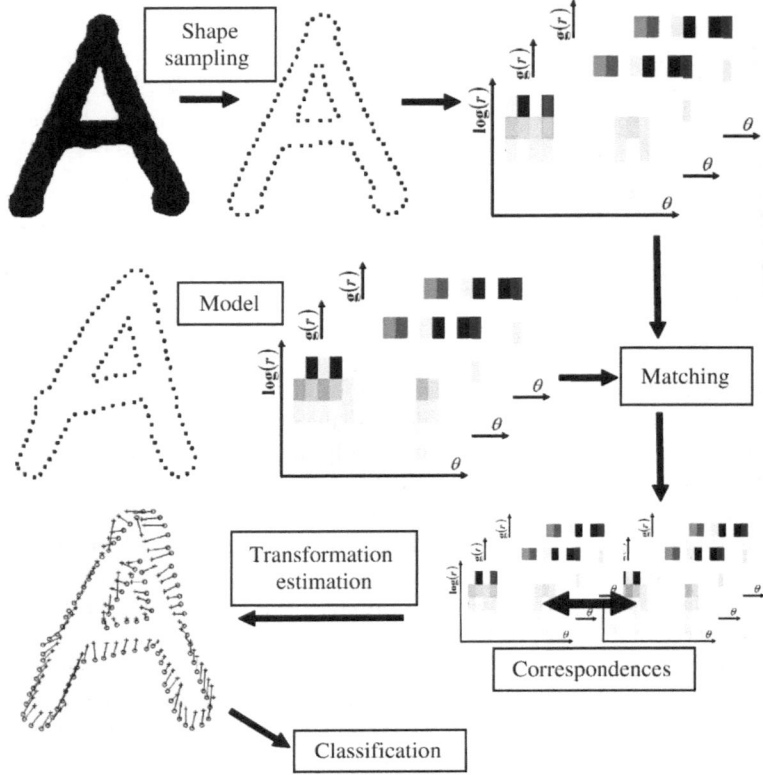

Fig. 7.10 Images taken from Belongie et al. [2]; © 2002 IEEE; with permission (illustrating the algorithm flow of the shape context method)

The shape contexts are calculated by detection of internal and external contour points of an object, e.g., with the help of an edge detector sensitive to rapid local changes of intensity. A preferably uniformly sampled subset of these contour points is chosen to be the set of landmark points for shape context calculation. At the location of each landmark point its shape context is calculated as a histogram of the log-polar spatial distribution of the other landmark points.

Correspondence finding can be achieved by comparing the distribution described by the histograms and thus calculating a measure of histogram similarity, e.g., with a χ^2 test metric.

Once the correspondences are established, the parameters of the transform that describes the mapping between the locations of the sampled contour points $\mathbf{x}_{S,i}$ in the scene image and their model counterparts $\mathbf{x}_{M,k}$ have to be estimated. Affine transformations given by $\mathbf{x}_{S,i} = \mathbf{A} \cdot \mathbf{x}_{M,k} + \mathbf{t}$ don't allow for local deformations. Therefore, transformations are modeled by thin plate splines (TPS). TPS are commonly used when more flexible coordinate transforms performing non-linear mappings are needed. Without going into detail, the transform is modeled by a low-degree polynomial and a sum of radial symmetric basis functions, thereby being able to model local deformations (details of the method can be found in [21]).

After estimation of the transformation parameters object classification can be done by calculating a measure of similarity for each object class. Details are given in Chapter 5 of [2].

7.5.1.3 Pseudocode

```
function detectObjectPosShapeContext (in Image I, in model
shape contexts dM , in model contour point locations xM,
in shape context similarity threshold td,sim, in position
similarity threshold tp,sim, out object position list p)

// shape context calculation
detect all edge pixels (e.g. with Canny detector) and store
them in list e
xS ← sampling of edge points e, preferably uniform
for i = 1 to number of landmark points xS
   // calculate shape context dS,i of landmark point xS,i
   for each landmark point xS,k located in the vicinity of xS,i
      increase dS,i at the bin of the log-polar spatial grid
      defined by the geometric relation between xS,k and xS,i
   next
next

// matching
for i = 1 to number of shape contexts dS
   find model shape context dM,k being most similar to dS,i
   if similarity (dS,i, dM,k) ≥ td,sim then // match found
      add correspondence c = [dS,i, dM,k] to list c
   end if
next

// generation of hypothesis
find all models with a sufficient number of correspondences
for m = 1 to number of thus found model indices
   estimate transformation tm based on all correspondences
   cm of c which support model m with thin plate splines
   // hypothesis verification
   err ← 0
   for i = 1 to number of cm
      increase err according to position deviation
      dist (xS,i, tm (xM,k)) (contour points defined by corresp. cm,i)
```

```
   next
   if err ≤ t_{p,sim} then
       add hypothesis [t_m, m] to list p
   end if
next
```

7.5.1.4 Rating

Shape contexts are a powerful scheme for position determination as well as object classification even when local distortions are present, because the possibility of local deformations is explicitly considered in descriptor design and transform parameter estimation. Compared to, e.g., Hausdorff distance-based schemes, the principle of matching the shape with the help of a rich descriptor is a considerable improvement in terms of runtime, as the descriptor offers enough information in order to establish 1-to-1 correspondences between two shape contexts. With the help of the correspondences, the estimation of the transform parameters can be accelerated significantly compared to the search in parameter space.

However, the method relies on the assumption that enough contour information is present and thus is not suitable when the objects lack of high-gradient information.

7.5.2 Variants

7.5.2.1 Labeled Distance Sets

Instead of summarizing the geometric configuration in the neighborhood of a contour point in a histogram, Grigorescu and Petkov [8] suggest to use so-called *distance sets* as descriptors of the contour points. A distance set $\mathbf{d}(p)$ is a vector, where each element $d_i(p)$ represents the distance between the contour point p (for which $\mathbf{d}(p)$ is to be calculated) and another contour point in the vicinity of p. The dimensionality of the vector $\mathbf{d}(p)$ is set to N, which means that the N contour points located closest to p contribute to $\mathbf{d}(p)$. The choice of N allows – to a certain extent – to control the size of the neighborhood region which contributes to the descriptors.

The dissimilarity $D(q, p)$ between a contour point q of a query object and a point p of a model object can be calculated by summing the normalized differences between the elements d_i and $d_{\pi(i)}$ of the sets:

$$D(q, p) = \min_{\pi} \left[\sum_{i=1}^{N} \frac{\left| d_i(p) - d_{\pi(i)}(q) \right|}{\max \left(d_i(p), d_{\pi(i)}(q) \right)} \right] \tag{7.10}$$

where π denotes a mapping function which defines a 1-to-1 mapping between the elements of the two distance sets under consideration. The denominator serves as a normalization term. As the dissimilarity between two sets should be a metric for the "best" possible mapping, we have to choose a mapping π such that $D(q, p)$ is

Fig. 7.11 Illustrative example for the construction of labeled distance sets for the character "1"

minimized. Efficient techniques exist which avoid a combinatorial test of possible mappings in order to find the minimum (see [8] for details).

When comparing the whole query object to a database model a matching coefficient based on the sum of the $D(q, p)$'s of all contour points q is calculated. As the mapping between the contour points is not known a priori, it has to be determined in the matching process by establishing a mapping for each q to the point of the model point set where $D(q, p)$ attains a minimum. Unmatched points can be considered by a penalty term.

In order to increase the discriminative power of the matching coefficient, different labels can be assigned to each point q and p. The labels characterize the type of the points, e.g., "end point," "line," "junction". An example is shown in Fig. 7.11, where the contour points are labeled as "end point" (blue), "junction" (red), and "line" (green). For each contour point, the distances to its neighbors are summarized in a vector (here, each descriptor consists of five elements; exemplarily shown for the two blue points in the right part of Fig. 7.11). In the case of labeled points, the dissimilarity between two points q and p is defined by calculating a separate $D_l(q, p)$ for each label l, where only points of identical type l are considered, followed by a weighted sum of all $D_l(q, p)$.

7.5.2.2 Shape Similarity Based on Contour Parts

The method proposed by Bai et al. [1] is based on the shape context descriptor, but works with contiguous contour parts instead of a discrete point set. It is a combination of a curve matching scheme with a descriptor-based approach.

It works as follows: after edge detection and grouping, the object contour is approximated by the discrete contour evolution algorithm presented in the last chapter (DCE, cf. [14]). Subsequently, it is split into segments, each containing at least two successive line segments of the polygonal approximation obtained by DCE. Each of the so-called visual parts, which is defined by the original contour between the two end points of the previously obtained segments, can be transformed by mapping the "outer" end points to coordinates (0,0) and (1,0) in a 2D coordinate frame. As a result, the transformed description of each part is invariant to translation, rotation, and scale. Subsequently, a polar grid is superimposed onto the center point of the curve in the transformed frame. Finally, the descriptor is obtained by counting the number of edge pixels which are located within that bin for each bin of the polar grid. The process is shown in Fig. 7.12.

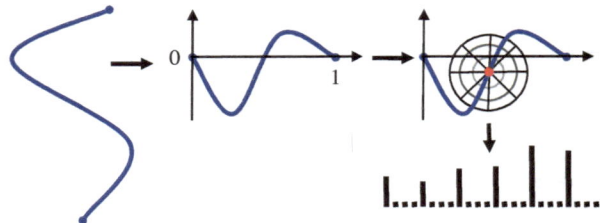

Fig. 7.12 Showing the process of calculating a descriptor for the center point (marked *red*) of a visual part

Please note that especially the invariance with respect to scale is difficult to obtain for a part-based representation as there is no a priori knowledge how much of the object is covered by a certain part. Therefore common normalizations utilized for closed contours, e.g., normalizing the arc length to the interval [0,1], don't work for parts.

The matching is performed with the help of the descriptors just described, which shall be called "shape contexts," too. For speed reasons, at first only one shape context of each transformed contour part, e.g., the context of the center point, is calculated and matched to a database of shape contexts of known objects in order to perform a fast pre-classification. All correspondences which are considered as similar in this step are examined further by calculating the shape context of each pixel of the transformed contour part and matching it to the database. The correspondence that passes this extended test with minimum dissimilarity can be considered as a matching hypothesis of the complete object.

7.6 Image Categorization

7.6.1 Appearance-Based "Bag-of-Features" Approach

The task of image categorization is to label a query image to a certain scene type, e.g., "building," "street," "mountains," or "forest." The main difference compared to recognition tasks for distinct objects is a much wider range of intra-class variation. Two instances of type "building," for example, can look very different in spite of having certain common features. Therefore a more or less rigid model of the object geometry is not applicable any longer.

7.6.1.1 Main Idea

A similar problem is faced in document analysis when attempting to automatically assign a piece of text to a certain topic, e.g., "mathematics," "news," or "sports". This problem is solved by the definition of a so-called codebook there (cf. [11] for example). A codebook consists of lists of words or phrases which are typical for a

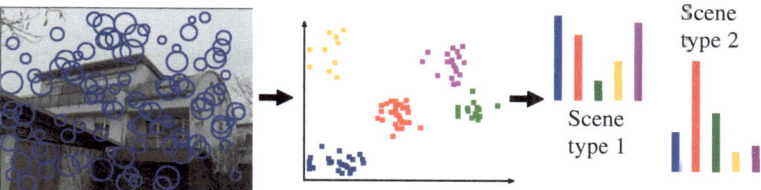

Fig. 7.13 Exemplifying the process of scene categorization

certain topic. It is built in a training phase. As a result, each topic is characterized by a "bag of words" (set of codebook entries), regardless of the position at which they actually appear in the text. During classification of an unknown text the codebook entries can be used for gathering evidence that the text belongs to a specific topic.

This solution can be applied to the image categorization task as well: here, the "visual codebook" consists of characteristic region descriptors (which correspond to the "words") and the "bag of words" is often described as a "*bag of features*" in literature. In principle, each of the previously described region descriptors can be used for this task, e.g., the SIFT descriptor.

The visual codebook is built in a training phase where descriptors are extracted from sample images of different scene types and clustered in feature space. The cluster centers can be interpreted as the visual words. Each scene type can then be characterized by a characteristic, orderless feature distribution, e.g., by assigning each descriptor to its nearest cluster center and building a histogram based on the counts for each center (cf. Fig. 7.13). The geometric relations between the features are not evaluated any longer.

In the recognition phase, the feature distribution of a query image based on the codebook data is derived (e.g., through assignment of each descriptor to the most similar codebook entry) and classification is done by comparing it to the distributions of the scene types learnt in the training phase, e.g., by calculating some kind of similarity between the histograms of the query image and known scene types in the model database.

7.6.1.2 Example

Figure 7.13 shows a schematic toy example for scene categorization. On the left side, an image with 100 randomly sampled patches (blue circles) is shown. A schematic distribution of the descriptors in feature space (only two dimensions are shown for illustrative purposes, e.g., for SIFT we would need 128 dimensions) is depicted in the middle. The descriptors are divided into five clusters. Hence, for each scene type a 5-bin histogram specifying the occurrence of each descriptor class can be calculated. Two histogram examples for two scene types are shown on the right.

7.6.1.3 Modifications

Many proposed algorithms follow this outline. Basically, there remain four degrees of freedom in algorithm design. A choice has to be made for each of the following points:

- Identification method of the image patches: the "sampling strategy"
- Method for descriptor calculation
- Characterization of the resulting distribution of the descriptors in feature space
- Classification method of a query image in the recognition phase

The identification of image patches can be achieved by one of the keypoint detection methods already described. An alternative strategy is to sample the image by random. Empirical studies conducted by Nowak et al. [25] give evidence that such a simple random sampling strategy yields equal or even better recognition results, because it is possible to sample image patches densely, whereas the number of patches is limited for keypoint detectors as they focus on characteristic points. Dense sampling has the advantage of containing more information.

As far as the descriptor choice is concerned, one of the descriptor methods described above is often chosen for image categorization tasks, too (e.g., the SIFT descriptor).

A simple clustering scheme is to perform vector quantization, i.e., partition the feature space (e.g., for SIFT descriptors a 128D space) into equally sized cells. Hence, each descriptor is located in a specific cell. The codebook is built by taking all cells which contain at least one descriptor into account (all training images of all scene types are considered); the center position of such a cell can be referred to as a codeword. Each scene type can be characterized by a histogram counting the number of occurrences of visual code words (identified in all training images belonging to that type) for each cell. Please note that such a partitioning leads to high memory demand for high-dimensional feature spaces.

An alternative clustering scheme is the k-means algorithm (cf. [19]), which intends to identify densely populated regions in feature space (i.e., where many descriptors are located close to each other). The distribution of the descriptors is then characterized by a so-called signature, which consists of the set of cluster centers and, if indicated, the cluster sizes (i.e., the number of descriptors belonging to a cluster). The advantage of k-means clustering is that the codebook fits better to the actual distribution of the data, but on the other hand – at least in its original form – k-means only performs local optimization and the number of clusters k has to be known in advance. Therefore there exist many modifications of the scheme intending to overcome these limitations.

If the descriptor distribution of a specific scene type is characterized by a histogram, the classification of a query image can be performed by calculating similarity measures between the query image histogram H_Q and the histograms of the scene types $H_{S,l}$ determined in the training phase. A popular similarity metric is the χ^2 test . It defines a distance measure $d_{\chi^2,l}$ for each scene type l:

$$d_{\chi^2,l}\left(H_Q, H_{S,l}\right) = \sum_i \frac{\left(h_{Q,i} - m_i\right)^2}{m_i} \qquad (7.11a)$$

$$\text{with } m_i = \frac{h_{Q,i} + h_{S,l,i}}{2} \qquad (7.11b)$$

where $h_{Q,i}$ denotes the value of bin i of H_Q and $h_{S,l,i}$ denotes the value of bin i of $H_{S,l}$ respectively.

An alternative method, the Earth Mover's Distance (EMD, cf. the article of Rubner et al. [29]), can be applied if the distribution is characterized by a signature, i.e., a collection of cluster centers and the sizes of each cluster. For example, the signature of the distribution of the descriptors of a query image consists of m cluster centers $\mathbf{c}_{Q,i}$ and a weighting factor w_i; $1 \leq i \leq m$ as a measure of the cluster size. A scene type l is characterized by signature $\mathbf{c}_{S,l,j}$ and $w_{l,j}$; $1 \leq j \leq n$, respectively. The EMD defines a measure of the "work" which is necessary for transforming one signature into another. It can be calculated by

$$d_{EMD,l} = \frac{\sum_{i=1}^{m}\sum_{j=1}^{n} d_{ij}f_{ij}}{\sum_{i=1}^{m}\sum_{j=1}^{n} f_{ij}} \qquad (7.12)$$

where d_{ij} denotes a distance measure between the cluster centers $\mathbf{c}_{Q,i}$ and $\mathbf{c}_{S,l,j}$ (e.g., Euclidean distance). f_{ij} is a regularization term influenced by w_i and $w_{l,j}$, see [29] for details.

The Earth Mover's Distance has the advantage that it can also be calculated if the numbers of cluster centers of the two distributions differ from each other, i.e., $m \neq n$. Additionally, it avoids any quantization effects resulting from bin borders.

Results of comparative studies for a number of degrees of freedom in algorithm design like sampling strategies, codebook size, descriptor choice, or classification scheme are reported in [25] or [34].

7.6.1.4 Spatial Pyramid Matching

A modification of the orderless bag-of-features approach described by Lazebnik et al. [15], which in fact considers geometric relations up to some degree, is called *spatial pyramid matching*. Here, the descriptor distribution in feature space is characterized by histograms based on a codebook built with a k-means algorithm.

Compared to the bag-of-features approach, additional actions are performed: spatially, the image region is divided into four sub-regions. Consequently, an additional distribution histogram can be calculated for each sub-region again. This process can be repeated several times. Overall, when concatenating the histograms of all pyramid levels into one vector, the resulting description is in part identical to the histogram computed with a bag-of-features approach (for level 0), but has additional entries characterizing the distribution in the sub-images

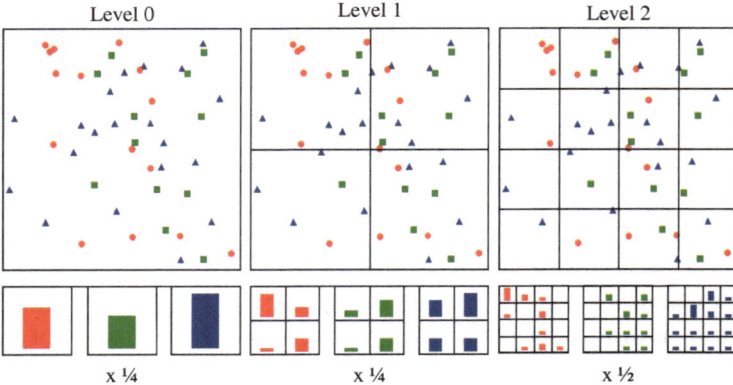

Fig. 7.14 Giving an example of the method with three descriptor types (indicated by *red circles*, *green squares*, and *blue triangles*) and three pyramid levels

The similarity metric for histogram comparison applied by Lazebnik et al. [15] differs from the χ^2 test. Without going into details, let's just mention that a similarity value of a sub-histogram at a high level ("high" means division of the image into many subimages) is weighted stronger than a similarity value at a lower level, because at higher levels matching descriptors are similar not only in appearance but also in location. Lazebnik et al. report improved performance compared to a totally unordered bag-of-features approach.

The proceeding is illustrated in Fig. 7.14, where a schematic example is given for three descriptor types (indicated by red circles, green squares, and blue triangles) and three pyramid levels. In the top part, the spatial descriptor distribution as well as the spatial partitioning is shown. At each pyramid level, the number of descriptors of each type is determined for each spatial bin and summarized in separate histograms (depicted below the spatial descriptor distribution). Each level is weighted by a weighting factor given in the last row when concatenating the bins of all histograms into the final description of the scene.

7.6.2 Categorization with Contour Information

Apart from the appearance-based bag-of-features approach, many propositions intending to exploit shape or contour information in order to solve the object categorization task have been made recently. Here, we want to identify all objects belonging to a specific *category* (e.g., "cars") in a scene image. Compared to scene categorization, the intra-class variance is a bit narrowed down, but still much higher compared to the task of object detection. The method proposed by Shotton et al. [30], where recognition performance is demonstrated by the identification of objects of category "horse," shall be presented as one example for this class of methods.

7.6.2.1 Main Idea

Shotton et al. [30] use an object representation which is based upon fragments of the contour and their spatial relationship. When dealing with object categorization, closed contours are not feasible due to the large intra-class variance within a specific object class. Therefore the contour is broken into fragments. This proceeding also circumvents the problem that closed contours are difficult to extract anyway. As far as the spatial relationship between the fragments is concerned, it has to be flexible enough to allow for considerable variations. In turn, the advantage of including spatial relationships into the model is the ability to determine the position of detected objects as well. An example of an object model showing contour fragments of a horse can be seen in Fig. 7.15.

In a training stage, contour fragments which are considered characteristic are learned in an automatic manner from a limited set of example images for each object class. To this end, edge pixels (edgels) are extracted from the original intensity images, e.g., with the Canny edge detector including non-maximum suppression (cf. [3] or Appendix A) and grouped to contour fragments.

During recognition, matching of a query image is performed by applying a modified chamfer distance measure between the edgel point sets of the query image contour fragments and the fragments of the model database. The basic principle of the chamfer distance has already been presented in Chapter 3; here the modified distance also considers orientation differences of the edgels and allows for comparing point sets differing in scale, too (see [30] for details).

The question now is which fragments have to be compared. The answer is as follows: At first, hypothetic object locations are sampled in scale space (i.e., hypotheses for locations are generated by sampling the $[x, y]$-position as well as scale s). For each hypothesis the modified chamfer distance is calculated for each contour fragment pair that is geometrically consistent with this hypothesis: the relative position of the fragment center to the object centroid (defined by the hypothesis) has to be similar to the position of the model fragment. As a result, a valid object position $\mathbf{x}_k$ for a specific object class m is reported by the system if enough evidence

Fig. 7.15 Taken from Shotton et al. [30] (© 2008 IEEE; with permission): the object model consists of four contour fragments. Their spatial relationship is modeled by the distance vectors (*blue arrows*) between the center points of the fragments (*red crosses*) and the object centroid (*green cross*)

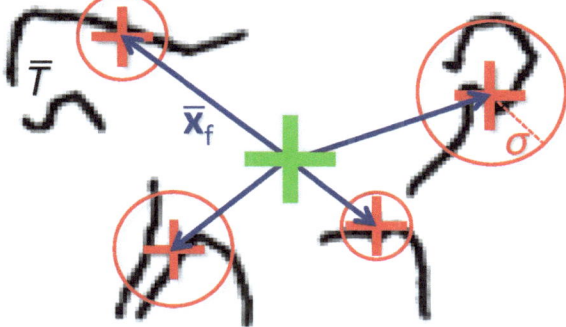

for the occurrence of an instance of this class at position $\mathbf{x}_k$ has been collected, i.e., several fragments showed low chamfer distance measures.

7.6.2.2 Training Phase

1. *Detection of edge pixels*: In the fist step, all edge pixels (edgels e) are detected by applying, e.g., a Canny edge detector to the original intensity image including non-maximum suppression. Only pixels with gradient above a threshold value t are kept. This process is performed for all training images.
2. *Grouping to fragments*: Initially, all edge pixels which are detected in the first step and are located in a rectangular sub-region of the object area defined by $[x_i, y_i, s_i]$ (spatial position $[x_i, y_i]$ and scale/size s_i) are considered to belong to a specific contour fragment F_i. Hence, there is no need to obtain connected sets of edgels (which sometimes is a problem, e.g., in noisy situations). Multiple fragments are extracted by randomly choosing the position as well as the size of the rectangles. Some examples of extracted contour fragments are depicted in Fig. 7.16. They contain characteristic fragments (like the horse head) as well as "noise fragments" (e.g., the fragment shown down to the right) which should be removed in the following cleaning step.
3. *Cleaning of fragments*: In order to remove non-characteristic fragments, the edgel density (number of edgels divided by the area of the rectangular region) is compared to two thresholds. All fragments with density below threshold η_1 are discarded, as they are not supposed to represent characteristic parts of the object. If the density exceeds a second threshold value η_2 ($\eta_2 \gg \eta_1$) the fragment is discarded as well, because it is assumed to contain a significant amount of background clutter. Even if this is not the case, it is advisable not to consider

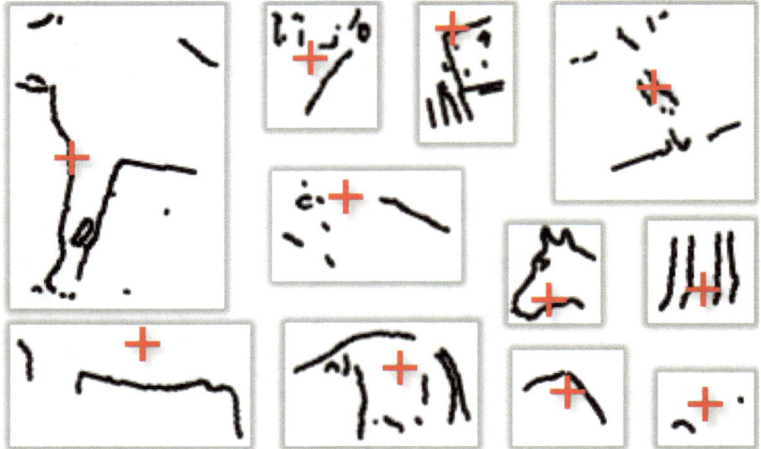

Fig. 7.16 Taken from Shotton et al. [30] (© 2008 IEEE; with permission) where some examples of contour fragments extracted from a horse image can be seen

the fragment as the matching step would require much computation time due to the large number of edgels.

4. *Virtual sample generation*: In order to capture sufficient characteristics of an object class and its intra-class variations, a considerable number of fragment samples is necessary. However, the system should also work in situations where only a few training examples for each object class are available. To this end, modified versions of the contour fragments are generated by scaling and rotating the edgels around the fragment center as well as rotating and shifting the fragment relative to the object centroid to some extent. The parameters for these transformations are chosen at random within some reasonable bounds.

5. *Fragment clustering*: Up to now, each training image has been processed separately. In the last training step, contour fragments which have similar occurrences in multiple training images are identified. To this end, a modified chamfer distance is calculated between pairs of two fragments of different training images. If several fragments originating from different training images show a low distance, they are supposed to share a characteristic part of the contour of the object class. Additionally, the center point locations of the bounding rectangles of similar fragments should build clusters in the $[x, y]$-plane. See Fig. 7.17 for an example with horse fragments: It is clearly visible that the occurrence of the pair of legs (upper left fragment) mainly splits into two clusters in the lower part of the image, whereas the head of the horse is clustered in the upper left part of the image. A fragment with no characteristic information about the horse object class is depicted in the lower right. No clusters can be detected for that fragment.

Hence, only the clusters are included in the model. For each of the found clusters, a prototype representation (the fragment of the cluster which has minimum overall chamfer distance to the other cluster members) is taken. Altogether, the model of a

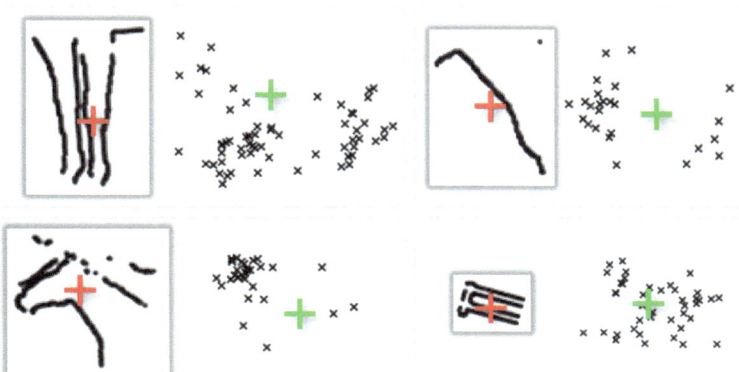

Fig. 7.17   Taken from Shotton et al. [30] (© 2008 IEEE; with permission) displaying the spatial distribution of occurrence for some example fragments (*green cross*: object centroid)

specific object class m consists of fragment data $F_{m,l}$ of each found cluster l. Each fragment data $F_{m,l} = \left[\overline{E}, \overline{\mathbf{x}_f}, \sigma\right]$ consists of (see also Fig. 7.15):

- The edge map $\overline{E}$ consisting of the edgels of the prototype representation of the cluster $F_{m,l}$.
- The mean $\overline{\mathbf{x}_f}$ of the distance vectors $\mathbf{x}_f$ of all fragments of cluster $F_{m,l}$ to the object centroid.
- The variance σ of the distance vectors $\mathbf{x}_f$ of all fragments of the cluster $F_{m,l}$.

7.6.2.3 Recognition Phase

During recognition, the system tries to find matches between contour fragments $\mathbf{F}_S$ in the scene image and the fragments $\mathbf{F}_M$ of the model database. To this end, the fragments $F_{S,k}$ have to be extracted first by applying the same process as used in training up to step 3. Next, the modified chamfer distance is calculated between the detected query fragments and the model fragments. To this end, the template fragments of the model database are shifted and scaled by uniformly sampling the $[x, y, s]$-space with carefully chosen stepsizes.

For speed reasons, not all template fragments are compared at all positions. Instead, a technique called *boosting* is applied. Suppose we want to examine the hypothesis $[x_i, y_i, s_i, m]$ (stating that an instance of object class m is present at position $[x_i, y_i, s_i]$). In principle boosting here works as follows: At first, the chamfer distance is calculated for only one fragment $F_{m,l}$: based on the supposed $[x_i, y_i, s_i]$-position of the object centroid as well as the distance vector $\overline{\mathbf{x}_f}$ of fragment $F_{m,l}$, a supposed position of its matching counterpart can be derived. Subsequently, the modified chamfer distance of a scene image fragment $F_{S,k}$ in the vicinity of this position is calculated (if some fragment close to the expected position actually exists). Shotton et al. [30] suggest a modification of the distance measure such that fragments are penalized if their location differs considerably from the hypothesized position.

If this distance turns out to be low, this is a hint that an object actually is present at the current $[x_i, y_i, s_i]$-position. If it is high, however, this is a sign of rejecting the current hypothesis. Subsequently, other fragments of the same object class m are chosen for further refinement of the hypothesis. In order to allow for object variations, there just has to be a rather coarse alignment between the positions of different fragments. The thus obtained measures either give evidence to weaken or enforce the current hypothesis. The process is repeated until the hypothesis can finally be rejected or confirmed.

7.6.2.4 Example

A recognition example is shown in Fig. 7.18, where the system aims at detecting all horses in a test image dataset. The appearance of the horses changes considerably from instance to instance, mainly because they belong to different breeds as well as

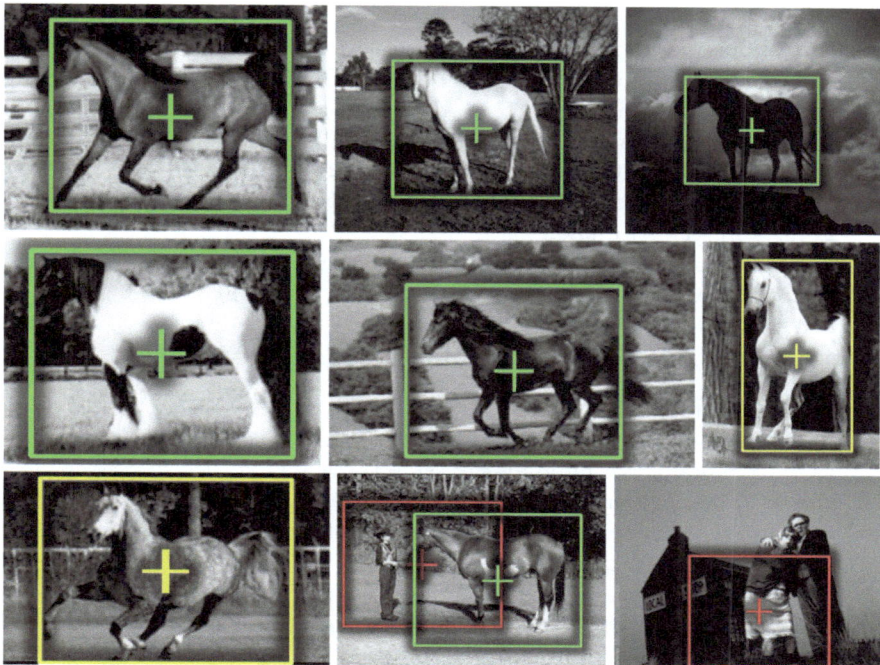

Fig. 7.18 With images taken from Shotton et al. [30] (© 2008 IEEE; with permission) illustrating the recognition performance of the method when applied to a horse test dataset

due to non-rigid motion of the horses and viewpoint changes. Some of the images show substantial background clutter. All correctly identified instances are marked green, the wrongly detected instances are marked red, and the horses missed by the system are marked yellow. Whereas most of the horses are correctly found by the system, some are also missed, especially in situations where the horse moves (look at the legs!) or the viewpoint is considerably different compared to training (which was performed with view from the side).

7.6.2.5 Pseudocode

```
function categorizeObjectsContourFragments (in Image I, in
model contour fragments F_M, in density thresholds η₁ and
η₂, in probability thresholds t_P,accept and t_P,reject, out object
position list p)

// contour fragment calculation
detect all edge pixels (e.g. with Canny operator) and arrange
them in list e
```

```
for i = 1 to number of random samples N
    // random sampling of position [x_i, y_i, s_i]
    x_i ← random (x_min, x_max)
    y_i ← random (y_min, y_max)
    s_i ← random (s_min, s_max)
    calculate density d_e of edgels in edge map Ē (Ē = all
    elements of e located within a region defined by [x_i, y_i, s_i])
    if d_e ≥ η_1 ∧ d_e ≤ η_2 then
        // accept current contour fragment
        add fragment info F_i = [Ē, x_i, y_i, s_i] to list F_S
    end if
next

// boosted matching
for k = 1 to number of position samples
    sample position: hypothesis x_k = [x_k, y_k, s_k]
    for m = 1 to number of model indices
        //init of probability that object m is at position x_k
        P(m, x_k) ← (t_{P,accept} + t_{P,reject})/2
        while P(m, x_k) ≥ t_{P,reject} ∧ P(m, x_k) ≤ t_{P,accept} do
            choose next model fragment F_{m,l}
            retrieve scene image fragment F_{S,i} closest to x_k,
            corrected by x̄_f of F_{m,l}
            calculate modified chamfer distance d_{k,i,l} between
            F_{S,i} and F_{m,l} (including penalty for pos. mismatch)
            adjust P(m, x_k) according to value of d_{k,i,l}
        end while
        if P(m, x_k) ≥ t_{P,accept} then
            // hypothesis is confirmed
            add hypothesis [x_k, m] to list p
        end if
    next
next
```

7.6.2.6 Rating

In their paper Shotton et al. [30] give evidence that fragmented contour information can be used for object categorization. Their method performs well even in challenging situations. The partitioning of the contour into fragments together with a coarse modeling of the relative positions of the fragments with respect to each other showed flexible enough to cope with considerable intra-class object variations. The advantages of the usage of contours are an effective representation of the objects (effective natural data reduction to a limited set of edgels) as well as increased invariance with respect to illumination and/or color changes. Compared to the usage of local image patches, contours can be matched exactly to the object boundary, whereas the mostly used rectangular or circular image patches of appearance-based descriptors inevitably include some part of the background, at least for arbitrarily shaped objects.

However, when restricting oneself to contours some potentially important information might be lost, especially if the objects feature smooth intensity transitions. Additionally the scheme is sensitive to out-of-plane viewpoint changes. Another point is that the method is inefficient for large databases as the chamfer distances have to be calculated separately for each model class/position hypothesis combination. In general, the computational complexity is rather high.

References

1. Bai, X., Yang, X. and Latecki, L.J.., "Detection and Recognition of Contour Parts Based on Shape Similarity", *Pattern Recognition*, 41:2189–2199, 2008
2. Belongie, S., Malik, J. and Puzicha, J., "shape Matching and Object Recognition Using Shape Contexts", *IEEE Transactions on Pattern Analysis and Machine Intelligence*, 24(4):509–522, 2002
3. Canny, J.F., "A Computational Approach to Edge Detection", *IEEE Transactions on Pattern Analysis and Machine Intelligence*, 8(6):679–698, 1986
4. Edelman, S., Intrator, N. and Poggio, T., "Complex Cells and Object Recognition", *Unpublished manuscript*, 1997, http://kybele.psych.cornell.edu/~edelman/Archive/nips97.pdf
5. Florack, L., Haar Romney, B.M., Koenderink, J. and Viergever, M., "General Intensity Transformations and Second Order Invariants", *Proceedings of 7th Scandinavian Conference on Image Analysis*, Alborg, Denmark, 338–345, 1991
6. Flusser, J. and Suk, T., "Pattern Recognition by Affine Moment Invariants", *Pattern Recognition*, 26(1):167–174, 1993
7. Freeman, W.T. and Adelson, E.H., "The Design and Use of Steerable Filters", *IEEE Transactions on Pattern Analysis and Machine Intelligence*, 13(9):891–906, 1991
8. Grigorescu, C. and Petkov, N., "Distance Sets for Shape Filters and Shape Recognition", *IEEE Transactions on Image Processing*, 12(10):1274–1286, 2003
9. Harris, C. and Stephens, M., "A Combined Corner and Edge Detector", *Alvey Vision Conference*, 147–151, 1988
10. Huang, C.-R., Chen, C.-S. and Chung, P.-C., "Contrast Context Histogram – An Efficient Discriminating Local Descriptor for Object Recognition and Image Matching", *Pattern Recognition*, 41:3071–3077, 2008
11. Joachims, T., "Text Categorization with Support Vector Machines: Learning with many Relevant Features" *Proceedings of 10th European Conference on Machine Learning*, Chemnitz, Germany, 137–142, 1998
12. Ke, Y. and Sukthanakar, R., "PCA-SIFT: A More Distinctive Representation for Local Image Features", *Proceedings of IEEE Conference on Computer Vision and Pattern Recognition*, 2:506–513, 2004
13. Koenderink, J. and Van Doorn, A.J., "Representation of Local Geometry in the Visual System", *Biological Cybernetics*, 55:367–375, 1987
14. Latecki, L.J. and Lakämper, R., "Shape Similarity Measure Based on Correspondence of Visual Parts", *IEEE Transactions on Pattern Analysis and Machine Intelligence*, 22(10):1185–1190, 2000
15. Lazebnik, S., Schmid, C. and Ponce, J., "Beyond Bags of Features: Spatial Pyramid Matching for Recognizing Natural Scene Categories", *Proceedings of IEEE Conference on Computer Vision and Pattern Recognition*, 2:2169–2178, 2006
16. Lindeberg, T., "Feature Detection with Automatic Scale Selection", *International Journal of Computer Vision*, 30(2):77–116, 1998

17. Lowe, D.G., "Object recognition from local scale-invariant features", *International Conference on Computer Vision,* Corfu, Greece, 1150–1157, 1999
18. Lowe, D.G., "Distinctive Image Features from Scale-Invariant Viewpoints", *International Journal of Computer Vision,* 60:91–111, 2004
19. MacQueen, J., "Some Methods for Classification and Analysis of Multivariate Observations", *Proceedings of the Symposium of Mathematical Statistics and Probability,* Berkely, USA, 281–297, 1967
20. Matas, J., Chum, O., Martin, U. and Pajdla, T., "Robust Wide Baseline Stereo form Maximally Stable Extremal Regions", *Proceedings of British Machine Vision Conference,* 1:384–393, 2002
21. Meinguet, J., "Multivariate Interpolation at Arbitrary Points Made Simple", *Journal of Applied Mathematics and Physics (ZAMP),* 5:439–468, 1979
22. Mikolajczyk, K. and Schmid, C., "An Affine Invariant Interest Point Detector", *Proceedings of European Conference on Computer Vision,* 1:128–142, 2002
23. Mikolajczyk, K. and Schmid, C., "A Performance Evaluation of Local Descriptors", *IEEE Transactions on Pattern Analysis and Machine Intelligence,* 27(10):1615–1630, 2005
24. Mikolajczyk, K. , Tuytelaars, T., Schmid, C, Zisserman, A., Matas, J., Schaffalitzky, F., Kadir, T. and Van Gool, L., "A Comparison of Affine Region Detectors", *International Journal of Computer Vision,* 65:43–72, 2005
25. Nowak, E., Jurie, F. and Triggs, B., "Sampling strategies for Bag-of-Features Image Classification", *Proceedings of European Conference on Computer Vision,* 4:490–503, 2006
26. Pinz, A., "Object Categorization", *Foundations and Trends in Computer Graphics and Vision,* 1(4):255–353, 2005
27. Rosten, E. and Drummond, T., "Machine learning for high-speed corner detection", *Proceedings of European Conference on Computer Vision,* Graz, Austria, 430–443, 2006
28. Roth, P.M. and Winter, M., "Survey of Appearance-based Methods for Object Recognition", *Technical Report ICG-TR-01/08 TU Graz,* 2008
29. Rubner, Y., Tomasi, C. and Leonidas, J.G., "The Earth Mover's Distance as a Metric for Image Retrieval", *International Journal of Computer Vision,* 40(2):99–121, 2000
30. Shotton, J., Blake, A. and Cipolla, R., "Multi-Scale Categorical Object Recognition Using Contour Fragments", *IEEE Transactions on Pattern Analysis and Machine Intelligence,* 30(7):1270–1281, 2008
31. Schmid, C. and Mohr, R., "Local Grey Value Invariants for Image Retrieval", *IEEE Transactions on Pattern Analysis and Machine Intelligence,* 19:530–535, 1997
32. Van Gool, L., Moons, T. and Ungureanu, D., "Affine/Photometric Invariants for Planar Intensity Patterns", *Proceedings of European Conference on Computer Vision,* 1:642–651, 1996
33. Witkin, A.P., "Scale-Space Filtering", *International Joint Conferences on Artificial Intelligence,* Karlsruhe, 1019–1022, 1983
34. Zhang, J., Marszalek, M., Lazebnik, S. and Schimd, C., "Local Features and Kernels for Classification of Texture and Object Categories: A Comprehensive Study", *International Journal of Computer Vision,* 73(2):213–238, 2007

Chapter 8
Summary

Abstract The last chapter summarizes the methods presented in this book by comparing their strengths as well as limitations. A brief rating with respect to several criteria, such as algorithm runtime, object complexity, or invariance with respect to intra-class object variation, viewpoint change, occlusion, is also given. Please note that such a rating can only be done at coarse level as algorithm performance depends heavily on the application context. Nevertheless the comparison should help the reader to asses which kind of algorithm might be suitable for a specific application.

One major concern of this book is to point out that in the field of object recognition a general purpose algorithm doesn't exist. The existence of numerous applications with characteristic requirements – ranging from industrial applications with good imaging conditions, but very tough demands as far as accuracy, reliability, or execution time is concerned to tasks like categorization of real-world scenes with difficult conditions like heavy background clutter, significant intra-class variations, or poor illumination or image quality – has lead to many different solutions with specific properties.

Global methods like cross-correlation or principal component analysis have the advantage of making no a priori assumptions about the object to be recognized and therefore are applicable to a wide variety of objects. In general, this also holds for feature vectors; however, it often is advisable to choose features which are most suited for specific properties of the objects under consideration. Furthermore, most of the global methods are straightforward and easy to implement.

However, the flip side of simplicity often is inefficiency, e.g., for cross-correlation extra calculations of the correlation coefficient for scaled and rotated templates are necessary at every position if scaled and rotated versions of the objects are also to be found. Additionally, many global methods are not very discriminative and can therefore be used to classify clearly distinct objects only. Please note also that many global methods pre-suppose a correct segmentation of the object from the background, which often is a difficult task and in particular problematic in the case of partial occlusion.

Transformation-search based schemes like the generalized Hough transform or methods based on the Hausdorff distance are applicable to a wide variety of objects,

M. Treiber, *An Introduction to Object Recognition*, Advances in Pattern Recognition,
DOI 10.1007/978-1-84996-235-3_8, © Springer-Verlag London Limited 2010

too. Although they are based on a global distance or similarity measure, they are able to deal with considerable occlusion, because the object representation is restricted to a finite set of points and each element of the model point set makes a local contribution to the measure. For that reason it is tolerable if some points are missing as long as there are enough points remaining which can be matched to the model correctly. Similar considerations can be made with respect to background clutter. This also implies that no segmentation of the object is necessary.

However, the process of scanning the transformation space leads to impractical memory demands (generalized Hough transform) and/or execution times (Hausdorff distance), at least if there is a large search space to be investigated (e.g., transformations with many parameters and/or a large parameter range).

Another point is that the reduction of the object representation to a finite point set is commonly achieved by edge detection, i.e., the calculation of intensity gradients followed by thresholding. This makes the methods robust to illumination changes to some extent, but not completely: minor reductions of contrast between training and recognition can cause some edge pixels, which still are detected during training, to remain below the gradient threshold, which has the same effect as partial occlusion.

The method proposed by Viola and Jones includes some alternative approaches, where local contributions to the overall match score are made by special haar-like filters instead of using point sets. The specific design of the filters allows for fast calculations when scanning the transformation space, but restricts the applicability of the method a bit. It is best suited for objects which show a more or less block-like structure.

The number of features typically utilized in correspondence-based schemes like graph matching is significantly lower than the cardinality of the point sets of transformation-search based methods. This leads to a much faster execution time, especially if the combinatorial approach of evaluating all possible correspondences is replaced by a more sophisticated strategy (see, e.g., interpretation trees for an example). Further speedup can be achieved through indexing (as implemented by geometric hashing), especially if large model databases have to be explored.

On the other hand, such a proceeding restricts the applicability of these methods to objects which can be characterized well by a small set of primitives/features. Additionally, these features have to be detected reliably. In general, this is the case for man-made objects, which makes these methods most suitable for industrial applications. This coincides well with the fact that the rigid object model these algorithms employ fits well to the objects to be recognized in industrial applications: they usually show little intra-class variation and are well characterized by the geometric relations between the features.

The usage of invariants or feature configurations which remain perceptually similar even in the case of perspective transformations allows for the design of methods which are able to detect objects in 3D space from a wide variety of viewpoints with only a single 2D intensity image as input for recognition. This is a notable achievement, and some methods could be presented which indeed have proven that a localization of objects in 3D space with aid of just a single 2D image is possible.

Table 8.1 Overview of the properties of some recognition schemes. Please note that only a coarse and simplified classification is given here as many properties depend on the context in which the method is used. Important properties like recognition error rate or accuracy of position determination are not reported here, because they heavily depend on the application context

Method	Computation speed	Suitable object complexity	Suitable intra-class object variation	Invariance respective		
				Image formation process	Viewpoint change	Occlusion and clutter
Correlation	Fast – slow	Simple – medium	Rigid	Low-medium	Low	Low
Feature vector	Very fast – medium	Simple	Rigid	Medium	Medium	Medium
Hough transform	Fast – slow	Simple – high	Rigid – medium	Medium – high	Low-medium	Medium-high
Interpretation Tree	Very fast – medium	Medium – high	Very rigid	High	Low	Low (occlusion) High (clutter)
3D recog./invariants	Fast – medium	Simple – medium	Rigid	High	Very high	Med. (occlusion) High (clutter)
Snakes	Medium	Simple	Very flexible	High	Med.-high	Low-medium
SIFT	Medium – very slow	Medium – very high	Rigid – flexible	High	Very high	Very high
Shape contexts	Medium	Medium	Flexible	High	High	High

The methods are restricted, however, to objects which can be characterized well by specific feature configurations. Additionally, it is crucial that these feature configurations, which usually are groups of some kind of primitives, can be detected reliably. This stable detection, though, is very difficult to achieve if multiple features are involved. Therefore the methods seem to be suited most for industrial applications, e.g., determining gripping points for lifting objects out of a bin. Yet personally I doubt that the recognition rates reported in the original articles are sufficient for industrial applications, where error rates usually have to remain close to 0%.

Active contour models like Snakes aim at locating the borders of deformable objects: they explicitly account for local deformations by fitting a parametric curve to the local image content at the cost of only a limited area of convergence. Therefore they have the necessity of a reasonable initial estimate of the object contour.

On the other hand they allow for the determination of a closed contour even in challenging situations where the contour is "interrupted" frequently, which for example, is typical of medical imaging. Given an estimate of a closed contour, it is possible to derive similarity measures which are related to perceptual similarity. Therefore they are able to identify objects as similar in situations where the contours show considerable discrepancies in a distance metric sense, but are considered similar by humans.

Recognition methods based on region descriptor matching are a major contribution of recent research. They are capable to cope with significant variety, as far as the intra-class variety of the objects themselves as well as the imaging conditions like viewpoint or illumination change or background clutter is concerned. Their design aims at focusing on characteristic data as the descriptors are derived from local neighborhoods around interest points considered significant in some way. Furthermore, the dimensionality of the descriptors is reduced intending to make them insensitive to "undesired" information change and retaining their discriminative power at the same time. In the meantime methods utilizing appearance information have come to a high degree of maturity, whereas methods evaluating shape information are beginning to emerge more and more.

A disadvantage of this kind of algorithms is the rather high computational complexity of most of the methods, no matter whether appearance or shape information is used.

A coarse and schematic overview of some properties of the recognition methods described in this book is given in Table 8.1.

A worthwhile consideration often is to combine different approaches in order to benefit from their contrary advantages, e.g., employing the generalized Hough transform as a pre-processing stage for a flexible model matching approach, which is capable to estimate the boundary of an object very accurately, but has only a limited area of convergence. Besides, this is one reason why older or simple methods like the global feature vectors shouldn't be considered out of date: They're still widely used in recent approaches – as building blocks of more sophisticated schemes.

Appendix A
Edge Detection

The detection of edge points is widely spread among object recognition schemes, and that's the reason why it is mentioned here, although it is not an object recognition method in itself. A detailed description could fill a complete book, therefore only a short outline of some basic principles shall be given here.

Edge points are characterized by high local intensity changes, which are typical of pixels located on the border of objects, as the background color often differs significantly from object colour. In addition to that, edge points can also be located within the object, e.g., due to texture or because of a rapid change of the object surface normal vector, which results in changes of the intensity of light reflected into the camera.

Mathematically speaking, high local intensity changes correspond to high first derivatives (gradients) of the intensity function. In the following, the Sobel Operator as a typical method of fast gradient calculation is explained. Additionally, the Canny edge detector, which in addition to gradient calculation, also classifies pixels as "edge point" or "non-edge point" shall be presented.

But first let's mention a few reasons why edge detection is so popular:

- **Information content**: much of the information of object location is concentrated on pixels with high gradient. Imagine a simple plain bright object upon a dark background: if its position changes slightly, the intensity of a pixel located near the centre will essentially not change after movement. However, the intensity of a pixel, which is also located inside the object, but close to its border, might change considerably, because it might be located outside the object after movement. Figure A.1 illustrates this fact for a cross-shaped object.
- **Invariance to illumination changes**: brightness offsets as well as linear brightness changes lead to differing intensities of every pixel. The first derivative of the intensity function, however, is less affected by those changes: constant offsets, for example, are cancelled out completely.
- **Analogy to human vision**: last but not least there is evidence that the human vision system, which clearly has very powerful recognition capabilities, is sensitive to areas featuring rapid intensity changes, too.

M. Treiber, *An Introduction to Object Recognition*, Advances in Pattern Recognition,
DOI 10.1007/978-1-84996-235-3, © Springer-Verlag London Limited 2010

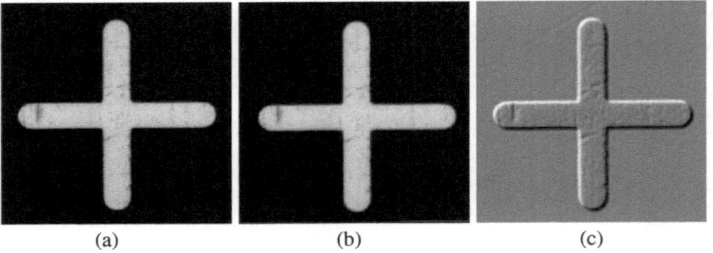

Fig. A.1 The gray value differences (image c) of each pixel between two the two images (**a**) and (**b**) are shown. Images (**a**) and (**b**) show the same object, but are displaced by 2 ½ pixels in x- and y-direction. Dark values in (**c**) indicate that (**a**) is darker than (**b**), bright values that (**a**) is brighter than (**b**)

A.1 Gradient Calculation

As we are working with digital images, discrete data has to be processed. Therefore a calculation of the first derivative amounts to an evaluation of the gray value difference between adjacent pixels. Because we have 2D data, two such differences can be calculated, e.g., one in the x-direction and one in the y-direction.

Mathematically speaking, the calculation of intensity differences for all pixels of an input image I is equivalent to a convolution of I with an appropriate filter kernel k. The first choice for such a kernel might be $k_x = [-1, 1]$ for the x-direction, but unfortunately, this is not symmetric and the convolution result would represent the derivative of positions located in between two adjacent pixels. Therefore the symmetric kernel $k_x = [-1, 0, 1]$ is a better choice.

Another problem is the sensitivity of derivatives with respect to noise. In order to suppress the disturbing influence of noise, the filter kernels can be expanded in size in order to perform smoothing of the data. Please note, however, that the size of the filter kernel affects the speed of the calculations. Edge detection usually is one of the early steps of OR methods where many pixels have to be processed.

Many filter kernels have been proposed over the years. A good trade-off between speed and smoothing is achieved by the 3×3 Sobel filter kernels $k_{S,x}$ and $k_{S,y}$:

$$k_{S,x} = \frac{1}{4} \cdot \begin{bmatrix} -1 & 0 & 1 \\ -2 & 0 & 2 \\ -1 & 0 & 1 \end{bmatrix} \text{ and } k_{S,y} = \frac{1}{4} \cdot \begin{bmatrix} 1 & 2 & 1 \\ 0 & 0 & 0 \\ -1 & -2 & -1 \end{bmatrix} \tag{A.1}$$

Convolution of the input image I with $k_{S,x}$ and $k_{S,y}$ leads to the x- and y-gradient I_x and I_y:

$$I_x = I * k_{S,x} \text{ and } I_y = I * k_{S,y} \tag{A.2}$$

Table A.1 Example of the Sobel operator

Intensity image	X-Gradient (bright=pos. val.;dark=neg.)	Y-Gradient (bright=pos. val.;dark=neg.)	Gradient magnitude (bright=high magn.)	Gradient orientation (coded as gray values)

An alternative representation to I_x and I_y is the gradient magnitude I_G and orientation I_θ (see Table A.1 for an example). Due to speed reasons, I_G is often approximated by the summation of magnitudes:

$$I_G = |I_x| + |I_y| \text{ and } I_\theta = \arctan\left(I_y/I_x\right) \tag{A.3}$$

A.2 Canny Edge Detector

One of the most popular detectors of edge pixels was developed by Canny [1]. As far as gradient calculation is concerned, Canny formulated some desirable properties that a good gradient operator should fulfil and found out that convolutions of I with the first derivatives of the Gaussian filter kernel in x- as well as y-direction are good approximations. After gradient filtering, the output has to be thresholded in some way in order to decide which pixels can be classified as "edge pixels."

Now let's have a closer look at the optimality criteria defined by Canny:

- **Good detection quality**: ideally, the operator should not miss actual edge pixels as well as not erroneously classify non-edge pixels as edge pixels. In a more formal language, this corresponds to a maximization of the signal-to-noise ratio (SNR) of the output of the gradient operator.
- **Good localization quality**: the reported edge pixel positions should be as close as possible to the true edge positions. This requirement can be formalized to a minimization of the variance of the detected edge pixel positions.
- **No multiple responses**: a single true edge pixel should lead to only a single reported edge pixel as well. More formally, the distance between the extracted edge pixel positions should be maximized.

It was shown by Canny that the first derivative of the Gaussian filter is a good approximation to the optimal solution to the criteria defined above. The convolution of the input image with such a filter performs smoothing and gradient calculation at the same time. As we have 2D input data, two convolutions have to be performed, one yielding the x-gradient and one the y-gradient.

Another desirable property of those filters is the fact that they show a good trade-off between performance and speed, as they can be approximated by rather small kernels and, furthermore, they're separable in the 2D-case. Hence, I_x and I_y can be calculated by a convolution with the following functions:

$$g_x(x,y) = \sqrt{2\pi}\sigma \cdot \partial g(x)/\partial x \cdot g(y) \tag{A.4a}$$

$$g_y(x,y) = \sqrt{2\pi}\sigma \cdot \partial g(y)/\partial y \cdot g(x) \tag{A.4b}$$

with $g(a) = 1/\left(\sqrt{2\pi}\sigma\right) \cdot e^{-a^2/(2\sigma^2)}$ being the 1D-gaussian function. Please note that the factor $\sqrt{2\pi}\sigma$ serves as a regularization term which compensates for the fact that derivative amplitudes decline with increasing σ. Numerically, a sampling of g_x and g_y leads to the filter kernels $k_{C,x}$ and $k_{C,y}$, with which the convolutions are actually carried out.

Overall, the Canny filter consists of the following steps:

1. **Smoothed Gradient calculation**: In the first step the gradient magnitude I_G is calculated. It can be derived from its components I_x and I_y (e.g., by Equation (A.3)), which are calculated by convolution of the input image I with the filter kernels $k_{C,x}$ and $k_{C,y}$ as defined above.

2. **Non-maximum suppression**: In order to produce unique responses for each true edge point, I_G has to be post-processed before thresholding, because the smoothing leads to a diffusion of the gradient values. To this end, the gradient of all pixels which don't have maximum magnitude in gradient direction is suppressed (e.g., set to zero). This can be achieved by examining a 3×3 neighborhood surrounding each pixel p. At first, the two pixels of the neighborhood which are closest to the gradient direction of p are identified. If one of those pixels has a gradient magnitude which is larger than those of p, the magnitude of p is set to zero.

3. **Hysteresis thresholding**: In the last step, the pixels have to be classified into "edge" or "non-edge" based on their gradient value. Pixels with high gradient magnitude are likely to be edge points. Instead of using a single threshold for classification two such thresholds are used. At first, all pixels with gradient magnitude above a rather high threshold t_h are immediately classified as "edge." These pixels serve as "seeds" for the second step, where all pixels adjacent to those already classified as "edge" are considered to be edge pixels as well if their gradient magnitude is above a second, rather low threshold t_l. This process is repeated until no more additional edge pixels can be found.

An example of the different steps of the Canny edge detector can be seen in Fig. A.2.

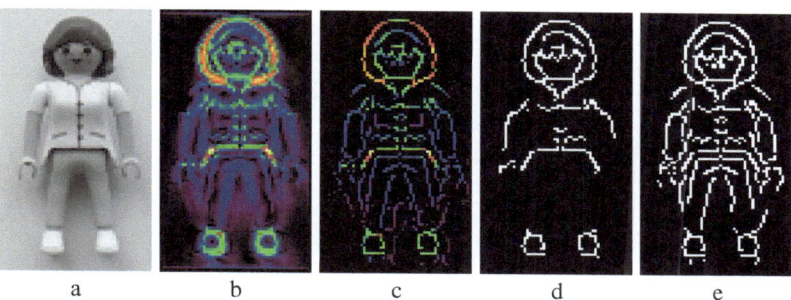

a   b   c   d   e

Fig. A.2 An example of the Canny operator is shown: (**a**) intensity image; (**b**) output of gradient filter in pseudocolor, the gradient magnitude increases in the following order: *black – violet – blue – green – red – yellow – white*; (**c**) gradient after non-maximum suppression in pseudocolor; (**e**) detected edges with high thresholds; (**f**) detected edges with low thresholds

Of course there are many alternatives to the Canny edge filter. Deriche [2], for example, developed recursive filters for calculating the smoothed gradient which are optimized with respect to speed. Freeman and Adelson [3] proposed to replace the gaussian-based filter by so-called quadrature pairs of steerable filters in Canny's framework. They argued that the filter derived by Canny, which is optimized for step-edges, is sub-optimal in the case of other contours, e.g., bar-like structures or junctions of multiple edges. Therefore they derived an energy measure form quadrature pairs of steerable filters as an alternative, which shows good results for a variety of edge types.

References

1. Canny, J.F., "A Computational Approach to Edge Detection", *IEEE Transactions on Pattern Analysis and Machine Intelligence,* 8(6):679–698, 1986
2. Deriche, R., "Using Canny's criteria to derive a recursively implemented edge detector ", *International Journal of Computer Vision,* 1:167–187, 1987
3. Freeman, W.T. and Adelson, E.H., "The Design and Use of Steerable Filters", *IEEE Transactions on Pattern Analysis and Machine Intelligence*, 13(9):891–906, 1991

Appendix B
Classification

In many object recognition schemes so-called feature vectors $\mathbf{x} = [x_1, x_2, \ldots, x_N]^T$ consisting of some kind of processed or intermediate data are derived from the input images. In order to decide which object class is shown in an image, its feature vector is compared to vectors derived from images showing objects of known class label, which were obtained during a training stage. In other words, a classification takes place in the feature space during recognition. Over the years many proposals of classification methods have been made (see, e.g., the book written by Duda et al. [3] for an overview). A detailed presentation is beyond the scope of this book – just some general thoughts shall be given here. Some basic classification principles are briefly discussed. However, this doesn't mean that the choice of the classification scheme is not important in object recognition, in fact the opposite is true! A good overview how classification can be applied to the more general field of pattern recognition can be found in [1].

B.1 Nearest-Neighbor Classification

A basic classification scheme is the so-called 1-nearest neighbor classification. Here, the Euclidean distances in feature space between the feature vector of a scene object and every of the feature vectors acquired during training are calculated. For two feature vectors $\mathbf{x} = [x_1, x_2, \ldots, x_N]^T$ and $\mathbf{y} = [y_1, y_2, \ldots, y_N]^T$ consisting of N elements, the Euclidean distance d in R^N is defined by

$$d(\mathbf{x}, \mathbf{y}) = \sqrt{\sum_{n=1}^{N} (y_n - x_n)^2} \tag{B.1}$$

If the distances $d(\mathbf{x}, \mathbf{y}_i)$ of the vector $\mathbf{x}$ derived from the scene image to the vectors $\mathbf{y}_i$ derived from the training samples are known, classification amounts to assigning the class label of the training sample $\mathbf{y}_k$ with minimum Euclidean distance to $\mathbf{x} : d(\mathbf{x}, \mathbf{y}_k) < d(\mathbf{x}, \mathbf{y}_i) \ \forall \ i \neq k$ ($\mathbf{y}_k$ is then called the "nearest neighbor" in feature space). This procedure can be simplified to calculating the distances to some

Fig. B.1 Different variations
of nearest neighbor
classification are illustrated

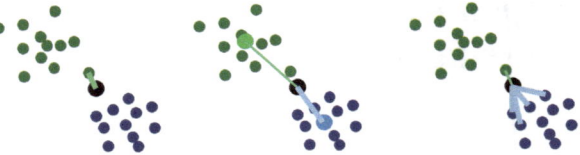

prototype vectors, where each object class is represented by a single prototype vector (e.g., the center of gravity of the cluster which is defined by all samples of the
same object class in feature space).

An extension is the k-nearest neighbor classification, where k nearest neighbors
are considered. In that case, the class label being assigned to a feature vector **x** is
determined by the label which receives the majority of votes among the k-training
sample vectors located closest to **x**.

The different proceedings are illustrated in Fig. B.1: In each of the three cases, the
black point has to be assigned to either the green or the blue cluster. In the left part,
1-nearest neighbor classification assigns the black point to the green class, as the
nearest neighbor of the black point belongs to the green class. In contrast to that, it
is assigned to the blue class if distances to the cluster centers are evaluated (shown
in the middle; the cluster centers are marked light). Finally, a 5-nearest neighbor
classification is shown in the right part. As four blue points are the majority among
the five nearest neighbors of the black point, it is assigned to the blue cluster.

B.2 Mahalanobis Distance

A weakness of the Euclidean distance is the fact that it treats all dimensions
(i.e., features) in the same way. However, especially in cases where different mea-
sures/features are combined in a feature vector, each feature might have its own
statistical properties, e.g., different variances. Therefore, distance measures exist
which try to estimate the statistical properties of each feature from a training
set and consider this information during distance calculation. One example is the
Mahalanobis distance, where the contribution of each feature value to the distance
is normalized with respect to its estimated variance.

The motivation for this can be seen in Fig. B.2: there, the euclidean distance to
the center of the green point set (marked light green) is equal for both of the two
blue points, which is indicated by the blue circle. But obviously, their similarity to
the class characterized by the set of green points is not the same. With a suitable
estimation of the statistical properties of the distribution of the green points, the
Mahalanobis distance, which is equal on all points located upon the green ellipse,
reflects the perceived similarity better.

Such a proceeding implies, however, the necessity of estimating the statistics
during training. A reliable estimation requires that a sufficiently high number of
training samples is available. Additionally, the statistics shouldn't change between
training and recognition.

Fig. B.2 The problems
involved with the Euclidean
distance if the distribution of
the data is not uniform are
illustrated

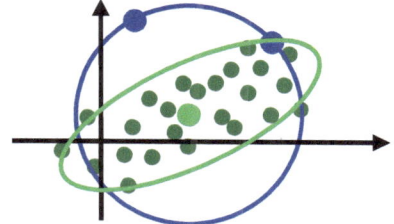

B.3 Linear Classification

Classification can also be performed by thresholding the output of a so-called decision function f, which is a linear combination of the elements of the feature vector $\mathbf{x}$. In the two-class case, $\mathbf{x}$ is assigned to class 1 if f is greater than or equal to zero and to class 2 otherwise:

$$f = \sum_{n=1}^{N} w_n \cdot x_n + w_0 \begin{cases} \geq 0 \rightarrow \text{assign } \mathbf{x} \text{ to class } 1 \\ < 0 \rightarrow \text{assign } \mathbf{x} \text{ to class } 2 \end{cases} \tag{B.2}$$

where w_0 is often called bias and the w_n are the elements of the so-called weight vector.

The decision boundary, which is defined by $f = 0$, is a $N - 1$-dimensional hyperplane and separates the N-dimensional feature space in two fractions, where each fraction belongs to one of the two classes. Figure B.3 depicts a 2D feature space, where the decision boundary reduces to a line (depicted in black). The location of the hyperplane can be influenced by the weights w_n as well as the bias w_0. These parameters are often defined in a training phase with the help of labeled training samples (here, "labeled" means that the object class of a sample is known).

If we have to distinguish between $K > 2$ classes we can formulate K decision functions $f_k; k \in [1, 2, ..., K]$ (one for each class) and classify a feature vector $\mathbf{x}$ according to the decision function f_k with the highest value: $\mathbf{x}$ is assigned to class k if $f_k(\mathbf{x}) > f_j(\mathbf{x})$ for all $j \neq k$.

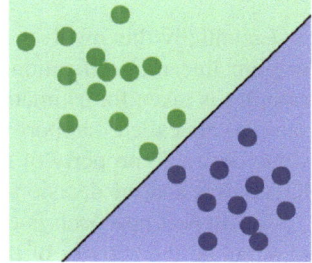

Fig. B.3 The separation of a
2D feature space into two
fractions (marked *green* and
blue) by a decision boundary
(*black line*) is shown

B.4 Bayesian Classification

Another example of exploiting the statistical properties of the distribution of the feature vectors in feature space is classification according to Bayes' rule. Here, the probability of occurrence of the sensed data or alternatively a feature vector $\mathbf{x}$ is modeled by a probability density function (PDF) $p(\mathbf{x})$. This modeling helps to solve the following classification problem: given an observation $\mathbf{x}$, what is the probability that it was produced by class k? If these conditional probabilities $p(k \,|\, \mathbf{x})$ were known for all classes $k \in [1, 2, ..., K]$, we could assign $\mathbf{x}$ to the class which maximizes $p(k \,|\, \mathbf{x})$.

Unfortunately the $p(k \,|\, \mathbf{x})$ are unknown in most applications. But, based on labeled training samples (where the class label is known for each sample), it is possible to estimate the conditional probabilities $p(\mathbf{x} \,|\, k)$ in a training step by evaluating the distribution of all training samples belonging to class k. Now the $p(k \,|\, \mathbf{x})$ can be calculated according to Bayes' rule:

$$p(k \,|\, \mathbf{x}) = \frac{p(\mathbf{x} \,|\, k) \cdot p(k)}{p(\mathbf{x})} \tag{B.3}$$

The probability $p(k)$ of occurrence of a specific class k can be estimated during training by calculating the fraction of training samples belonging to class k, related to the total number of samples. $p(\mathbf{x})$ can then be estimated by the sum $\sum_{k=1}^{K} p(\mathbf{x} \,|\, k) \cdot p(k)$. Hence, all terms necessary for calculating Equation (B.3) during recognition are known.

B.5 Other Schemes

Several other classification schemes are also trying to exploit the statistical properties of the data. Recently, support vector machines (SVM) have become very popular (cf. [2], for example). SVM's are examples of so-called kernel-based classification methods, where the input data $\mathbf{x}$ to be classified is transformed by a non-linear function $\phi(\mathbf{x})$ before a linear decision-function is calculated:

$$f_{\text{SVM}}(\mathbf{x}) = \mathbf{w}^T \cdot \phi(\mathbf{x}) + b \tag{B.4}$$

Essentially this involves making the decision boundary more flexible compared to pure linear classification. During training, only a small subset of the training samples is taken for estimating the weights, based on their distribution. The chosen samples are called "support vectors." Such a picking of samples aims at maximizing some desirable property of the classifier, e.g., maximizing the margin between the data points and the decision boundary (see [2] for details).

A different approach is taken by neural networks (NNs). Such networks intend to simulate the activity of the human brain, which consists of connected neurons.

Each neuron receives input from other neurons and defines its output by a weighted combination of various inputs from other neurons. This is mathematically modeled by the function

$$f_{NN}(\mathbf{x}, \mathbf{w}) = g(\mathbf{w}^T \cdot \phi(\mathbf{x})) \tag{B.5}$$

where $g(\cdot)$ performs a nonlinear transformation.

Accordingly, a neural net consists of multiple elements ("neurons"), each implementing a function of type (B.5). These neurons are connected by supplying their output as input to other neurons. A special and widely-used configuration is the so-called feed-forward neural network (also known as multilayer perceptrons), where the neurons are arranged in layers: the neurons of each layer get their input data from the output of the preceding layer and supply their output as input data to the successive layer. A special treatment is necessary for the first layer, where the data vector $\mathbf{x}$ serves as input, as well as the last layer, where the output pattern can be used for classification. The weights $\mathbf{w}$ as well as the parameters of ϕ are adjusted for each neuron separately during training.

References

1. Bishop, C.M., *"Pattern Recognition and Machine Learning"*, Springer-Verlag, 2006, ISBN 0-387-31073-8
2. Cristiani, N. and Shawe-Taylor J., *"An Introduction to Support-Vector Machines and Other Kernel-based Learning Methods"*, Cambridge University Press, 2000, ISBN 0-521-78019-5
3. Duda, R.O., Hart, P.E. and Stork, D.G., *"Pattern Classification"*, Wiley & Sons, 2000, ISBN 0-471-05669-3

Index

A

Accumulator, 44
Active contour models, 118–126
AdaBoost, 61
Alignment, 92
Anisometry, 26
Anisotropic diffusion, 125
Association graph, 76

B

Bag of features, 171
Bayesian classification, 195
Bias, 194
Binarization, 158
Bin picking, 96
Boosting, 178
Breakpoint, 72

C

Canny edge detector, 8
Canonical frame, 110
CCD, *see* Contracting curve density
CCH, *see* Contrast context histogram
Center of gravity, 26
Centroid distance function, 28
Chamfer matching, 60
Chi-square (χ^2) test, 166, 172
Circular arc, 70
City block distance, 29
Classification methods, 24, 192
Class label, 12
Clique, 77
Clutter, 5
Codebook, 170
Collinearity, 97
Conics, 110
Contour fragments, 175
Contracting curve density,
    126–131

Contrast context histogram, 162
Cornerness function, 156
Correlation, 11–22
Correspondence-based OR, 70
Correspondence clustering, 151
Cost function, 81
Covariance matrix, 35
CSS, *see* Curvature scale space
Curvature, 72
Curvature scale space, 135–139

D

DCE, *see* Discrete contour evolution
Decision boundary, 194
Decision function, 194
Depth map, 96
Descriptor, 9
    distribution-based, 160
    filter-based, 160
Differential filters, 162–163
Differential invariant, 163
Discrete contour evolution, 133,
    169
Distance sets, 168–169
Distance transform, 54–55
DoG detector, 148

E

Earth Mover's Distance, 173
Edgel, 8, 74
Edge map, 123
Eigenimage, 33
Eigenvalue decomposition, 33
Eigenvector, 33
EMD, *see* Earth Mover's Distance
Energy functional, 118
Euclidean distance, 192
Euler equation, 120

F
False alarms, 5
False positives, 5
FAST detector, 157–158
Feature space, 24, 192
Feature vector, 24–31
Feed-forward NN, 196
Fiducial, 27
Force field, 122
Fourier descriptor, 27–31
Fourier transform, 18
    FFT, 19
    polar FT, 29

G
Gabor filter, 160
Generalized Hausdorff distance, 59
Generalized Hough transform, 44–50
Generic Fourier descriptor, 29
Geometrical graph match, 75–80
Geometric filter, 74–75
Geometric hashing, 87–92
Geometric primitive, 71
GHT, *see* Generalized Hough transform
GLOH, *see* Gradient location orientation
    histogram
Gradient, 188–189
Gradient location orientation histogram, 161
Gradient vector flow, 122–126
Graph, 75–87
GVF, *see* Gradient vector flow

H
Haar filter, 60–61
Harris detector, 158
Hash table, 87
Hausdorff distance, 51–60
    forward distance, 51
    partial distance, 52
    reverse distance, 51
Hessian detector, 156–157
Hessian matrix, 156–157
Homogeneous coordinates, 43
Hough transform, 44–50
Hypothesis generation, 104
Hysteresis thresholding, 71, 190

I
Image
    plane, 5
    pyramid, 17–18, 50
    registration, 18
    retrieval, 4
Indexing, 88

I
Inflection point, 137
Integral image, 61
Interest points, 9, 145–181
Internal energy, 119
Interpretation tree, 80–87
Invariance, 5
Invariants, 108
    algebraic, 109
    canonical frame, 109

K
Kernel-based classification, 195
Keypoint, 146
K-means, 172

L
Labeled distance sets, 168–169
Landmark point, 164
Laplacian of Gaussian, 98
Least squares solution, 77
LEWIS, 108–116
Linear classification, 194
Linear classifier, 63–64
Line segment, 69–70
Local jet, 162
Log-polar grid, 162
LoG, *see* Laplacian of Gaussian

M
Machine vision, 3
Mahalanobis distance, 193
Maximally stable extremal region, 158–159
Metric, 51
Moment invariants, 27, 163
Moments, 25–27
    central moments, 26
    gray value moments, 26
    normalized moments, 25
    region moments, 25
MSER, *see* Maximally stable extremal region
M-tree, 141
Multilayer perceptron, 196

N
Nearest neighbor classification, 192–193
Neural networks, 195
Non-maximum suppression, 45

O
Object
    appearance, 5, 7
    categorization, 184
    counting, 3
    detection, 3

inspection, 3
scale, 5
shape, 7
sorting, 3
Occlusion, 5

P

Parallelism, 97
Parametric curve, 117–118
Parametric manifold, 33–34
PCA, *see* Principal component analysis
PCA-SIFT, 160
Perceptual grouping, 97–101
Phase-only correlation, 18–20
Planar object, 43
POC, *see* Phase-only correlation
Point pair, 74
Polygonal approximation, 71
Pose, 3
Position measurement, 3
Principal component analysis, 31–38
Probability density function, 195

Q

QBIC system, 24

R

R-table, 44
Radial basis functions, 167
Range image, 96
Region descriptor, 145–181
Relational indexing, 101–108

S

Scale invariant feature transform, 147–155
Scale space, 147
Scaling, 43
Scattermatrix, 33
Scene categorization, 4, 145, 147
SCERPO, 97–101
Search tree, *see* Interpretation tree
Second moment matrix, 156
Segmentation, 25
Shape-based matching, 20–22
Shape context, 164–168

SIFT, *see* Scale invariant feature transform
descriptor, 149
detector, 147
Signatures, 28, 172
Snakes, 118–126
Sobel operator, 187
Spatial pyramid matching, 173–174
Steerable filter, 163
Strong classifier, 64
Subsampling, 17–18
Subspace projection, 32
Support vector machines, 195

T

Tangent, 72
Template image, 11
Thin plate spline, 166
Thresholding, 25, 158
Token, 139–143
TPS, *see* Thin plate spline
Transformation, 41–67
affine transform, 42
perspective transform, 42–43
rigid transform, 43
similarity transform, 42
Transformation space, 41
Turning function, 131–135

V

Variance
inter-class, 5
intra-class, 5
View-class, 101
Viewpoint, 5
Viewpoint consistency constraint, 98
Virtual sample, 177
Visual codebook, 171
Visual parts, 134, 169

W

Wavelet descriptors, 29
Wavelet filter, 160
Weak classifier, 64
Weight vector, 194
World coordinates, 95